SIMPLE
TIPS
SMART
IDEAS

Erica Wolfe-Murray

SIMPLE TIPS SMART IDEAS

FREE IDEAS ★ SMART THINKING ★ SIMPLE ADVICE
QUICK TIPS ★ REAL CASE STUDIES TO HELP YOU
BUILD A BETTER, MORE RESILIENT BUSINESS

SMALL COMPANIES, SELF-EMPLOYED, FREELANCERS,
SIDE HUSTLERS... THIS BOOK IS FOR YOU!

Build a Bigger, Better Business

First published in 2018 by Lola Media Ltd

ISBN 978-1-911195-98-6

Also available as an ebook
ISBN 978-1-911195-99-3

Page design by Austin Taylor
Cover design and illustration by Alice Clarke, concept by Patternity
Printed and bound by OZGraf

To Faye, Xander, Christopher and Robin,
for your belief and love

Erica can look a business right in the eye and tell it what it needs to do to grow.

Mark Bonner, GBH, London

About me

Having left home at 16 and supported myself since, I am well aware of how tough working for yourself or running a small business can be.

Although I worked for larger organisations in my early 20s, much of my career has been spent running companies with a maximum of 50 employees. Latterly, most of my clients also run companies with fewer than 50 employees, and very many have fewer than 10.

Rather than being a limitation, on the contrary this gives them tremendous freedom. They are masters of their own destiny, can make decisions quickly, turn ideas into new services or products fast and outmanoeuvre much larger enterprises. But make no mistake – these are not inconsiderable companies. Many have a turnover per head that larger companies can only aspire to, while some have a global influence that far outweighs their size.

Although my career has largely seen me work in the creative industries, I have always been intrigued by the different ways smaller businesses change, develop, flex and grow. I am just as fascinated by how a plumbing business runs as how a design company operates – and what each can learn from the other. I watch, talk, ask endless questions around what their ambitions are, what commercial models they use, what it is they love about working in the way they do.

Unusually, I have been both the creative head of a design company and the financial director of a well-respected independent production company making documentaries for the BBC, Channel 4 and international broadcasters, so I really understand how all aspects of a business need to work together to harness opportunity smartly when it presents itself.

As a working mother of four children, I was very aware of how I had to structure my work and business needs around their lives, school and other commitments. Now they are adults, I see myself supporting company directors using similar methods to those I discovered for combining an involving work life with a rich and noisy home life.

I have really enjoyed writing this book. In the process, I've been reminded of some of the fascinating people I'm lucky enough to work with. I hope you can share this delight, along with the book's range of ideas, tips and new ways of approaching an issue, to help your own venture grow.

Erica Wolfe-Murray

CONTENTS

....

Introduction 12

HOW TO DRAW A BUSINESS PLAN 17

GROWING YOUR BUSINESS 47

The four business factors you can influence 49

Introduction

Growth

This book is about helping your business grow.

It's packed with ideas, new approaches to old problems, old approaches you can apply to new issues... There are diagrams, case studies, quick tips and the odd statistic to give you a wider picture.

And the best thing about it? Pretty much everything in here costs little or nothing to do and develop. But many of the ideas can help you get your business on track for its next phase – whatever that is.

The book cover refers to 'building a business' but this will look different to each person who picks this up. You might want to make yourself more profitable. You could be planning to expand, or want to find new revenue streams. Perhaps you just want to refresh how you approach customers. Or are you thinking there might be exciting untapped markets out there? This book can help you with all of these and more.

Whether your company is a start-up, is at an early stage of growth or you've been trading for 15–20 years, there's lots to make you think differently about your goals.

But most importantly, all of the methods and ideas have been used in companies already, in some way or other. They work. So find one, two or more that fit what you need, adapt them to suit your venture – and crack on.

I've tried to ensure that the wide gamut of ideas can be applied across all sorts of commercial endeavour. Whether you are a self-employed master craftsman, are launching an app with a great team, have a dispersed global workforce, or run a shop, each and every type of company can find ideas here to help them approach their business with fresh eyes.

And it's been kept simple on purpose.

There are plenty of brilliant minds out there offering exceptional advice – people who've worked hard for MBAs, write economics and accountancy books, or run high-level programmes to build 'unicorns' (companies worth $1 billion+). I am not one of those – I've devised this book for hands-on owner/managers who want to make their smaller business grow better and smarter, using the experience I've gleaned from working with well over 200 companies of all sizes and complexions.

You are likely to know about some of the ideas already – if so, move on to another section. Some of the contents will be more relevant to people starting out – where you once were. Or perhaps you feel some parts will be more use to you once you're further ahead than where you are today – fine. Mark these sections to come back to in a couple of months.

This book is aimed at the 5 million+ companies in the UK who employ 10 people or fewer. There are 5.2 million companies overall, and you form the bulk of them. The country depends on you. The economy depends on you. Your families depend on you. Yet growing your business is tough. That is why I have written this book. For you.

Good luck.

How to use this book

In pretty much any way you want.

Most books start at the front and you work your way through. It can feel like a bit of a mission. You don't have to do that here.

Use it to dip in and out of at any time you need a bit of a boost, or want to take a fresh approach to a meeting, or a problem that's been taxing you overnight.

Just a few of the notebooks containing all my meeting notes, ideas and plans from my work with growing small and medium enterprises over the last few years. Their contents have been ransacked for this book.

There are diagrams you can adapt as necessary to better suit your company framework. There are easy tips to widen your thinking. And ways of helping your team contribute differently.

Please make notes in this book, draw in the margins and use it every day. It's meant to be a workbook – enjoyable to use, a place to store your own diagrams, thoughts, tips and plans. It should be messy, colourful and filled with good ideas you've torn out of magazines, scribbled-down URLs or web pages that could help you. Staple in business cards, photos of good things you spot on your travels, anything that triggers a business 'aha' moment...

Photocopy the diagrams and stick them on the wall. Draw on them, get everyone else to draw on them. Great ideas aren't the sole preserve of company founders. Friends, family and other people involved with you and your business might have a killer insight.

While writing this, I've talked about it as a 'workbook' to friends and clients. Everyone has smiled, remembering how much they enjoyed starting a new project, a new workbook at school. How their 'rough' book held all their jottings, notes, drawings and doodles. Things they could refer back to. You can use this book in a similar way.

But first, a question...

What do you want from your working life?

As we all know, most of us spend the bulk of our working life doing just that – working. For some it's highly enjoyable; they relish the challenges, love what they do and go to work with a smile on their faces. For others –, working is a means to an end. That could be anything from putting food on the table and a roof over your head to growing and selling the company, and everything in between.

But it is important to reflect occasionally about what you want from the work that you do. If you are building a business, you will have very different factors driving you, compared to someone who is comfortable just 'doing what they do'. Neither is any better than the other – just different. So take a moment to find three things that you want from your world of work...

1 ---------------------------------------

2 ---------------------------------------

3 ---------------------------------------

Are you achieving them or at least on the road to achieving them? What can take you along this road faster or more smartly? And if you aren't on the right road for you yet – how can you get to it? What steps do you need to take? Life is long, rich and complicated, but is infinitely better if you are doing something you enjoy. Whatever that is.

My father learned how to do joinery when he was 45. He came out top of his joinery class – much to his delight. And while he was never the most artistic joiner, or even the best joiner in his neighbourhood, he was surely the happiest. He scraped by, having odd holidays, looking after his dogs but loving every minute of working with wood. So what is it that you want to be doing if not what you do already?

Core ideas and diagrams

Throughout this book there are several core ideas and diagrams that I suggest you have a look at. The aspects of your work that you unpack through using these diagrams lead you in all sorts of different ways of thinking and give you lots of new ideas and ways to grow your business.

By using these, you will have a fabulous toolbox to work with. Experiment with them when you feel inspired and ready to go for it.

You can find them on the following pages:

- How to Draw a Business Plan: pages 21–39
- SPICK + Span: pages 55–59
- Cake: pages 86–91
- Target: pages 143–151

Towards the end of each section, you will find a 'Let's talk about...' heading. Each of the paragraphs under here goes into things we never really talk about in business. Maybe we're embarrassed, or it seems unprofessional. But understanding them, grasping these particular nettles, is really vital. They can give your business an emotional intelligence that everyone will welcome.

But make them yours and use them regularly.

I draw up a business plan **every year** in that dead time between Christmas and New Year – not because I've forgotten what I've done, but because it never fails to surprise me **how much** I have done and how one or two projects can change the focus of how I approach the future. Or new clients or projects or ideas.

About one-third of your life is spent working, so it's important you enjoy it!

Seemingly simple, this business planning
process will give you an effective,
unassailable edge over your competitors,
helping you to build a more successful
venture. Although this is not a plan for
sharing with your financial advisors or
bank manager, it gives you a powerful
framework through which you can develop
a unique offering for your business, leading
to growth in a range of ways.

How to Draw a Business Plan

One of the first things that individuals, start-ups or small companies feel they need to do as they launch a company, develop a new product or go for growth is to write a business plan. How can their venture be taken seriously without one?

Hours will be spent at the computer poring over text, figures, marketing, sales projections and so on – culminating in long Word documents and endless Excel spreadsheets.

But, once written, most business plans never see the light of day, staying in the computer and perhaps being referred to very occasionally. While I completely agree that it is vital to have a plan if you are seeing the bank manager or seeking investment, most of us aren't. Yet we go through this tortuous process while missing out on some key thinking that could simply and easily set our company ahead of the competition – with little or no effort.

At my company whilst working with our clients, what struck us in the early days was how unique everyone's story was. As we mapped their individual history, we realised that the greatest potential for success lay in that uniqueness. If we could build their business based on this life trajectory that no one else could ever, would ever, be able to share, the opportunity to do something really different was enormous. It could set a company apart from its peers, give it a unique proposition – because effectively no one could compete.

After lots of practice, we developed a very simple mapping process to do just this. Don't underestimate it because it looks easy. The power lies in the work you put into it, and how you interpret what then emerges. The flow diagram on page 24 will take you through the process.

And we will also return/refer to the work you do in this mapping process throughout the book, so it makes sense to do it thoroughly first time round.

But first we need to look at **why** we are doing this...

Hopes and dreams

When was the last time you were asked what your hopes and dreams are?

Last week? Lucky you.

Last month? Good, they're somewhere near the top of your mind.

Last year? Hmm – are they still the same ones?

Never? How does that make you feel? A sense of confusion? Loss? Lack of direction?

Whoever I work with and support through this business mapping process, I always start by asking them what their hopes and dreams are. Always.

If you don't know what your ambitions, innermost drivers, or ultimate daydreams are – why are you starting,

A successful growing company was about to start on the business plan process when I asked them about their hopes and dreams. One young board member piped up that money was all that mattered. Others in the room commented how this individual's imperative impacted on them all – every day – driving them harder.

But as we started to work through the background mapping steps, it emerged that abject poverty was part of this person's early life experience – including going to school one day wearing flip-flops because their only pair of shoes was nowhere to be found. The teasing lasted all day...

This had a profound impact. At no point did they ever want to be back there – at school with no shoes, owing to lack of money. Money was security, it was a home, it was warmth, food. It was two pairs of shoes.

By being open and so direct, the whole team rallied round, recognising that this was not greed, as previously thought, but a deeply personal dream that informed and underpinned the everyday. This was a team member who would never, ever risk the company's finances or safety, because the alternative was too painful to contemplate.

building or running a business? And how can you hope to achieve success when you don't know what that means to you?

Yes, I appreciate it is different for bigger or publicly listed companies who have shareholders, investors and the like, but most of the companies in the UK are not in that big bracket. They are just like you.

So take some time at the start of the mapping process to ask yourself, and everyone else in the room, about your hopes and dreams.

They can be anything from 'financial security' or 'I want to take a holiday/ buy a house' to being internationally recognised for your contribution in a given field of expertise or being able to buy a pair of Joseph boots when you want. Personal, company, public... your hopes and dreams can and should be a mixture of all.

Be aware of these as you go through the process outlined below. It will help you understand yourself and your colleagues better.

Individual, company/board or product map?

Depending on whether you are an individual looking for a career change, run your own business, are part of the board of a growing company or are doing it for a product, you may need to adapt the questions and therefore the content accordingly.

However, be assured this process works for all of these situations.

AS AN INDIVIDUAL

If you are looking to change career, are feeling stale or have reached a place in life where you are asking 'Is this it?' – please do this mapping exercise.

Or perhaps you are mid-to-late 30s, 40s or 50s and are feeling lost, not sure what career steps to take next, or have younger employees snapping at your heels... Maybe you have retired but don't want to slip gently into irrelevance? Please don't lose heart – if you go through this process honestly and thoroughly, so much will emerge – you could see an inspiring future role you never envisaged.

AS A COMPANY DIRECTOR OR BOARD

This exercise seems quite prosaic at the outset. I've had several directors sigh heavily about how the hours spent working on it could be better utilised. However, by the time the process is well underway, with new company potential/value revealing itself, they become its strongest supporters.

The contributors to the process need to be honest and share experiences for it to work fully. Many board members will sit in a room with colleagues for years, knowing little about each other. They might feel competitive or combative with them, rather than recognising that by understanding one another's past – their history – the pooling of experience builds an infinitely stronger environment to allow the company to flourish.

If you are the only director of your company – that's fine. I've done this process almost every year for ages. It's still as useful now as it was in the early days, because each year things change, a new slant emerges.

AS A PRODUCT

This model can also be adapted to look at the life of a product and think

Quick tip... If you're mapping as an individual, it's a good idea to create this map with a friend or acquaintance. Someone you know and trust, but probably not your partner. Why? Because with them we often self-limit or edit ourselves, which is the last thing you need to do here.

Quick tip... A facilitator to ask the questions and write up responses works best with two or more participants. This allows each participant to hear what the others are saying, rather than focusing on capturing what was said.

This way of working is also good for a department, a team or a an SMT (senior management team).

through where it has potential. The questions will need modifying, as will the outcomes, but they allow you to explore both the history and trajectory of the product's life cycle to date in a different way from merely looking at sales figures.

Guidelines

• Don't rush this process – do it when you have time and are relaxed.
• Enjoy it – have fun. It's your story, after all.
• Use coloured markers – make it look good.
• Do it together as a team or with a friend.
• If you feel a facilitator would make it easier to focus, bring one in. And someone with nice handwriting – even better.
• Try to complete the 'Internal' and the 'External' sections of the plan in one sitting, or each of them in one sitting, rather than breaking the process down into a series of short sessions, where you lose the flow.

Preparation: What you will need

Take either:
• several **big** sheets of paper and mount end to end on the wall, or
• a roll of Magic Whiteboard, or
• a roll of brown paper/lining wallpaper and stick it horizontally to the wall.
Big is best.

Drawing up this plan large on the wall and in colours, rather than doing it on a computer, brings different parts of your brain into play and will also help you see different patterns, ideas, etc.

Don't use flip charts, as you need to see the plan as a whole as it emerges, rather than having to flip pages back and forth.

Use lots of coloured pens. It gives your eye a break and also helps you differentiate the columns, or thoughts you are writing up.

Drawing the outline

Draw a horizontal line from the left-hand edge to two-thirds of the way across, about two-thirds of the way down the sheet (see the diagram on pages 24–25).

Mark the top half of the page **Internal** and the bottom half **External**.

The top half of the page will be all about you; the bottom half is to record the market you are operating in and the external factors at play.

Start with the 'Internal' section...

STEP **1** BACKGROUND
On the left-hand side of the 'Internal' section, put the heading **Background**.

Now, going round to each individual in turn, ask a wide range of questions about their background, turning the answers into short bullet points, using the list of questions provided on the next page as guidance. Write these up under the heading.

You can use a different colour for different people if you want.

Do **not** be judgemental. Listen to each other's answers. It is likely you will learn a huge amount about both yourself and your colleagues, which ultimately will be helpful to your business. The more you understand each other, and are able to work constructively together, the more your business will thrive.

Everyone will answer as best they feel able. If they don't want to share particular facts, parts of their life or stories, that is their choice. Respect this.

Although to some people the questions may seem intrusive, much of how you run a company is based on behaviour learned as children. Obvious elements may emerge, such as the impact of your sibling position, but extraordinary other influences also emerge – the impact of which can only be seen once the process is complete.

It is likely that the bullet points answering these questions will take up lots of space. So just use as much paper as you need. Although you may not be aware of it, there will be much in everyone's backgrounds that can really help shape the company moving forward.

The 'internal' part of the map is all about you...

BACKGROUND questions

Where were you born? Are there any regional, national or other influences in your family?

What brothers and sisters do you have, and are they older or younger?

How did you get on with your siblings? Do you have an extended family?

Tell us a bit about your parents. What was your relationship like? What did they do?

Where did you grow up?

What was that like?

What hobbies/sports did you enjoy as a child? What activities did your family enjoy?

How did you find your early school years?

Did anything major happen in your family as you were growing up? Positive or negative.

Was there anything that impinged particularly on your childhood?

Where did you go on holidays?

What things were important to your family? Sport? Money? Creativity? Culture? etc.

What sort of child were you? How did this manifest itself?

How did you find secondary school? What subjects did you enjoy?

Were your family supportive?

Were there any teachers that meant more to you than others? Why?

How did you spend your holidays?

Did you work outside of school to earn cash, or volunteer? Paper round or your own small venture?

What GCSEs did you study and how did they go?

What happened next? A-levels, leave, sixth-form college?

What did you do in your spare time? What did you enjoy/hate doing?

Did you have any major illnesses?

Did you go on to university? After a gap year? What did you study? How was that?

Did you work while at uni?

What was your first job? And how long did you stay?

How did your career develop – whether paid or unpaid?

Where did you live and work?

Have you travelled, and, if so, to where?

How many languages do you speak?

How do you spend your leisure time now?

What family do you have? Partner? Children? Pets?

Other than family/teachers, were there any other major influences in your life?

internal

1. Background
This is about your history. p22

3. Paid to Do
What have you actually been paid to do in your career? p27

5. Recent Developments
What has impacted on your life recently? p31

2. Clients
Who has paid you during your career? p27

4. Passions, Skills & Talents
What do you really love, what have you learned and what are you good at? p28

external

6. The Market
What does the world you are trading in look like? p31

8. Competition
Who is stealing your lunch? p33

10. Recent Developments
What has impacted on the market recently? p33

7. Trends
What are the behavioral changes that could/will impact on your business? p32

9. Market Positioning
Where are you in the competition? p33

11. Strengths

S

If your team has put its heart or soul into this process, this bit should be rich or diverse. p35

12. Weaknesses

W

These emerge through discussion or interpretation but can be hard to see. p36

13. Opportunities

O

Really look in-depth at the market and trends to see where you can spot new areas that are growing. p37

14. Threats

T

Don't, don't, don't under estimate where threats can come from. p39

Spend time really thinking through your answers to the points each heading raises

case study

USING YOUR UNIQUE CHARACTERISTICS TO BUILD A COMPANY

CEO of a small company working with the arts, Caroline had spent a fascinating childhood moving around with her father, who was involved in a large corporation. Most similar families moved every two or so years. However, her father's career meant that Caroline moved pretty much every year. So each autumn there was a new house, a new school, a new set of children whom she had to befriend, already aware that she would be saying 'goodbye' to them the following autumn.

There was also a new culture, city, landscape and language to explore.

For some, this constant disruption could be perceived as a difficulty, but for Caroline it elicited a sense of wonderment – that places could be so different, have such different cultures, influences and people, even though they were not necessarily that distant.

And she always saw places with fresh eyes. She never got used to being anywhere, yet had to make herself feel at home quickly, becoming hyper-aware of what keys you need in order to unlock somewhere and get quickly under its skin.

As we worked together to determine what Caroline's new business would be, through closely unpacking her background, we realised that her childhood had given her a rich set of skills in understanding cultures, their impact and their influence on both those who live in a place and those who visit. These two groups have very different needs. We harnessed this knowledge to build a company that works with cultural institutions, helping them explore the requirements of the local, regular visitor as well as the occasional visitor or traveller.

STEP 2 CLIENTS/CUSTOMERS WHO'VE PAID YOU

Once you have finished unpacking your background, the next heading to write on the sheet of paper is **Clients**.

Everyone contributing to this process now needs to list **all** the clients and companies that have **ever** paid them for work.

This could include mentions of teenage bar work, or pool lifeguard work, but make sure to list all the company names once you started your career proper.

If you have worked for a company who in turn has clients, put both the name of your employer and also the actual clients on whose businesses you've worked. List within reason. If you have lots of individual clients, put down some of their key characteristics (for example: are they homeowners, or commuters?).

So, for example, in my late teens/ early 20s, I worked for ad agency *Foote, Cone & Belding* on clients *British Airways, Newsweek, Dairy Crest* and *London Transport*. All of these would feature in my list.

If you have worked in different capacities for a range of organisations, just name the organisations or the clients. Equally, if you ran a café or were self-employed, add in who was paying you – even if it was just 'members of the public in Leicester'.

Remember to list any unpaid voluntary work too. This is as important on your list of clients as paid work.

At this point, do not list what you were actually paid to do – just who paid you.

The reason this list is so potent becomes clear when we mix up everyone's client list. You will see common threads and groups you may not have realised anyone had. It may mean you can offer a service to a new sector.

When I listed this out a few years ago, reflecting on my career, I identified that I could add 'luxury goods' to sectors I knew about. This only became apparent once I had regrouped the companies I had worked with/had as clients.

STEP 3 WHAT YOU HAVE BEEN PAID TO DO

The next step we need to unpack is what you have actually been paid to do.

This sounds very easy and rather glib, but it is vital that you look carefully at each company and client that you listed under 'Clients' to really interpret what you did.

It is also critical that you break the link between the client and the work. Keeping them linked means that you limit your own and your company's potential.

What do I mean by this?

Some years back, I undertook some work for Knightsbridge store Harvey Nichols.

Just by mentioning their name as a client, potential clients assumed it was work involved in the fashion industry. In fact, we were paid to do work completely unrelated to fashion... First, we were asked to help them recover/map their archive. This had been lost due to two centuries of development and building work, as well as changes in owners, staff and a lack of interest. Second, we were asked to help them pull together a TV strategy to deal with the constant requests from broadcasters and production companies for access to film on the shop floor.

By listing these two activities under the 'What you have been paid to do' heading, we could clearly see these two services could have value to a range of other clients.

Some companies I have worked with dismiss this section lightly... 'I run a café, so I am paid for beverages and food, but also sell deli products. It's not complicated.'

But running a café business is not just about being paid to make coffee. It is also about creating the environment people want to pay to be in; they are paying for your knowledge and passion for food, for hospitality, for cake-baking. So really think carefully about what you are actually paid to deliver. It may surprise you how far it could be from what you consider to be your core business.

By now, your piece of paper should really be starting to fill up. If there are several of you contributing to this process, you will have learned a lot about your colleagues that perhaps you were unaware of. This voyage of discovery is an excellent bonding process, as it is likely that you will share both the good and the difficult stuff.

You will also see what a talented lot you are. Past experience, clients, skills and roles will all be revealed. The only other time this ever emerges is in a CV – and most CVs are forgotten about once the person is appointed. Yet they are a treasure trove of riches, too often overlooked.

Now, on to Step 4...

STEP 4 PASSIONS, SKILLS AND TALENTS

For some reason, when I write this heading up it elicits a sigh, a groan or a comment about how difficult it is. Perhaps it is our British reserve in not wanting to talk about ourselves. Passions are very personal things. Or perhaps people feel they may expose too much.

You just have to ignore this feeling and do it.

So let's unpick this a little further...

Passions – These are things you really, really love. Things you may have loved since childhood... interests you may have recently discovered...

Food and cooking often features on people's lists, as do travelling, motorsport, football and making things. This list should also include elements of your work – entertaining people, music, design.

case study

BEN WILD

Ben Wild is a really talented history teacher. In fact, to give him his full title, he is Dr Benjamin Wild, FRHistS, with a PhD in medieval history. His degree, ongoing studies and career have focused on history and passing on his love of the subject to teenagers studying for GCSEs and A levels. But over lunch one day, Ben confessed that history wasn't his greatest passion.

When pressed, he revealed a deep, long-standing passion for art and men's fashion. Neither came as any surprise – Ben dresses beautifully in tailored suits, plumage-colour socks and accessories. But what was so sad was that his real love was getting hidden, swamped by the need to be the history teacher, with all its demands.

So we hatched a plot.

Ben would continue to work in his day job, using his undoubted skills to teach history – but during weekends, holidays and whenever he got the chance, he would develop a parallel career focusing on art and menswear fashion, but from a historical perspective.

Three weeks later he wrote his first blog post – and more followed in quick succession. Each picked up on a contemporary theme, linking it back through sartorial history, illustrated with photographs and works of art showing how we always recycle ideas. (For example – one blog post revealed how today's young men wearing low-slung jeans/tracksuit bottoms to expose their underwear links back to the hose and codpieces worn by Henry VIII as an expression of virility and manliness, as seen in paintings by Hans Holbein.)

As Ben's blog developed, it grew increasingly popular, attracting lecture and speaking engagements from the Condé Nast College of Fashion, the V&A Museum and the National Portrait Gallery. Two books have followed – one on Cecil Beaton's clothing in imagery, to accompany an exhibition, and an academic book on the history/importance of fancy dress. And he still teaches history.

So if you have a passion – what can you turn it into?

www.benjaminwild.co

Try to find about 5–10 passions that absorb you, that you care deeply about.

Skills – These are things you have learned to do, such as computer programming, car mechanics, a language or whatever else. They are areas where you have an above-average aptitude.

Talents – Different from skills, talents are inherent in who you are, what you do. They are the things you find easy. So you may have listed speaking French as a skill, but the natural ability to pick up languages, allowing you to speak three or four, would be a talent.

Sometimes you are unaware of them until they are pointed out by another person. Discovering new talents can also happen at any age in pretty much any place – you won't realise you have a talent for something until you are called upon to use it, then it will just seem natural, part of who you are.

case study

AGA ENGINEER

I have an elderly Aga in my home, which, like a boiler, needs regular servicing. One day, Aga serviceman Phil turned up to check it out, replace the wick, etc., as usual. When he had finished, we stood chatting while he drank his mug of tea. He was mulling over moving on from his current employer and going freelance. This thought was largely prompted by the imminent arrival of his fourth child and the need to have greater flexibility as a parent to support his partner.

We talked more about how he and his partner were going to manage four small children, with both of them working. He laughingly mentioned how much he loved baking and cooking on his own Aga, so he'd be happy to spend more time as a male 'Mary Berry'. And that was when it struck us... here was an Aga engineer who not only knew how to get the best from his oven mechanically, but knew how to maximise its potential for cooking healthy, nutritious meals for a big family. He even came up with a super-smart title for a cookery book and food blog.

So what recent developments are happening in your life that could trigger an opportunity you haven't seen before?

STEP 5 RECENT DEVELOPMENTS

The final part of the 'Internal' section is listing the recent developments in your own, your team's or your business's life.

Think back over the last 12–18 months. What big things have happened?

Have you become a parent? Fallen in love? Moved home? Bought a flat? Started a business? Learned to drive? Launched a new product? Had a friend or family member die? Opened a shop? Whatever was a big deal in your life – list it here.

Why?

When something big happens in your life, it absorbs you and exposes you to experiences you may not have encountered before. You will be aware of the pinch points, the new things you learned, loved, hated. These will all have become part of the fabric of you, more easily recalled than earlier events in your life.

Surprisingly, they can be useful moving forward to the next steps in the business planning process – this exposure to the new will have made you more open to exploring different ways of working.

Moving on to the 'External' half of the plan...

The top half of the plan was all about you, your past work, your clients, the areas you excel at.

The bottom half of the plan is totally different. It is about what is going on in the world that you operate in – your market.

We complete it in exactly the same way, using a series of headings as prompts. Whereas the top was about you as an individual, or coming together as a board, a team or whatever, pooling all of your past experience, the bottom is about contributing knowledge around what is going on in the world your business is – or will be – operating in.

There are five steps in this section, which we will look at in detail.

STEP 6 THE MARKET

Using simple bullet points again, list some of the main features of the market or markets that you trade in. These will be different for every single company – the only commonality being that they must all be external factors.

What sort of markets do your client companies operate in? Are they in different sectors? What is happening in their worlds? Is the market expanding or contracting? What was the impact of the recession, or other key challenges?

...ie market potential growing?

Keep the points brief, but be aware they should be based in fact, not supposition.

I always take the view when I draw a plan for my business that – if asked – I could provide hard stats to back up the market points. It is useful to be disciplined in this way

And really do think about how many markets you might be involved in... Often they overlap with each other.

STEP 7 TRENDS

If the market is about hard reality, in 'Trends' you are listing behavioural shifts... Some may be very early, some may be more mature. But identifying how your customers, potential customers and those who are not even on your radar are changing their behaviour is critical.

This is not a science – it is about you and your team having your radar switched on, about being curious – endlessly curious. It's wanting and needing to understand the 'why' as much as the 'what'; the 'how' as well as the 'who'.

Trends can be about a whisper you overheard, about a thread you spotted, about seeing that 1 + 1 can equal 3. It is

Quick tip... Don't forget the weekend/Sunday papers... Because most people now do their research online, they are subject to a linear mechanism that is also geared to a search engine's algorithm, which by its very nature is feeding you what you want to see – your 'bubble'. Double linear, and potentially very limiting.

Get your team to buy all or a selection of the weekend's papers. And read them thoroughly. Sports pages, business sections, problem pages – the lot. Get them to bring in any articles, points, ideas that catch their eye, to talk about.

Why?

By doing this regularly, it is your brain, not Google's algorithm, that makes interesting, useful connections – helping you identify behaviours, trends, new ideas, markets. Keep your mind open, and tear out articles that stand out. Use these to prompt discussion in your company.

I regularly also buy magazines I've never read (or even heard of, sometimes), just to get other perspectives.

about putting you ahead of the game.

Trends can start anywhere, everywhere. What matters to your business is recognising them early so you can ride the upswing, or avoid them if they may cause you damage.

But also remember that, just like you can spot a trend, you can start one too.

STEP 8 COMPETITION

OK, so who is your competition? Who do you dread seeing on a client's pitch shortlist?

Who is stealing your customers? And why?

Who is eating your lunch? Are they the obvious characters or a company that has come from nowhere? Did you miss a trend, and you're up against the company that spotted it – or even started it?

Make sure you list not only companies but also departments or even specific job roles within companies if they are taking potential work from you.

In the early days of running my company, I realised that commercial directors of companies represented both a target market and also my competition. Some clearly told me there was nothing I could offer that they weren't already doing!

You need to add other industries to this list, too, if it looks like they are encroaching on you and your territory.

STEP 9 MARKET POSITIONING

When drawing up this plan with clients, at this point they sometimes suggest 'market positioning' should feature on the 'Internal' half of the diagram. But where you sit within your market and in relation to your competitors – whoever they are – is an external factor in your business.

Drawing up bullet points for this step is likely to evoke a discussion around all sorts of aspects of the company – such as target market, marketing strategies etc. Allow this to ebb and flow, but distill it down into the key points. Even if they feel pretty brutal.

STEP 10 RECENT DEVELOPMENTS

Just as we unpicked new events from the last 12–18 months in the 'Internal' section, we need to do the same for the 'External' part of the plan.

Factors that could really impact your market(s) need to be listed. They are the things featuring large on your audience's, customers' or clients' radars. They can range from changing import/ export rules and tariffs to the growth of the Uber food delivery service, or a new plant opening.

So that is the bulk of the 'heavy lifting' completed.

You will probably all be pretty tired, so go out for some fresh air, get something to eat. Come back to it either after a good break or perhaps on another day.

How to interpret what you have mapped

The work that you have just completed will have immense value to you moving forward in the growth of your business. You may not see how or why quite yet, but as we head through the interpretation process, you will start to see value in it in so many ways.

Throughout this book we will return to this work on several occasions, but now we are going to start looking at how best to interpret it. (Refer to the diagram on pages 38–39 to give you an idea of how to draw up the next part.)

SWOT analysis

For those unfamiliar with the term 'SWOT analysis', it is an acronym for **S**trengths, **W**eaknesses, **O**pportunities and **T**hreats, and forms a core part of every business plan or report.

However, one of the key weaknesses in most SWOT analyses is that they never unpick/unpack the individuals/company far enough back to really deliver a unique plan of difference. I see this the whole time – huge chunks of experience, services and skills are missing, yet these could be the springboard that launches your company into new markets, ways of working or finding revenue streams you had overlooked.

One of the main points in developing

Quick tip...

Sometimes, it is not just the positive aspects of your background that you can draw on for strengths. Bad stuff happens to lots of us, and even these awful times can help us develop beneficial strengths for the company.

One client admitted to being emotionally abused as a child by a parent. Just hearing the story was painful.

But in fact all that pain morphed into a company strength. It instigated strong, supportive HR policies for every team member and their families, encouraging talented employees to stay a long time, contributing to the company growth and profitability. This stable working team brought clients who were interested in long-term relationships, too; they knew that their creative teams would not up sticks and head for a rival agency anytime soon.

case study

I recently worked with an individual who had spent the first five years of her life in China, speaking Mandarin. While she can't really recall much of it now to speak, she understands a fair bit, but also knows how to behave in Chinese circles. She subsequently lived in India and a number of other countries. This ability to feel at home on several continents and, importantly, to show clients she understands them at a very visceral level puts her on a totally different footing to her competitors. It is a great strength, which only emerged because we mapped her background thoroughly. Needless to say – one of her talents is understanding/speaking seven languages!

a kick-arse SWOT analysis is to recognise that your strengths and weaknesses come from the top, 'Internal' section of your map, and *only* the top section – whereas the opportunities and threats can *only* be driven by the bottom, 'External' section.

So by using all the work in Steps 1–10, we are going to do a SWOT analysis, unlike one you have ever done before...

See the diagram on page 39 as to where to draw up each of the four areas.

STEP 11 STRENGTHS

We're going to start by listing your strengths. Go back to all the points you wrote up under 'Background'. Really stand back and look carefully at what is hidden in there.

Does your team have an international perspective because of where they grew up? Can you spot a strong volunteering/caring theme? Do you have extensive high-level creativity? List as many as seem to jump out at you.

Now look for hidden strengths in the 'Clients' list. Perhaps when you all group your lifetime clients together, you can see a real penchant for transport clients, or beauty. Or do these clients all speak to the same audience?

Add all these seemingly unrelated things to your 'Strengths' list.

The same goes for your areas of expertise.

Then think which aspects of you or your team's passions, skills and talents could feature on your 'Strengths' list.

By the time this is complete, you should have around 10–12 strengths, all of which have been drawn from your experience over many years.

Quick tip... Add up the sum of your work experience... a small PR company with just four directors, all in their late 20s/early 30s, will already have over 36 years of commercial PR experience between them.

Bear in mind – it is precisely this level of experience you are now activating. Don't underestimate its weight.

STEP 12 WEAKNESSES

Now we turn to weaknesses – those things we spend our lives trying to hide. By writing them up on the wall and acknowledging them openly, this process allows them to be addressed.

First and foremost, remember this – **no** company has **ever** been built on its weaknesses.

So build your company **only** on your strengths.

If you focus on your strengths, many of your company's weaknesses will automatically become irrelevant. It is extraordinary how this happens.

But there are some weaknesses that you cannot ignore and we'll come to those in a minute.

As you look across all of the work you have done on the 'Internal' half of the map, you will see a weakness here and there, but you will also know them yourself in your heart of hearts. Be honest and write them up. A skilled facilitator will also be able to help you here.

The other thing about weaknesses is that sometimes you simply can't see them. Lack of diversity of thought is a classic one.

Quick tip... Diversity of thought can be a real game changer for companies. It is inspiring, vital and makes you relevant today, tomorrow and next year.

A weakness I see time and again is the lack of diversity of thought – people start companies with others similar to them and appoint staff similar to them because it's what makes them feel comfortable.

But this is a huge weakness... A spectrum of sexuality, education, intellectual strengths, nationalities, ages, skills and ethnicities will add so much to your company in so many ways. Not least the bottom line.

So do a diversity of thought audit on a range of different spectrums to see how you stack up and whether you need to list it as a weakness.

Try to think of the weaknesses you can't see – perhaps using the term 'drag' might be useful here. What is 'dragging' on your business, causing it to go slower than you'd like – is that a weakness you've not really identified?

So what are those weaknesses you simply can't ignore?

Being adept at financial management is on lots of people's minds. It would seem there are a whole host of company owners that list numbers/money as their top weakness.

This is worrying and – to a certain extent – simple to solve. See page 129 for the section on money. But it's not as hard as you might think. Believe me – if you can run your household finances, then you are capable of running a small company's finances.

The other thing that often shows up, albeit as an unacknowledged weakness, is legal issues.

Do you have Terms and Conditions for contractors, clients, suppliers? Do you have all the necessary employment policies in place for health and safety, risk assessment, first aid, etc? Does your website meet all of the legal requirements? Do you have the right insurance for your area of work?

The list will vary depending on your line of work, but **does** need to be dealt with. If you don't have these things in place and something goes wrong – your business could risk being closed down.

Other easy-to-spot weaknesses might include being overly reliant on one client, one business model, or working in areas where you have minimal expertise, rather than using all the great experience you have. (It is surprising how many companies don't realise they have huge experience in areas outside what they consider to be their core offering!)

STEP 13 OPPORTUNITIES

Just as the strengths and weaknesses emerge from the 'Internal' half of the map, the opportunities and threats are to be found in the 'External' half.

The prime opportunities lying ahead for your venture will emerge from your breakdown of the market and those trends you have identified. So start listing them clearly and simply.

Focus on the competition – are they doing anything you should be doing too? Or have they missed out on something you believe could be a sizzling-hot revenue generator?

Try to think about the opportunities inventively, with optimism... Pull in other members of your staff, as they may well read the map differently to you, identifying areas you haven't spotted.

Be ambitious, be excited. And for a little inspiration as to what those opportunities could bring, reread your hopes and dreams. Are there enough opportunities up there to deliver all of those wonderful things in your mind's eye?

　　　　　　　　HOW TO DRAW A BUSINESS PLAN

11. Strengths

S If your team has put its heart or soul into this process this bit should be rich or diverse. p35

12. Weaknesses

W These emerge through discussion or interpretation but can be hard to see. p36

13. Opportunities

O Really look in depth at the market and trends to see where you can spot new areas that are growing. p37

14. Threats

T Don't, don't, don't under-estimate where threats can come from. p39

15. Your Vision(s)

What do you want your company to be?

16. Your USP

What will you be famous for?

STRENGTHS/
WEAKNESSES
COME FROM THE
INTERNAL HALF
OF YOUR PLAN,
OPPORTUNITIES/
THREATS FROM
THE EXTERNAL.

STEP 14 THREATS

Now we turn to threats...

Sadly, unlike weaknesses, many of which may well just go away if you focus on your real strengths, the same cannot be said of threats.

You ignore threats at your peril. They have an ability to come from nowhere and bite you very hard in the bum. They can take your business down in a variety of ways, through clients, supply chain wars, skill shortages, import/export law changes – the list is endless.

Think how Kodak ignored digital cameras, how BlackBerry failed to appreciate the rise of the smartphone, how Diageo didn't appreciate the impact our growing coffee culture would have on pub revenues....

Keeping on top of these is paramount. It is good to do this list now, but also regularly revisit it to ensure you haven't missed something or have turned a blind eye.

Check out all new technologies, read the papers' business pages, skim through useful e-bulletins/blasts... Ask your staff what they think might pose a threat – whether in the near future or the longer term.

Defining your vision(s)

The next step is to encapsulate all you are thinking, feeling and have discovered into a big vision for the company.

This is for internal consumption only – a horizon for the company to work towards.

It is also likely that by this point some fundamental changes will have taken place in how you view your business. Lots of new ideas will have come up, opportunities have emerged, weaknesses been exposed. You will also start feeling a profound groundswell of excitement... The possibilities you have unearthed will be inspiring and new.

Harness that big map of your totally unique set of experiences, clients, work and strengths to develop a company vision that is absolutely and totally aligned with what you want to be and do.

No other company in the world, now or in the future, can match this. So use it richly, inventively and creatively.

Come up with a vision that is uniquely yours.

It can be one big statement or several statements – and remember, it's for internal consumption only. This is what **your** vision(s) is/are for **your** company. Don't worry about the detail – we'll get to that in other parts of this book.

It is often useful to go back to the hopes and dreams you set out at the beginning. Will your big vision help you to get to these? Will it support you on your road to achieving them?

Put your vision up big on the wall. Walk away from it. And revisit it several times. If it needs editing or changing – then change it. Nothing is written in stone.

Once you have got as close to your master vision as possible, relish it. Love it.

You may also have given yourself confirmation that yes, you are on the right path for you, your team, your company. You had it right all along – that's a good place to be, too.

When I launched my current company, I thought I knew what I wanted...

I had formulated the original idea during hours spent painting the skirting boards of my home after a leg operation. Not being able to walk, I was scooting round on my bottom doing that mindless task, allowing my thoughts to roam freely around some form of new business.

Once I started working on my business plan and drew up my map, totally unanticipated strengths started to emerge, with a few surprising weaknesses too.

When I reached the company vision step, it was pretty far removed from the concept I'd started with. But I knew there was real truth behind my new vision. It was based on everything I

could bring to the table, in an expanding selection of markets.

I didn't get the wording totally right first time. In fact, if I am honest, crafting it took me quite a while. But the sense of relief and delight when you have got that vision true for your enterprise is fab!

So, what's next...?

Nailing your USP

If your vision is determining the internal direction of travel within your company, the next step that will emerge from this huge amount of work you have done is to nail your USP.

What is USP? It is an acronym/phrase that is bandied around, with everyone being told they need one.

A Unique Selling Point/Proposition is the offer statement that differentiates your product/service or whatever as widely as possible from the competition.

A useful way of thinking about it is that your USP is what will make you famous.

What is it that only your company can offer that no one else can challenge?

By really pegging this very firmly in all the work you have done in the plan to date – those experiences, that client list, the reasons they hire or use you, your strengths – it should be relatively easy to come up with a USP.

Write it up and then ask 'Could this be applied to anyone else/any other company?' If you think it could – go back and redo it. Until it really is unique.

My own USP is genuinely that – an offer, a proposition that no one else can match. And the more companies I work with, the further ahead of any potential competitors I get.

Some companies say they are in a 'me too' business. They are running a digital agency, a farm, a clothing company, like many others. That may be the case – but why is it that someone will choose to spend their money with you and not your competitors?

If it is price – that's fine, but then build your USP around that. Originally, department store John Lewis set themselves up as 'Never Knowingly Undersold'. Much of the merchandise they sold wasn't different from that of their competitors, but knowing that you would not be able to buy it cheaper elsewhere – or if so they would refund the difference – set them apart. (Obviously this has had to change in today's online world, but before the internet, that was their USP summed up in a tagline.)

Once you have your USP, how you build out from it, talk about it, ensure your prospective customers know about it, is all down to marketing.

We will come back to the different elements of your plan several times and in various ways as you dip in and out of this book. Keep everything to hand so you know where to find it. Pin it up on your wall, print out a photo of it and carry it round with you.

We want to add some GOALS to it for the next 12–18 months, but until you have considered some of the other factors around your business, let's leave it as it is.

You can't affect the external market, but you *can* affect what you sell (p.51), the money side (p.129), your team (p.192) and how you market (p.232)

Let's talk about...

Passion

This book is largely aimed at smaller companies, the nearly 5 million smaller companies who operate in the UK. Most of them are owner-managed, from farms through to plumbers, tech start-ups to freelance tree surgeons. The range is huge. We are all working in them in order to earn money to pay for the lives we lead or want to lead. But it strikes me that one of the underpinning themes is how passionate many who work in small companies are about what they do. Really passionate.

Some of you could go and get jobs in bigger companies, or have already had them. But actually, what you want is only achievable by starting your own small venture. And one of the hidden strengths of this venture will be the passion you bring to the table.

Don't ever underestimate what a powerful tool for business passion is. Facebook was started because Mark Zuckerberg, its founder, was passionate. The same with the team at Apple. What other brands – big and small – make you feel they are passionate about what they do? And deliver on it?

Ask yourself what role passion plays in your business. Ask what it can bring to clients. How can you make your passion felt, seen, heard? Just talking about it can inspire others. But just **saying** you are passionate isn't enough – you have to show it, do it.

Who wants a partner in their life who professes to be passionate, but then is cool, off-hand, uncaring? Certainly not me!

And if it's not there – why not? Perhaps you have been running your company for a while, falling out of love with it during the day-to-day grind. Well, if you have fallen out of love with it, you can be sure your staff, your clients and your suppliers will all have noticed. So you need to ask whether you still want to be doing this, or would you really rather be doing something else?

SWOT analysis: The best and the worst...

Strengths, Weaknesses, Opportunities, Threats – a SWOT analysis is a great way of understanding your business's potential 'place' in the market. It forms one of the core planks of a business plan and is used widely.

Because a SWOT analysis functions on many levels, it can also be drawn up around a product, or you can do a SWOT analysis on a service you provide. It doesn't have to be about the whole company.

However, most companies don't draw up their SWOT analysis widely enough – particularly small companies

case study

FALLING BACK IN LOVE

The founders of a small video content platform targeted at a very specific market had fallen out of love with their business. The two partners had done extraordinary things in just 18 months. They had learned how to build a platform, had produced a wealth of material for their market and were selling it to both schools and individuals. They had even brought on a very well-known investor to help their growth.

But in talking about the breadth and depth of their achievements, tears slid down the face of the managing director. The hard work had taken its toll, they weren't bringing in the revenue they had anticipated, their investor was getting antsy and worst of all, they felt they had lost the passion that had got them this far.

Standing back and looking at their achievements, we assessed the position.

The content was fantastic, a real market leader. The platform was well designed and robust. The finances were shaky due to the lower take-up – revenue generation and market-building frequently take a lot longer than many organisations realise. And they were both exhausted. But underneath, they really loved and cared about what they had done.

We knew we had to come up with new ways to utilise the content, find other ways to earn money for it – and fast. We used the SPICK model (see page 55) one afternoon. And there, sitting in one of the columns, was a golden opportunity just waiting for exploitation.

At that point, knowing there was a future for their business, it was time for one of the directors to take a holiday. Just a week away, somewhere hot. She returned, eyes sparkling, with a plan for the new idea in place. She had always been passionate about her business, but she had just fallen back in love with it.

who are reliant on their founders and a small leadership team. If you only focus on factors within the business for your strengths and weaknesses, you will build self-limiting factors into the plan.

By widening the remit and delving into the background of your team, their past experiences, clients and roles, it is then that the real strengths begin to emerge. Too often, SWOTs are only about the recent past, and overlook the riches to be found in the earlier careers of the founders, or in the early stories of the products you offer.

Quick tip...

Remember: Strengths and weaknesses come from inside a company, your supply chain, customer base, team, products. Build your business *only* on your strengths, while acknowledging and addressing any weaknesses.

Opportunities and threats are to be found in the market in which you are operating. They are external factors that can provide you with a fertile landscape or produce worrying competitive factors.

Valuing your skills

Working with companies across a wide sector, it often amazes me how both individuals and companies undervalue their own skills and knowledge. Yes, really.

Founders, directors and managers often have far higher levels of skill in certain areas than their clients, yet their clients still believe that they know more and demand ways of working that waste that knowledge. The old saying 'Why keep a dog and bark yourself?' springs to mind.

A client company will invariably know more about its own business than you do. Understandably. But that client is working with you because you are an expert in **your** field, you have levels of skill in an area they don't, or you have a vision/offer a service they want to harness. It is vital you recognise why they are coming to you – look at their motivations and ensure you are seen as an equal partner in the deal.

I do realise that in supply chains where price is an important factor in decision-making, this can be hard. So 'adding value' becomes crucial, otherwise you get involved in the dreaded 'race to the bottom' on price.

If you drew up your business plan as shown in the last chapter, various parts of it can be used in different ways – we will come back to all these unique elements repeatedly the whole way through this workbook.

Growing Your Business

11. Strengths

S If your team has put its heart or soul into this process this bit should be rich or diverse. p35

12. Weaknesses

W These emerge through discussion or interpretation but can be hard to see. p36

13. Opportunities

O Really look in depth at the market and trends to see where you can spot new areas that are growing. p37

14. Threats

T Don't, don't, don't under-estimate where threats can come from. p39

15. Your Vision(s)

What do you want your company to be?

16. Your USP

What will you be famous for?

These feed into Your Vision & USP

You can affect 4 aspects of your business moving forward – each is covered by a section in this book.

Book Section 1: What You Sell

Book Section 2: Value & Finances

Book Section 3: Your People

Book Section 4: Your Markets

Four controllable factors

The four business factors you can influence

Take a long look at the plan you have just drawn up ... Are you happy with it? If not, don't hesitate to think through how you'd like to change it, and why.

However, there is one really important point to bear in mind. **You cannot change any of the 'External' parts of the plan – at the moment.**

The 'External' part of the plan is the world you inhabit. The market, the competition, the place that creates opportunities and threats for your business. You have no ability whatsoever to control that. Period.

However, you can affect 'Internal' aspects of your business.

The 'Internal' half is about your **past** (which you can use, but can't change), your **present** (which you are in, so provides the springboard) and your **future** – which is yours for the making. And you **do** have the ability to change a whole raft of factors about **your** business – and in some cases this can lead to changes in the marketplace itself. Think how Facebook totally changed the market.

There are **four** key parts of your business you can adapt, change or just tweak. I've pulled together a section on each as, individually or together, they can impact what you do, your customer base, what trends and markets you map against, in a variety of ways.

Each section has some tools, some case studies, some ideas, some tips. Use them just as you would the sliders on a mixing deck, or the ingredients in a cupboard. Some will be right for you, others not. It's a real pick'n'mix, but pretty much all of them are easy to implement.

So the four factors you can affect in your business are:

1 What you sell – whether that's a product, a service or whatever.

2 Your value, how you charge and everything to do with money.

3 The people you engage with... these will be your staff, your friends, suppliers, as well as past/present clients.

4 How you market yourself to the outside world.

At the end of each section, I've asked you to write some **GOALS** for you to achieve.

Choose to go through these sections in any order you want. If you feel that your business could do with some new ideas around what you sell, head for that section. Or perhaps you'd like some fresh ways of charging – there are 50+ in the money section. Just bite off the bits you want, that float your boat, or that might be right for the meeting you are about to head into. Or photocopy a paragraph to give to the team at a Friday afternoon brainstorm. Ask a client or two what they think...

case study

PODSTORE

Mark Glanville has been running Pod Packaging for a number of years when we sat down to draw up the business plan you've seen mapped out over the last few pages. Talking at length about his 'journey to here', he explained that he'd worked as a photographer, as a map maker, as a sales director to packaging print companies liaising closely with design companies. Yet he didn't seem to view himself as a creative person, more a businessman.

His current venture, Pod Packaging, supplies promotional giftware to large scale distributors, who work for the end client companies such as Google or Virgin. Pod's particular speciality was supplying lightweight aluminium corporate gifts, such as water bottles, or small pots for desktop gardens. Mark was interested in how to develop a business growth plan.

As we talked about his company, it became increasingly clear that Mark was passionate about the green credentials of the recycled aluminium that made up the bulk of his stock. He knew so much about it, understood its merits and worked closely with his suppliers, often visiting their factories.

In between our meetings, the image of the turtle with a plastic straw piercing its nose from a BBC documentary went viral. The clamour to move towards the elimination of single use plastics grew. When Mark and I next met, as we looked at the various recycled aluminium bottles he'd put on the table, we realised with a palpable sense of excitement that we were holding the answer to replacing plastic in some areas.

Just six months after our first meeting together, Mark launched PodStore, an online shop aimed at conscious consumers who want 'sustainability with style'. Stocking eco-friendly, recycled and recyclable products, Mark worked with leading global pattern design team, Patternity, to apply their recognisable patterns to the launch range – small refillable bottles that can be used when travelling. And this is just the start... with lots more eco-friendly products to come.

https://podstore.net

WHAT YOU SELL

When you think about what you sell – it's pretty obvious. You might sell your time, you might sell books, you might sell expertise, or access to an event. There are millions of individuals and businesses across the globe, all selling in countless ways.

Adapting what you sell is a key way of growing your business – obviously. You can add versions of what you sell, or make it more cheaply or sell it for a higher price. You can be really good, a market leader, selling only one thing or a variety of things. All of these are just fine.

Just as you can alter who you employ and what roles they fulfil, you can also alter what you sell to your clients and customers. And what markets you are in.

You may well have invested in machinery, plant, premises or other big-ticket items, but there are **always** ways you can find new markets and revenue streams.

Each business's 'offering', or 'offer', can be unpacked in all sorts of ways to help you grow – whatever that means to you. This section of the book looks at how you can do this – no matter what you do – in order to find growth in surprising ways.

Play with some of the ideas you'll find here. There is no hard-and-fast rule about which one will work for you, but they are intended to start you thinking in inventive ways. Business growth isn't always linear – there may be something hidden somewhere in your way of working that could prove to be next year's top revenue earner. But until you look, explore, you won't know...

I've also included a big section about intellectual assets and intellectual property (IP). Everybody switches off when you mention this area as it seems complex. But if you are running a business – whether you are self-employed or have 250 employees – you need to know about it, as it under-pins what you sell.

> **Play with some of the ideas you'll find here. There is no hard-and-fast rule about which one will work for you, but they are intended to start you thinking in inventive ways.**

What are you really selling?

Do you really understand what it is you are actually selling?

This seems obvious – of course you do. But when was the last time you asked yourself this question? Or asked your customers?

If you run a picture-framing business, you sell mounts, frames and glass in a range of different colours and styles. But you are also 'selling' a way to enhance memories, protect the precious things in a person's or family's life, or adding to the interior style of their home.

In the next few customer engagements, look closely at why each of those people is buying from you... The reason could prompt a new service or provide a way of talking about your business that could generate growth. And it will cost you nothing.

WHAT DO YOUR CLIENTS WANT FROM THEIR 'CONVERSATION' WITH YOU?

Some organisations need have little conversation with their customers – for example, if you go into a supermarket, newsagent or other retail outlet, you can buy what you need without having any interaction with the seller whatsoever.

But there are many other companies that really have to understand what their customer needs before any form of engagement or transaction takes place.

For example, if you run a plumbing business, it is crucial that you have a clear vision of your customer's lifestyle, their family size, their fuel supply, etc., before you think about what water or heating system you are fitting or adapting. So the conversation you have with them will be about the benefits your work will bring them, rather than the detail of the joints and pipe lengths.

case study

SMITH'S GYM

Smith runs a small local gym. It is populated with the normal range of equipment, which his customers can use on a drop-in basis or through a structured personalised training programme he develops for individuals. He is well known locally for resolving biomechanical issues and getting you fit, really fit.

At the start of every new client engagement, Smith asks them to complete a questionnaire. This includes the normal health and fitness range, but at the bottom he has added a simple final question: 'What are you hoping to achieve through working with me?' There's plenty of space for an answer. Sometimes one or two obvious words are completed – 'strength', 'fitness'. However, at other times answers are longer, deeper and much more personal. Smith is tapping into the fundamental reasons clients are working with him, and allowing them space to unpack those reasons.

One woman wanted to be able to have the composure and strength to physically dominate any room she entered. On asking more about this unusual request, Smith learned she was launching a new business, which would require working with male-dominated company boards and speaking at big industry events. She needed to be able to 'own the room' quickly and effectively. Now he knew the real reason behind her work with him, he structured a really tight, hard programme that gave her poise, strength, centredness and balance.

He also realised there was scope to add new 'business-focused' services to his gym's offer, rather than just talking about fitness training.

Quick tip... Allow room to explore fully the reasons why your clients are looking to engage you – either in a simple questionnaire, or by spending time talking to them about what issues they are looking to resolve. It may be that what they then go on to buy from you is rather different from what was on their original 'shopping list'.

And remember to go back to your existing clients regularly to ask them how they are getting on, if new needs have come up or whether there are other ways you can help.

It is unlikely in any case that a plumbing company's customers will understand the trade terminology used by the company. Not because they are obtuse or stupid, but the plumbers work in their field 100% of the time so know the vocabulary – whereas their customers don't.

So ensure you really understand what **your** clients are looking for. What are the benefits you sell?

Of course, there could be less obvious reasons for engaging you. It might be that you are fulfilling a particular step in their business growth, their personal goals, but it is important to understand and unpack what motivates and underpins the discussion.

Why your passions, skill and talents really matter

I've written about passion elsewhere in this book (see Let's talk about... on page 43) – it's a recurring theme because, no matter what you do, you need to approach it with profound care and an intention to deliver. You can always tell those businesses where passion is not at the heart of what they do and how they work.

So have a think about which companies or brands really engage you when you buy from them or work with them. What is it that inspires you about them? Makes you want to come back repeatedly, work with them more closely? Encourages you to choose them over anyone else? Does what you sell – your product or service – encompass this and show your passion off to best advantage?

If passion is driving a business, to be frank it doesn't matter whether that business's offer is big or relatively small. The employees love it, they pour their passion into it. But you can't just start a company on passion – to make it deliver, grow and survive, you have to have a skilled team turning that passion into actions. And then there is the talent, that sparkling pixie dust that really marks out one business from another.

Although these three – passion, skill and talent – seem such 'soft' ingredients to a business, they are the reasons we buy.

So if you didn't do the 'passions, skills and talents' breakdown from the business plan section, have a go at it now. By itself. Do it in detail about you, about your team. Are you bringing all of those passions, skills and talents into your business – and can your clients feel and see them?

Don't sell 'products' to a customer, sell the 'benefits' they will gain and how this will make them feel

SPICK + Span: An easy way to look for new things to sell

This acronym is one I invented to help you understand that, although your business may do one thing, you could have all sorts of other areas of knowledge or intel/data that can create further income streams for you.

SPICK stands for the five things that people pay or are paid for:

- Services
- Products
- Intel/data
- Clients/Customers
- Knowledge.

It may be that your business is already earning money in more than one of these areas, but why waste an opportunity to find other revenue streams that could reduce your reliance on a single revenue model or major client? In all the years I've used this breakdown, there hasn't been a single company I've known that hasn't been able to find **at least** one new way of growing and earning complementary revenue using this model.

So let's go through each one to ensure it's clear, and then use the diagram overleaf to help generate ideas.

SERVICES

When people are paid for a service, they are either selling their time or an outcome.

So you might be running a taxi business, a branding company or are paid to fix mobile phones. The way you charge will depend on your level of skill, the complexity of the project and other factors such as your reputation. Generally, payment is made after the 'service' has taken place.

PRODUCTS

We are all familiar with the idea of a product. It could be a pair of shoes, a cabbage or a car. Mostly, a company produces a product upfront and you pay for it before you get access to it or when it is yours to use. I also include events under the 'product' heading, as someone has to prepare it before you participate.

INTEL/DATA

This way of earning revenue has become much more prevalent recently, with the rise of the internet. Companies earn revenues through selling the way their subscribers **behave**, their activities, their potential activities or the insight this behavioural understanding gives.

For example, the Tesco Clubcard gives the company data on how their shoppers behave, what they purchase, their frequency of product purchase, their predilection for utilising offers, and it also allows them to interpret what customers might be in the market for next. This is of value to manufacturers looking to market a new product or the like.

While most of us small company owners may not think we have much intel/data, it is really surprising, when you unravel it from the other areas of what you sell, just how much data there is for you to use or to drive new revenues from.

CLIENTS/CUSTOMERS

Most businesses are familiar with buying a mailing list – someone earning revenue from someone else's client/customer list. The value of it is likely to be determined by the quality, the quantity and how you access it.

A blog that earns its creator substantial revenues is really about 'selling' access to the blogger's followers to other companies.

KNOWLEDGE

Most of us sell knowledge in some way or other, but it can be wrapped up in a service. A newsfeed, an online university course and a coaching programme can all be tucked under this heading.

HOW TO GET STARTED

You can either draw this diagram big on the wall, or use an A4 piece of paper, but it is much better drawn than just using a computer spreadsheet. It activates other ways of thinking. Similar to the business plan, doing it with a others makes it easier and also more fun.

1 Create five columns, as per the above diagram.

2 Write the name of whichever SPICK model you earn most revenue from at the top of the left-hand column. So if you sell a product, put 'Product' at the top of that column. If you run a dental practice,

put 'Service' at the top of the column.

Then, taking the four other SPICK models, write one at the top of each remaining column (the Span bit of the name!). See below for an example.

For the purposes of this diagram, I am using my business – so I have put 'Service' at the top of that left-hand column.

Service	Clients/customers	Products	Knowledge	Intel/data

Service	Clients/customers	Products	Knowledge	Intel/data
business growth coaching	– SMEs – owner/manager	Book? ↑ ‎	– wide understanding of _different types of biz_ – how to spot & remedy – seeing through their |potential| – making change happen – inspiring leaders of teams	– triggers for _contact_ in |IP issues| Talks? ↗

ways to earn more revenues →

3 Now what you have to do is write just **one** of the products you sell, the services you offer, or the knowledge you earn money from in that left-hand column.

I've put 'business growth coaching' in my starting column.

4 Focus only on this one aspect of your business, and start to really pull it apart. You will find that you can start listing various aspects that contribute to it under the other different headings.

So in order to offer 'business growth coaching' as a service, the 'Knowledge' I need to have includes:

• a wide understanding of different types of business
• how to spot and remedy underperformance
• how to identify trends and their potential
• ways of making change happen
• how to inspire leaders and their teams.

I'm also aware of the key triggers that direct company owners to get in touch with me, so those go into my 'Intel/data' column.

Do this across all the columns that you can for your company. Don't worry if some of the columns are empty – that's fine.

5 When you have exhausted the elements of the first product or service you have unpacked, take a fresh sheet and move on to the next thing you sell, and do exactly the same again, going on as long as you want. If you feel it would be helpful to get other members of your team to add to your sheets, pass them round.

6 When you've decided you've done enough, take a highlighter pen and work your way through **every single entry in every column**. Ask yourself or your team whether there is a nugget of gold in it. Can you take this behavioural data, this piece of knowledge, this client list and turn it into a new revenue stream? Either for your existing customers, or for a completely new market?

Be inventive and play with the ideas. Think of what will be happening in the marketplace in two years' time. Look at the 'trends' list that emerged if you did the business plan drawing. If you sell your knowledge now – can you turn this into a product later?

There are lots of great examples around of how other companies have done this – big and small. One of my favourites was the car part distribution company Unipart. They delivered car spares to large and small repair garages and mechanics across the UK, either the same or next day. Using their knowledge of getting parts sourced and delivered on time, they launched a logistics planning consultancy... Obvious, really.

But you don't have to be big to do this. You can be small and inventive. Look for easy wins that can slot in to your existing business with ease. Longer-term, big plans will take time to grow and mature, so will need you to allocate resources and time.

In my chart, I identified that I could harness the knowledge I have of business growth to produce a product to sell... the book you're now working with.

Talk about some of the new ideas and see which ones will have traction. Work out a plan as to how much work each one might take to come to fruition, what investment is needed, who are the likely customers are and whether there are enough of them. Just because you've come up with some cracking ideas doesn't mean that you can afford to ignore all the other factors around them. You will need to really explore these carefully, but this process can certainly provide you with a springboard to fresh ideas.

Don't under-estimate your knowledge – if you make a product, you will have a deep knowledge of materials, your supply chain and distribution

case study

Vicki owns barre exercise studio Barreworks in Richmond, the UK's original dedicated barre and ballet workout studio. She has been teaching barre training for around ten years and was looking to see how to develop the business.

Most companies in the fitness industry look to opening more outlets using the same model to widen their customer base. However, after some reflection, Vicki decided that running a portfolio of studios would simply follow the industry 'norm', and crucially dilute what was so special about Barreworks – namely, the personal attention clients receive from her and her team. Having developed Barreworks' programme from scratch, and with a maverick attitude to building her business, the last thing she wanted to be was a manager of several outlets, or to blindly follow the competition. She also felt that if the Regent Street store Liberty & Co. was able to trade for many decades with one single flagship outlet (and become a destination) then she must be able to come up with something similar.

After a couple of coaching sessions, I asked Vicki to draw up her own SPICK diagram. She struggled with it, but then between us we got into the flow. When

Process mapping: New revenues from how you work now?

Despite several similarities, most small businesses work in myriad ways.

They find clients in their own way. They engage with people through processes they've developed themselves. They run their relationships with their customers in whatever way best suits them and their business.

But what I find intriguing is that, despite all these differences, when you unpick the 'paths' that a client takes in their relationship with a business, there are frequently areas where the business owner could find new 'value'. These paths, or 'customer journeys', are a great place to look for pointers to give you a new service to offer or product to sell.

One of the easiest ways to do this is to map the actual process route that a customer takes through your business. (I will look at **how** customers find you under marketing – this idea is about their route once they are engaged with you.)

● To start with, just take a piece of paper and plot a **map** of the whole process –

we listed out her clients, they included ex-Royal Ballet dancers, professional polo players, triathletes and rugby players – and a gold-medal-winning Olympic team and their physio. Impressive! Her knowledge included the development of her unique training programme, which was just about to secure CPD accreditation and was attracting a number of ex-professional dancers keen to develop their skills. And one other point in the table caught my eye – a number of local physiotherapy clinics sent their recovering clients to Barreworks to strengthen joints and help regain movement.

As we talked, it became clear that Barreworks could add new consultancy services to its current offer, targeting specific new groups with well-thought-out adaptations of the existing barre training programme. Barreworks for Physio, Barreworks for Elite Sports and other programmes are now in the pipeline – all of which will be industry accredited.

www.barreworks.co.uk

Barreworks

Ballet barre-based exercise

from the 'hello' moment to the time they say 'thank you and goodbye'.

It will be different for each type of business – whether you are an online store, a florist shop and delivery service, or someone who sells your time as a service, such as an accountant or lawyer.

What you are looking to do is to see **where**, **when**, **how** and **who** in your business engages with your customer, to ask the question **why** and then understand **how** you can make it more effective and more profitable for you. This doesn't necessarily mean you charge the customer more – it could be

something simple like registering their name, email address and phone number so you can make contact with them if you have a spare appointment to fill up your less busy times.

Depending on your business, you may have several routes, but take each one. A good way to do this is to look back at some of your key customers and projects over the last year or so. Is there any way you could have improved this? Or is there another service you could offer them along the way? Are you giving something away to them, when in fact you could charge them for it?

Quick tip... If you work in the service industries, selling your time, often the first part of a project is doing a raft of research before you can actually get cracking. When you quote for the job, ensure you allow a fee for this time. Although it is research and may well involve 'thinking time', it is time being focused on that particular client and should therefore be part of the budget. Any actual development work can then be done as part of the next stage.

case study

JAKE EASTHAM PHOTOGRAPHY

Jake Eastham is a professional photographer capturing images of country life for clients such as Land Rover, Barbour and Mulberry. His wife, Lou, worked with him for years. A delightful, laughing person, she frequently went on shoots with him, or organised them at their restored Wiltshire cottage. As we talked about how work came in and flowed through the business, she made a passing comment about how she often had to raid the local shop to pick up props, or her garden for flowers. It soon became apparent that Lou was in fact acting as a stylist for Jake's clients. And doing it brilliantly. So there and then they made the decision to charge out Lou's time on projects that require additional input for styling and set dressing. Not only did it bring in more money, but it gave Lou a real stake in the business.

www.jakeeastham.co.uk

JAKE EASTHAM
PHOTOGRAPHER

case study

BUSINESS MANAGEMENT PROCESS

With another client, my client and I decided to focus on mapping their clients' journeys as a project evolved. One of the real headaches for the agency was that they had agreed to report back to the client every single month. Fine when you are handling a few clients, but when there are 20 or so, it becomes hugely disruptive for the workflow. We also became aware that sometimes the online reports weren't even opened by the clients for several months in succession.

There had to be a way to work smarter. We looked at our process map very carefully and identified a big potential 'win'.

All new clients were given a quarterly (not monthly) report, each of which focused on very different aspects of the client/agency relationship.

Report 1: 3 months: This focused on the agency's research findings about the client's digital profile, based on what they had inherited from their previous digital marketing team.

Report 2: 6 months: This was to show how the activities of the agency had started to really deliver against the brief.

Report 3: 9 months: This was the report where we really shifted the thinking...

Being paid on a monthly retainer agreed annually, the agency found it hard to plan ahead as each client approached the latter part of the contractual year. It was hard to get clients to focus on signing up for the year ahead. So we decided to change the nine month report into a big review meeting.

By the time the client arrived for the review meeting, the agency had already prepared a raft of new ideas for the business – including intriguing suggestions for joint products/services they could offer, ways of generating new audiences and revenues.

Invariably, following this highly proactive nine month review meeting, the agency had its next year's retainer confirmed.

Report 4: 12 months: This just became a confirmatory round-up of the performance against the year's key performance indicators (KPIs, see page 272) and setting new ones for the following year.

So in a really simple mapping process we had improved their client wins and also their client retention. It was all there in their processes the whole time!

case study

I was working with a small digital agency when we process-mapped their clients' 'journey' through the company.

One of the first points they raised was that during the credentials presentation, some potential clients were offered a comprehensive social media audit. They could pay a (relatively) small sum for the audit, which didn't commit them to any longer-term relationship with the agency. They were still free to place their business whereever they chose.

The mapping process illustrated that about 30% of the potential client companies took up the offer of the audit – a good level. But the process then showed that of this 30%, **every single one of them**, pretty much 100%, then became clients immediately or some months after the audit...

Yes, of course one could speculate that they were more likely to become clients anyway. But this was disproved by one or two of them initially appointing other agencies before returning to my client, who had ready proven capabilities through a simple audit system.

What was surprising was that not all potential clients were offered this effective business winner... So steps were then taken to ensure that it became regular practice.

'Hidden' expertise

This is a jaw-droppingly simple way of finding new ways to earn revenues from your business...

• Go back to the 'Clients' list you did when you drew up your business plan. If you missed that bit, you can find the instructions on page 27.

• Stick the list up big on the wall and stand well back. Ask a colleague or two to join you. Anyone that can look at it with fresh eyes.

• Taking a variety of coloured pens, highlight the clients from anywhere on the list that have any form of similarity or connection, no matter whose they were or even if they were from years past.

These might include areas of expertise such as transport, or statistical analysis, or even working with heritage locations. Perhaps coaching/mentoring experience is involved. Just find out all of those overlaps between the clients on the list – sometimes they are wonderfully obvious, other times less so. But believe you me, there will be overlaps.

• The exciting thing about doing this is that all of this capability is already in your company. So now all you have to do is to see whether you can turn each connection, similarity or expertise grouping into a new service or product!

Underused expertise

This is just as ridiculously easy as the above idea...

• First list all the clients you are working with now, are about to work with or have potential to work with in the next few months.

• Now go to the list on your business plan, where you detailed all the things you and your team have **ever** been **paid to do**. (If you didn't write that list, get to it now by following the instructions on pages 27.)

• Go through that 'Paid to do' list carefully. These are all the capabilities you/your team have and have earned money from in the past. Highlight those that are in alignment with your existing business.

• Now ask: How can you offer this range of in-house expertise to your list of clients?

Not all will be right for every client, but some will be a valuable offer and can bring in useful new revenues. They could also build a new arm to your business, spreading its capabilities wider and improving commercial resilience.

The easiest way to do this is to draw up a grid, with chargeable 'Capabilities' along the top and your clients listed

	Capability 1	Capability 2	Capability 3	Capability 4	Capability 5
Client 1	★	★	★	n/a	★
Client 2	★	★	★	★	n/a
Client 3	★	★	Next year	n/a	★
Client 4	n/a	★	n/a	n/a	★
Client 5	n/a	n/a	n/a	★	n/a
Client 6	n/a	Next year	★	n/a	★

down the side. Just tick the box if there's a match!

Of course, what emerges may not prove right for your business now – but if there is an unusable opportunity, do you know someone else who might be able to pick it up? (And could you possibly earn a concept or introduction fee?

Linked thinking

When you work across a wide range of clients, it is fascinating how many of them start talking about the same area of concern, opportunity or way of working within just a few days of each other. It feels as if they've all picked up on the same prompt, been reading the same paper, or have identified exactly the same new trend to benefit their business... even if they are in totally different worlds. It can feel a little bizarre – as if they've all been talking to each other behind your back!

If this happens to you, it can be a very neat way to think through how you could potentially apply this thinking to other clients. Because if three or four of your clients are picking up on it – sure as eggs are eggs, others will be too.

You could bring them all together for a mini conference to address their concerns. Or if the issue addresses a pinch point, find a team to solve it and offer the solution to all your other clients.

It doesn't have to be a complex new product or service – this is about hitting that moment in time when something is on everyone's radar.

Selling to your competitors

Hah! Someone once told me that this was the most bizarre suggestion I'd ever made to them. And asked me: 'Why would I want to sell to my competitors?'

Let's get one thing clear – you are probably **not** going to be selling marketing advice to them, or something that will put them ahead of you on your current playing field. But suppose you have a pinch point in your business, your industry, that pretty much every other operator is also likely to have... if you solve that problem for yourself, there is the potential for you to sell that solution to them too.

This next case study illustrates a good example.

case study

MASS PARTICIPATION EVENT MANAGEMENT

Working with a small company who helps stage and manage mass participation events, we were reviewing their SPICK diagram that we'd just spent two hours completing.

What became clear was just how much knowledge the company director had to have in order to fulfil his role on each project. But also how he had to keep teams of people informed, whether that was local councils, marshalls, health and safety support, volunteers, participants, friends and family, etc. – many of whom had limited experience of running or attending this type of event.

As we talked about this depth of knowledge, we realised that there was a rich opportunity to develop an online health and safety portal for all of these different roles for each event. Setting up the portal would be a big one-off cost, but it would be devised so that it could be used for lots of events under different organisers, and would include all the info they needed. There could be a unique log-in system depending on your role or participation level for each event, linking to the appropriate online H&S training and other information you needed, such as maps, road closures, safety instructions, parking directions, post-event care, etc.

And of course, not only would this online portal have immense value to him in his day-to-day work, but he could sell the service/access to his competitors, as it was something of real use and value to them too.

This was an offer very similar to one the BBC runs for independent production companies. Once you have signed a programme-making contract with the BBC, your team has to do an online health and safety training course (for which you pay) to gain the appropriate certification, which is then linked to your production.

What industry knowledge sits in your business that you could offer to your competitors to enhance your own business?

Intellectual property – and why it matters...

Depending on what the nature of your business is, IP will mean different things. Many different things. But across the spectrum it can – in some way or other – help you to generate more revenues for your business and, equally importantly, mean you can defend yourself against aggressive competitors. It doesn't matter whether you are a freelancer, a partnership, a company, a start-up, a medium size or even multinational: IP is important.

There is research saying that 80% of the value of a start-up can sit in its IP as part of its intangible assets. And we've all watched the BBC TV show *Dragon's Den*, where the 'dragons' ask about what IP is owned by a company – they know a company's IP needs to be secure to

ensure the company can be grown.

IP can also really affect both **what** you sell and **how** you sell it, which is why it's in this section of the book.

Most people think IP is complicated... Yes, sure, if your product is complicated, the IP can be too, but for most of us, understanding and ensuring IP is secure is relatively simple.

DEFINITION OF IP

For a good definition of IP, let's take a look at the World Intellectual Property Office (WIPO) definition displayed opposite: it states unequivocally how you – as the creator – should be able to profit from what you create.

Because I do a lot of work with creative people and their companies, I love this definition and frequently use it in talks I give, whether at Google Campus, at the Design Business Association, or to a group of companies in Beirut. When I tell them that the World Intellectual Property Office recognises their creativity, everyone sits up a bit straighter, acknowledges with pride what it is they do, and sees that IP is not a dull, legal necessity, but a rich world just waiting for their input. Sexy – yes. Fulfilling – yes. Rewarding – definitely.

But it's not just creative companies that own and can benefit from IP – as I've mentioned above, **all** companies own IP. The pages that follow tell you how to understand what you own and

'Intellectual property (IP) refers to creations of the mind such as inventions; literary and artistic works; designs; and symbols, names and images used in commerce.

IP is protected in law by, for example, copyright, trademarks and patents, which enable people to earn recognition or financial benefit from what they invent or create. By striking the right balance between the interests of innovators and the wider public interest, the IP system aims to foster an environment in which creativity and innovation can flourish.' World Intellectual Property Office (WIPO)

use it to fuel your growth.

And the ability to profit from your creation is at the heart of why IP should matter to you. Knowing that you own and can profit from what you have created – if you so choose – puts you in such a good place. No matter if you decide you want to keep your work, sell it, license it, share your creation in the spirit of Creative Commons or give it away – that should be your choice and no one else's. Don't let others make that decision for you, or force you to lose your rights.

YOU NEED TO KNOW ABOUT IP BECAUSE YOU ALREADY OWN SOME

In a book like this, there is no way I can cover all the areas of IP each type of company might own individually, but the following pages should provide you with an understanding of the fundamentals. And there are some clear steps that all businesses or freelance individuals can take to ensure they own what they create. It is up to you to adapt the ideas to your own situation.

I've tried to include some different case studies to give you a wider picture of IP, as well as tools and ways of thinking to help you, whether you are a design company, an arts organisation or involved in a totally different world. Being inventive is what we humans are good at, and while many of us spend time expending our creative energy on work for clients, now it's your turn to be inventive for yourself, for the benefit of your own company.

So why should IP matter to you?

• The key reason is that if you own intellectual property you can generate revenues from it in some way or other.
• You can protect it to stop other people or companies from passing it off as theirs, and earning revenues in your place.
• You can license it to someone else in return for royalties or a fee.
• It is an asset, so you can sell it – just like you can a property.
• You can use it to defend against competitors' activities and threats.
• It means that you can be credited as the creator.

Every single business owns some form of IP – without exception

BREAKING DOWN THE WIPO DEFINITION

It's worth repeating that WIPO definition to clarify some of the points, as these will crop up later.

Intellectual property (IP) refers to **creations of the mind** such as inventions; literary and artistic works; designs; and symbols, names and images used in commerce.

IP is **protected in law** by, for example, **copyright, trademarks and patents**, which enable people to **earn recognition or financial benefit** from what they invent or create. By striking the right balance between the interests of innovators and the wider public interest, the IP system aims to **foster an environment in which creativity and innovation can flourish**.

As you will see, I have highlighted some key phrases, so let's look at them in a bit more detail...

'creations of the mind...' When you design a pattern, illustrate or draw a picture, write a book, blog or article, develop a cartoon character, you are creating something that did not exist before. It's your original work. It is yours to do what you want with. It is this that IP rules are there to protect. But remember – you cannot protect an 'idea', only an actual thing.

Quick tip... If creativity is particularly important to you and your business, write the WIPO definition of IP up and stick it on your studio wall, your fridge, your computer, or even post it on Instagram. Then go and help your creativity flourish!

'protected in law...' Yes, that's right. What you create is protected by the law of the UK, of Europe and of the World. Some creations you need to register, others are automatic. But you are effectively protected. (Note: Some of them need to be registered before they are disclosed to the public, otherwise you lose your rights.) Should you build your business using IP, defending and proving a case in the courts is a different matter, however.

'copyright, trademarks and patents...' This list has left out design right, which is also part of IP protection – and there is more about each of these later on.

'earn recognition or financial benefit...' If creativity is the cornerstone of your business, being attributed as the author of a book, as the photographer, as an inventor or whatever is a crucial part of what you do. Whether that is just for popular acknowledgement as the writer of a blog, or the creator of a play – if it emerged from your imagination, you want it to be known as yours. And

certainly, if there is money to be made from it – that should come to you.

'foster an environment in which creativity and innovation can flourish...' This is an important, rich-sounding phrase at the end of the definition. The IP laws are there to help the things we do, the things we originate, the things we invent to 'flourish', to grow, to enrich our world. Of course, that is just how it should be – it is too sad that sometimes this gets forgotten or omitted along the way in the mayhem and greed of everyday life.

OWNING AND MANAGING IP

Owning IP is all very well. But like those old ingredients in your store cupboard that are well past their 'use by' dates, it is not worth much if you do nothing with it. IP can only really bring you rewards if you choose to make use of it.

This could involve selling it, exploiting it, or, with the vast range of platforms now online, making it available to others who can utilise it in some way – with your permission.

I own several trademarks and have a plan for each of them, which is why I registered them. In the fullness of time, when I have developed each of the plans, they will earn either recognition or financial reward, but at the moment they are sitting in my store cupboard. I've bought them but am not actively doing anything with them in the marketplace. Yet.

Although all of the companies I work with own IP, most of them don't actively manage it. Often, they don't see the value, as it may be rather old, out of favour/date or belong to a past incarnation of their company. But never ever underestimate when it might come in useful again.

On the other hand if it really is of no use, and is unlikely to be again, then make that decision and move on; don't waste money. It is important to audit your IP regularly, just like any other aspect of your business.

case study

MARKS & SPENCER

To celebrate its 100th anniversary in 1984, Marks & Spencer collected together the many historical items from all over the company to create the M&S Company Archive. Based in Leeds, the building houses M&S's clothing and graphics archive. As a member of the public, you can visit to look round; as a school, you can see how people dressed 30, 40 or 50 years ago; or – if you are Alexa Chung – you can have the freedom of roaming the archive and choosing some iconic pieces, to create a range for M&S's current customers... (Which generates the rather nice thought that in 25 years, her designs channelling the designs from the 1970s will be used to inspire other collections. A sort of 'pay it forward' model.)

Through this, M&S can repurpose fabric designs, clothing ranges, graphics for future merchandise.

Although most of us will never ever have sufficient material or the public profile to open a public archive, it is crucial not to lose or undervalue your own creative history. It can have value in surprising places.

marksintime.marksandspencer.com/home

M&S

EST. 1884

case study

LOUISE YATES

Multi-award-winning writer and illustrator of children's books Louise Yates is a perfect example of how important it is to nurture your own IP. Louise first came up with her character 'Dog' and the idea for a book just after leaving university. Discouraged by initial attempts to find a publisher, she developed her career in a different direction as a film/theatre costumier. But her belief in her original creation was undimmed. Supporting herself through part-time tutoring, she created another character and storyline, which won her an agent and publisher. When asked whether she had developed any other characters, she revealed 'Dog', her earlier creation. This became her second published book, *Dog Loves Books*, which debuted as a *New York Times* bestseller, has been made into a musical, was read on CBeebies by Dolly Parton and has been commissioned for production as an animated TV series.

All from a few sketches, ideas and etchings she'd reserved in the hope that one day they might be appreciated. www.louise-yates.com

DOG LOVES BOOKS

A brief guide to the different types of IP

....

This is a really simple guide to the four different types of IP that exist in law, namely:

- copyright
- trademarks
- registered and unregistered design rights
- patents.

In addition to the legally protectable IP detailed below, you may well own intellectual assets/capital that you can repurpose to create new IP. Yes, I know that sounds confusing... so this will be covered on pages 84–85, together with information about **trade secrets**.

Imagine your intellectual assets/capital are like the ingredients in your store cupboard. You can create all sorts of different things with them and try things out, but it is only when you cook the ingredients that they cannot be changed. This is effectively what happens to them when you protect them with a legal IP 'wrapper'.

It's easy to say that learning about IP is dull and not for you – yes, that's how IP is always seen, but you could not be more wrong. Just as learning a new app or computer program is a bit laborious,

once you 'get it' you can see how it adds to your ability to do new things. Understanding the basics of IP is pretty much the same. So make a cup of tea and get your head around the rest of this chapter. We'll be referring to these terms in other places in this book.

COPYRIGHT

I did a talk one evening at Google Campus in London to a roomful of 160–180 start-ups across all sorts of different business areas. To kick the evening off, I asked them who thought they owned any copyright... Only three people put up their hands. This really drove it home to me how little people understand this very basic IP right. Every company in that room owned some copyright works, but only three of them knew it. Scary. So read on...

- Copyright is an automatic, free right. But it can only protect what is recorded on paper, digitally or in materials (e.g. sculpture or print). In other words, what is actually made or recorded in some way. That could be a drawing, a script, a book, a design, a photograph, a model, a sculpture or a pitch document. It can be a recipe key to your food business. It can be your instructions manual. Or a blog.
- There is no register of copyright in the UK or Europe. If you create something using your own skill, not copying – you own it.

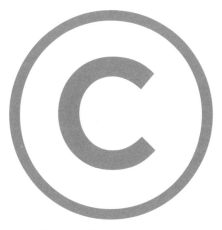

This is the copyright symbol you can use on what you originate.

- You cannot protect the concept or idea itself, it is only the physical embodiment of the idea that copyright protects, whether that is literary, dramatic, musical, artistic, film/broadcast or publishing, illustration, typographical styles or photography.

   So, for example, if you had an idea for a film, told someone about it and they went off with your idea, under European law you could not go after them for copyright infringement. However, if you showed them a script, or a printed synopsis, and you then discover that they whipped your idea, provided you can prove you had created the script first as well as shown it to them and they had copied your script, then you do have grounds for copyright infringement.

- Software, computer programmes, databases and the content of a website are also protected by copyright.

- It is a property right – the originator owns it – **unless** your contract says otherwise.

- If you create something, you should mark it with the copyright symbol, the name of the owner, and date it. You can either lodge a copy of this in your bank, or post it to yourself/your solicitor without opening it so the date stamp is proof of when it was created.

- Since 1970, any copyright you own is, in general, protected for 70 years after your death.

- The protection afforded by the copyright law means that no one **except you** can copy a substantial part, distribute copies whether for free, rent or sale, perform, adapt or put your work on the internet – without your permission.

Infringing copyright

If someone copies the work you have created, and it is substantially like your work, you can sue them for infringement of copyright.

   This means that they have taken your work and are selling it or using it in place of yours, saying it is theirs. The infringement is assessed through its various qualitative elements of copying.

Copyright and the pitching conundrum

Companies who sell their creativity and design skills often ask me how they can protect the ideas they present to potential clients during pitches. This is a really tricky area. You pitch for the work and you invest time/money in coming up with some original ideas to help you show your skills during the pitch. But then you don't actually win the business, only to see your work resurface for the client via another route some time later. Some ways you can approach this are:

1 Always refuse to do creative pitches for potential clients. Show them your thinking, not your creativity.

2 If you decide to do creative work for the pitch, never **ever** sign an agreement handing the work to them. If you do – they will then own it. Instead, show them a slide deck (or however you pitch), with absolute statements at the front that all of the work they are about to see is owned by your company. Any copying or adaptation may not occur without your express permission. Mark it all with a copyright symbol.

3 And never send through the slide deck for them to forward to 'other team members'. Ask for a meeting so you can present to them instead.

• Copyright protection starts when the work is created, and lasts for various lengths of time, depending on what it is you have created. (See the IPO website for further information: www.gov.uk/government/organisations/intellectual-property-office.)

• You can use your copyright works yourself, you can license someone else to use them, you can use them to raise finance, or you can sell them – as the owner, this is your choice. If you license works to others to use, you can register this with societies who can collect money owed to you on your behalf.

• If you create a copyright work, you also own the moral rights – these cover your right to be identified as the author, and the ability to object to how something is being performed, represented or changed.

• Your copyright is yours to defend if

you think someone is using it without permission or in a defamatory way. There is now a Copyright Tribunal run by the IPO to which collecting societies can apply if they think your copyright is being infringed.

TRADEMARKS

Somehow, trademarks seem to be understood more readily than any other form of IP. Perhaps this is coloured by the fact that we are generally familiar with concepts such as logos from brands we buy out shopping, from websites we use, etc. But a trademark can be so much more than just a registered mark.

• Trademarks are used to differentiate one company and its products and services from another's. But they can also be a really useful way of developing your own business. For example – do you have a product or service that you offer to a particular market segment that you could name, and then protect with a trademark?
• Trademarks also help stop companies 'passing off' your goods as theirs, as they ensure the goodwill and reputation you have built up stays with you and cannot be commercialised by someone else.

We all use trademarks regularly every day – for example, the icons on your smartphone are all individual company trademarks.

The key points to be aware of with trademarks are:

• They can be words, a graphic symbol, or words together with a graphic symbol, as well as a sound, colour, shape or any other 'sign' that distinguishes the services or products of one company from another.
• A trademark can be two-dimensional or three-dimensional – the tail fin designs of different airlines' jets are generally trademarked.
• A trademark should be registered. There are a number of different ways that a trademark can be registered in the UK. It can also be deceptively technical to do and an easy way to waste money without obtaining the desired protection. While you can file an application either online or via a paper submission through the Intellectual Property Office, who keep an easy-to-

This is the trademark symbol you can use on what you have already trademarked to avoid any confusion. It is particularly useful in written text.

search library of registered trademarks, it is recommended that you seek assistance from a good commercially focused attorney.

• A trademark generally lasts for 10 years once registered and can be extended ad infinitum.

• When you register a trademark, you have to decide which of 45 classes you want your trademark to be applied to. Classes 1–34 relate to goods and 35–45 relate to services. You can choose as many as you want when you first register.

Infringing trademarks

There are two types of infringement rules – 'passing off' and actual infringement.

'Passing off' protects your unregistered trademark. So if you have been trading under a name and trademark for some time, when another company comes along offering the same services in a way that may cause the public to think there's some connection or association with you – this is 'passing off'.

If your trademark has been infringed then you should seek quick legal advice, because infringing a trademark registration can be a criminal offence in the UK.

If you want to add classes later as your business develops, a new application will need to be filed. (This classification system is internationally agreed, but you can apply for a trademark in individual countries, across Europe or globally.)

• There are certain internationally recognised symbols that you can't register as a trademark or part of a trademark. These include flags, hallmarks, official symbols and other emblems, as well as the names or abbreviations of international organisations.

• Your trademark is not registerable if it is descriptive, is not sufficiently distinct, is a geographical reference, a common name, or – of course – if someone else already has it registered for the goods/ services (or similar) that you provide.

• Applying for a trademark can be relatively straightforward. The IPO website is clear and helpful, allowing you to search what has already been registered. (However, by using a trademark attorney to apply on your behalf, you will get valuable advice that can save you time and money down the line if you need to contest anything.)

I have helped lots of companies with their simple trademark applications. However, wherever complexities are involved, I always direct them to a trademark attorney.

A word of warning...

If you have a really great name for a product or service or company, ensure you register the trademark **before** you register the URL for the website; but try to do both consecutively. You can always adapt the URL slightly, whereas if you can't get the trademark, you're scuppered. You should also be aware that some unscrupulous companies monitor new applications and will file blocking URLs or trademarks to try to force you into paying them.

This has happened to me twice. Once, I lost a really fabulous name for a children's 360 brand for a TV series, with the potential to extend across platforms and through to the supermarket shelves. We had been developing an idea with a well-known global brand, who'd wanted to repurpose their content for use in new markets. One day they told me proudly they had registered the URL. I insisted they register the trademark too – and fast. To my horror, someone in the British Virgin Islands spotted they had registered the URL and took out a global trademark – pretty much the next day. Whether they thought they could leverage a purchase from the brand, I don't know. I was gutted.

The second time, it worked the other way. I had come up with an ace name for a training programme we were running, when I saw that the URL had been registered by a local design company who knew what I was doing. Hmm? Why? So rather than mess about, I went on to the IPO website to register the trademark for my programme. The design company ended up not being able to do anything with the URL because they would have infringed my trademark. So be careful out there...

Equally, just because you have registered a company name at Companies House, it does not automatically follow that you will be able to trademark the name or logo. You need to check everything in tandem. And remember – registering a company name does not give you any positive rights to that name as either a trademark or a URL.

case study

WITHOUT STUDIO

Based in Leather Lane, London, Without is a small design studio developing communication strategies and inventive creative work for well-known brands. I first met them a couple of years back, when we agreed to work together on a plan for growth.

As we explored their market and how they worked, it became obvious that their clients' end customers all had a similar attitude, behaved in a recognisable pattern and seemed to have a fair bit in common. But no one had really identified them as a homogenous group. And there was no marketing term to define them. It was an attitude of mind that linked them rather than anything else.

Without started to talk about their company's affinity with this group at their new business pitches. On seeing the success Without's actual clients were enjoying, these potential clients were keen to discuss this new group.

To protect Without's thinking, we decided to give the group a name: *Urban Adventurers™*. And we trademarked it in every class we thought appropriate, plus a few more to boot.

By owning this very clear trademark, Without is boosting their business by talking about all aspects of an urban adventurer's life, their understanding of this group and how clients can benefit from their behaviours. They are also publishing a guide to urban adventurers, available to the company's clients.

www.without.studio

DESIGN RIGHTS

Design right was developed historically as a form of industrial copyright. It protects the shape and/or appearance of something. It can be both 2D and 3D. This protection is intended to ensure no one can make, offer, put on the market, import or export copies for which you own the design right for their commercial gain.

- In the UK, unregistered design right protects your design for 10 years after it is first sold.
- A registered design can protect the design for 25 years.
- The design you do has to be new and to have its own characteristics.
- Design right protects the shape,

colours, decoration, materials and its configuration. So if you have something that can change shape (e.g. the toys Transformers, which start as a folded model that can be unfolded into something else), you need to ensure all stages of the shape change are documented, and from all sides.

• You need to be able to prove when you created a design. You should keep the original dated drawings. Alternatively, you can join ACID (Anti Copying in Design), a lobbying organisation that allows members to store their designs in their design library.

• You can also register a simple graphic design.

• You can register shape, pattern, texture, colour, materials and ornamentation – as long as they are all graphically represented.

• This can cover words, designs, letters, numerals, the shape of goods and their packaging. It *cannot* cover smells, ideas or concepts.

• The registration covers the appearance, physical shape, configuration and decoration. By registering it, you can get up to 25 years' protection, although this needs to be renewed every five years.

• To do this, it's vital that your design is new, belongs to you, isn't offensive and like trademarks, doesn't incorporate flags or other international symbols.

The main protagonist of the *Tomb Raider* video games, Lara Croft, is protected by design registration. So if you have characters or landscapes included in your creative work, you may well want to ensure they are similarly protected.

Some products are protected by both design registration and trademarks. A Mars bar, for example, has IP protected in a number of different ways. The font type is on the design register, as is the packaging colour.

Infringing design rights

As of October 2014, intentional copying of a registered design became a criminal offence – so the rip-off merchants could end up in prison.

If you think your design rights have been infringed by a third party, you can obtain an injunction (a legal restraining order) to stop them selling the goods and apply for compensation, which could include damages (to your reputation and profits), financial reparation and missed royalties, as well as paying for costs. You will need an IP attorney to help with your defence.

PATENTS

A patent protects the concept behind an idea. It can be a process, a formula, a computer programme, a system, a new use of something, or some other concept. It can take time for the patent process to go through, but your rights start from when the original application is filed. But a patent can really build value into your company if you succeed in your application.

Patents are absolutely the territory of patent attorneys. I know how to spot a potential patent – whether in data/algorithm or in a product – but when I think I may have identified one, I get a friendly patent attorney in to analyse and talk about it further. With patents, it is very important that you obtain good commercial advice and that the patent filing strategy meets your commercial needs and doesn't incur any more costs than necessary.

The key points to be aware of if you think you may want to apply for a patent for a product are as follows:

- It **has** to be new. Yes, I know that may seem obvious, but I have had clients wanting to apply for a patent to defend their approach to a product that should be covered by copyright. **NOTE:** 'new' means that it cannot have been disclosed to the public, including by you before the application is filed.
- It **has** to involve an inventive step.
- It **has** to be capable of being made/used in some kind of industry.
- The IPO website has really useful information about patents so you *must* read it if you think you may have a patent.

Useful websites

The Intellectual Property Office website has a range of tools, information and search functions as well as support to help you apply for a trademark online. The website is **www.gov.uk/government/organisations/intellectual-property-office.**

The Chartered Institute of Patent Attorneys (CIPA) is the professional body and can help you find a company or person to advise you. Their website is **www.cipa.org.uk.**

case study

In autumn 2013, I met bright, bubbly Melanie Goldsmith at a club opening. We chatted about the board game dating evenings she was launching with her partner, Emile, hosted in East London pubs. Then she offered me a fruit pastille from the plate she held.

'We make these cocktail pastilles to break the ice at our events. Don't have more than five if you're planning to drive, as we make each one with a half-shot of alcohol.' 'Like cherry liqueur chocolates?' I asked. 'No,' she replied, 'they don't have any active alcoholic content. These do. We don't know others like them.' After trying one, I gently pointed out that the sweets should be the focus of their new business rather than the dating evenings.

Over a coffee and a chat a couple of days later, it became clear the pastilles were their business. A few weeks later, their stall in Soho's Berwick Street sold out daily in the lead-up to Christmas. New year... new packaging, new website, and a new client: Harvey Nichols no less, where they were the only food product on the alcohol shelves.

Protecting what they did became crucial. Their process was new, was secret, was unique (the inventive step), and gave them a market advantage in manufacturing a product no one else offered. Shortly after, I suggested Mel talk to a patent lawyer I trusted. The firm looks after patents for the likes of Wrigleys, so I knew she would be in safe hands. And yes, as I write this, their patent application is pending and going through due process.

www.smithandsinclair.co.uk

SMITH & SINCLAIR

Gaining a basic understanding of IP isn't complicated. But it has the potential to really help you grow your business in ways that you may not have realised – so you need to get to grips with it. As I have mentioned before, the IPO website is a mine of useful information. And it is also wise to get support from a good trademark or patent attorney. Try to find one that has a strong commercial approach.

Cake: The difference between intellectual assets/ capital and IP

When I start working with companies, the term 'intellectual assets' mostly draws blank looks. What on earth am I talking about? (For the purpose of this book, I will use the term 'intellectual assets' – they are also called 'intellectual capital'.)

So what are intellectual assets? Where do you find them and how are they different from IP – intellectual property?

INTELLECTUAL ASSETS

As a company, the easiest way to understand your intellectual assets is to recognise they are *all* the elements of your business that has got it to where it is now. Everything. Pretty much

without exception.

It is the **knowledge** within your team. It is your **customer database**. It is all the factors that make up what you sell, from the **understanding of the materials** to the **machine expertise** you need to make a product. It is your ability to **create characters** and **tell stories**. It is the **animated landscape** they inhabit. It is the **processes** you have developed to deliver a service. It is the **big and small data** you map. It is the **premises** you occupy. Your **customer understanding**. Your **trade secrets**. Everything.

Imagine your company as the store cupboard in your kitchen. It is full of ingredients. Your intellectual assets are the 'ingredients' within your company.

But rather than opening a cookbook to see what recipe you want to make, using your assets is more like opening your store cupboard door to ask: 'This is what I've got, what can I make?'

In the same way you can combine your store cupboard ingredients in myriad ways to make savoury and sweet dishes, you can combine your intellectual assets to create new services or products to offer your clients. But just as we get used to making our favourite recipes with ingredients, companies rarely look at combining intellectual assets in inventive ways to find new revenue streams or additional audiences.

Look at the 'Cake' model on the next page to understand how this analogy can really be pushed further. You have the skills to be able to do this in your company. But first you need to understand and map your intellectual assets.

INTELLECTUAL PROPERTY

If the intellectual assets are the ingredients, your intellectual property is the cake, or the pie – the final dish that you have chosen to make with a selection of the ingredients. For your company, it could be an app, or a brand, or a new handbag. It could be a machine tool, a range of beauty products or handprinted scarves. Your IP rests in the finished 'thing' rather than in all the elements that go into it.

Yet it is all of these ingredients – these intellectual assets – that can help you to create new products, services, or chargeable models. They can build resilience into your business in a unique way, because only your company has those particular assets. It is for this very reason that understanding what intellectual assets you own is so important.

The other fascinating part of harnessing your intellectual assets in new ways is that individuals and small companies can be just as successful with this as big companies. In fact, because they can flex and pivot more readily, sometimes they can be **more** successful. This is partly why, in today's market, we see adaptable small 'pretenders' outmanoeuvring larger corporations.

How many usable exciting intellectual assets are hidden in your files, your past records, your way of working? Don't underestimate their value.

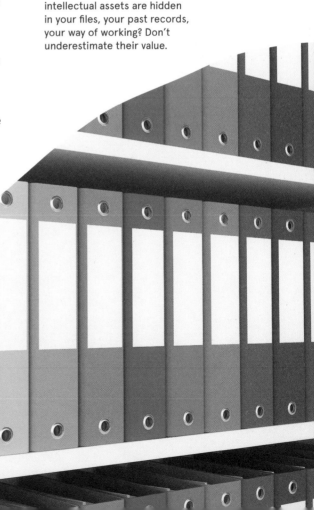

Cake

When I first started helping companies understand their intellectual assets/IP, to create more with what they owned and then exploit these assets to build greater internal resilience, many people found the notion hard to grasp. Or to explain to their teams.

So I came up with a way of showing what I meant by using cake-baking as an analogy – it is an easy way of explaining what I mean and how it can make a difference.

If you want to make a simple **Victoria sponge cake** at home, you need...
● Ingredients: 2 eggs, 250g caster sugar, 250g self-raising flour, 250g butter

But you also need...
● Know-how: baking

The cake you make is likely to appeal to...
● Target audience: family at home

It will most likely be eaten...
● Reason for consumption: teatime
● Time of consumption: let's say between 4 and 5pm

And if I put my sponge cake up for sale at the village fete, it would probably sell for...
● Value: around £2

But if you take just two of the ingredients from the sponge cake and add a little cream, you can make a plate of **meringues** or a delicious **pavlova**...

- Ingredients: 2 eggs, 250g caster sugar + added cream

You are calling on the same knowledge base...
- Know-how: baking

But the appeal of your freshly made meringues is wider than that of the cake...
- Target audience: family, friends, dinner

And also when they are consumed...
- Reason for consumption: dessert at lunchtime or dinner
- Time of consumption: there are two time frames now – 1–2.30pm and 7–10pm

And these freshly made meringues will also have increased the value...
- Value: now around £3–4

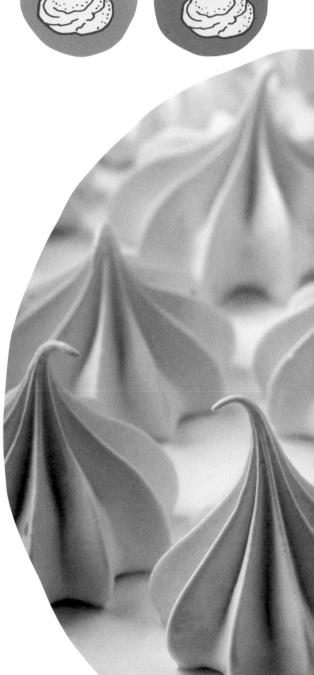

Let's go back to our basic ingredients again but just add some pretty cases and decorations to produce a box of **cupcakes**...
● Ingredients: 2 eggs, 250g caster sugar, 250g self-raising flour, 250g butter + cases + decorations

Once again you are calling on that well-practised knowledge base...
● Know-how: baking

But those eye-catching cupcakes have a completely different audience...
● Target audience: children, friends, colleagues

And also when they are consumed...
● Reason for consumption: at parties, as a gift, perhaps an office treat, impulse purchase
● Time of consumption: this will really vary, depending on why, where and who they are made/bought for

And the amount that they sell for will have risen substantially...
● Value: 8 cupcakes selling at £2 each = £16 in total

But the other element to bear in mind is that cupcakes emerged as part of a fast-growing trend following the recession, when we all wanted to go back to basics. It was a time when baking, making and repurposing really took hold. This interest also triggered TV shows like *The Great British Bake Off*.

There are times when your intellectual assets can fit with a rising trend – identifying it, then making sure you have the right offer for that growth market, means keeping your eye on the ball and being imaginative.

So far we have really just played around with our intellectual assets using our baking know-how. Most companies have a range of know-how – or skills – that they use in plying their trade each day.

But if you align your know-how with someone else's, you can get some very different and exciting results...

In 2013, a games development company, Maverick Software LLC, in the US produced a very 'simple' game called *Cupcake*. This game allowed you to create, bake and decorate a tray of cupcakes, using much of the smartphone interactivity. It was easy to use, a bit of fun, but done with wit and delight. It was hugely successful and downloaded by hundreds of thousands of smartphone owners.

- Ingredients: None
- Know-how: baking + digital app development
- Target audience: smartphone owners – particularly those with children
- Reason for consumption: fun gameplay, filling an idle moment
- Time of consumption: anytime, anywhere

Decorate the Cupcakes with Sweet Candies!

Value: the cost of the app when launched was $1.99. However, unlike our baked goods, the investment in the development will have run to many thousands of dollars. But this is a digital product so can be sold repeatedly across the globe from the app stores.

Let's go back to baking for our final example of how you can take your intellectual assets and develop them into different products and ways of working to find additional markets and revenues.

Unlike a cake, meringues or cupcakes, **pancakes** have a much wider potential audience. They can be eaten for breakfast, lunch or supper. They can be eaten as a meal, or a snack on the go. But in addition to this, they can be filled with savoury or sweet stuffings.

- Ingredients: Plain flour, milk, butter, an egg + filling or sprinkled sugar/ lemon juice
- Know-how: baking, but then...

If you know how to make pancakes, this could lead to a fast-food cart at a festival, or perhaps a small restaurant... Hospitality and management skills will need to be introduced (among many other areas) to your operating know-how.

- Target audience: could grow and vary widely
- Reason for consumption: a tasty filling meal or snack, sitting at the table or while on the go
- Time of consumption: a breakfast, lunch, tea or supper
- Value: the basic value of a pancake will probably never be high, although that can be tweaked depending on how it is served, the branding attached to it and then the way you choose to take it to its audience.

As your pancake brand develops, you could package it and offer it as a wholesale product to delis, supermarkets or other restaurants.

One of the other aspects of pancakes that I love is the traditional link of eating pancakes on Shrove Tuesday. This stems from the religious habit of using up butter, fat and eggs before Lent begins. It allows this product to tap into cultural history, but also the fact that, for some, Pancake Day was a treat day as a child. Don't underestimate how powerful this link is.

HAVING YOUR CAKE AND EATING IT

By using this analogy, I hope you can see how some of the very simplest intellectual assets or 'ingredients' can be repurposed to create new value and appeal to different audiences, and how their time of use can be extended and new markets can be found through additional know-how or tapping into emergent trends.

Sometimes, going back to the absolute basics, or lowest common denominator, can allow you to create a totally different product from the ground up.

So, looking at your own business, are there ways you can use the Cake idea to:

• take just a few of your own assets (see the next page to work out what you own) and **combine** them differently to offer a new service or product?

• make your assets valuable to other audiences at **different times** of day, months or seasons of the year?

• repackage or repurpose your assets to appeal to people in a **new venue or place**?

• take advantage of **new trends or behaviours**?

And if you feel your know-how/ knowledge base is limited, would running a hackathon and introducing **new know-how**, perhaps some **digital capability**, give you new ways to grow?

Be inventive... have fun... take your thinking a bit off the rails to see where you could go. Dream wildly. How can you push the envelope in a totally new way? What potential might you unlock?

While this may not seem a 'businesslike' way of working, just playing around with ideas and taking them to the outer limits can initiate trains of thought that just won't go away, because somewhere in that thinking could be a really smart idea. Giving it time to grow in your mind then talking it through with others could be your first steps on a new product development path.

Each business or person will have their own 'store cupboard' of intellectual assets, experiences and backgrounds which will allow them to create new products or services. Or even an exciting new career. So get planning!

How to understand what IP and intellectual assets you own

Rather than start with your assets, let's audit and list what IP you actually own.

First and foremost, don't do this sitting at your computer. Find a big sheet of paper, spread it out on the table or stick it to the wall, then set to with some big marker pens – drawing stuff up helps you access different parts of your brain. You see the bigger picture. If you can, get a team of people together to work with you. Short sharp bursts of activity are better than long heavy meetings.

Now you need to be methodical – write up headings...

- Copyright
- Trademarks
- Design Rights
- Patents

(If you have no patents, which will be the case for most companies, then don't worry about that one.)

Under each heading, list out what IP you think you own.

For me, for example, under the 'Copyright' heading I would list this book, the series of slides I use to illustrate my talks, the diagrams I use to work with clients, my workshop materials, the articles I have written, the blog posts on my website, my client and contact database, my 50+ spreadsheets of different business models used across the creative industries, etc etc.

Now do the same for 'Trademarks'.

Most companies know what trademarks they own, but interestingly enough, this exercise always shows up what trademarks they **don't** own, and others that they probably need to register. Sooner rather than later. It also reveals trademarks that they no longer use.

Continue with listing 'Design Rights' and 'Patents', if applicable. And, of

Copyright	Trademark	Design Right	Patent
Book	LOLA	n/a	n/a
Slides for talks	Intelligent Creativity		
Blog posts	Growth school		
Workshop materials			

> **One of the most important reasons to map your assets/IP, is that you realise either how much you *do* own or how much you *don't* own**

course, remember to think about whether you have any trade secrets that you need to protect through supplier or employee contracts.

As you extract all of this information, you'll probably realise you own rather more IP than you thought.

Many companies of all shapes and sizes think they own little or no IP. This will depend on how they run the business and if they understand how they can retain, develop or exploit their assets. However, it is still really critical to do this exercise – knowing how **little** you own is just as important as knowing how **much** you own, but gives you added impetus to start building assets.

This should give you a really good sense check on what IP you have or ought to ensure you secure. So if you need to take action – do it now. Sooner is better than later.

Asset unpacking model: SPICK + Span

The SPICK diagram shown on page 55 effectively helps you to map the assets your business already owns.

If you have already completed it – great stuff. However, if you have just started to look at IP/intellectual assets we will go through it again here. The diagram can really help you work out what your IP/intellectual assets are and what IP you own, and then identify the potential to develop new ways of earning money. It is simple but very effective. The more effort you put into it, the more you will get out of it.

Before we start charting your intellectual assets, let's just remind ourselves of the basic premise that underpins it.

People and companies pay for only **FIVE** things:

They pay for a **PRODUCT**... This can be a dress, a documentary, a can of paint, a cabbage, a car. Something that they can own or use.

They pay for a **SERVICE**... This can be babysitting, design, chauffeuring, accountancy, party organisation, art direction. You are exchanging your time and ability for money.

They pay for **KNOWLEDGE**... This can be a newsfeed, a university course, a coaching programme, your expertise – and is often combined with a service.

They pay for what I call **INTEL/DATA...** This is different from knowledge – it is about behavioural patterns to be found in customer purchasing habits, usage or dwell-time on your website.

And finally, what I bracket as:

CUSTOMERS/CLIENTS... This is about who your audience or your end user is. If you are a blogger with a big following, brands will pay you for your audience's eyeballs. A television station is paid by advertisers for its clients' attention during the commercial breaks. Or it could be that you sell access to your mailing list, or you bring attendees to a corporate event.

By unpicking each of these in turn across the diagram, you will start to see all the different intellectual assets that you perhaps didn't realise you do or could own.

Again – draw this up big on the wall and get your team to contribute. Diversity of thought (see page 36) really makes a difference here.

1 To start... In the left-hand column heading, write whichever of the five SPICK categories is your core business. Then add the other headings in whatever order you choose.

2 In the same left-hand column, under your core business heading, list out all the different aspects of your product, or your service.

If you are a PR company, it is likely that 'Service' will be in your left-hand column. So start detailing what service(s) customers pay you for. If you make films, 'Product' will be in that left-hand column heading.

List all the things you can think of in that column that you are paid for or to do.

Staying with the original column – unpick this further. If your product is a documentary, you will own the rushes, some photographic stills, the music. If it is an app, you will own the user interface, the build, the images.

3 Focusing on just **one** of the items in the left-hand column, move across the other columns, unpicking what knowledge you need in order to be able to provide that one item, what service its creation or provision might involve, what intel/data you have built from it or whether it has garnered you more clients.

The aim is to unpack more assets from your core business than you realised you even owned.

If you are rigorous in this exercise, for each line in the left-hand column you should have a variety of elements across the four other columns. Now the fun part begins...

Look at each of the other columns, taking each line one by one. Ask yourself who *else* might value this nugget of knowledge, or who would find this service useful? Where could this piece of behavioural intel find a new market? How can you develop your customer/client base to provide new revenues?

What will emerge is a whole new approach to understanding what there is of value in your organisation. Sometimes the realisation of just how much you actually own can be breathtaking. But the realisation is not enough by itself – you also have to come up with some smart ideas as to what you could do with all of these newly discovered assets!

Service	Clients/customers	Products	Knowledge	Intel/data

case study

FULL FAT PR

Full Fat is a leading boutique PR company attracting clients with a strong focus on contemporary culture, such as festivals, new restaurants and drink brands, with a dynamic team led by Megan Thomas and Ella McWilliam.

When Full Fat committed to unpacking their intellectual assets, they could not believe how many areas there were that could potentially be harnessed to produce new revenues.

By putting 'festival p.r.' in the left-hand 'Service' column, they started to list what 'Knowledge' they had just to deliver one of the core offerings. The list went on and on. They then looked at how they could turn just some of this knowledge into something saleable – perhaps a product or two. The two leading ideas that emerged were the continued development of a previously shelved app idea and the creation of a major industry report.

wearefullfat.com

Full Fat

case study

THE BUSINESS CREATIVE

When companies start to unpick what intellectual assets they actually own, they can overlook those they are needlessly passing across to their clients. Brighton-based design and experiential company The Business Creative produce events and entertainments for some of the world's leading leisure-centre brands. As part of their work, they were often asked to create short videos to entertain/teach children new activities and skills, supported by a trained host provided by the leisure centre itself.

These videos were only ever seen by a small audience, geo-limited to those visitors in that location. Yet these films had the potential to earn repeat revenues through being offered to a wider audience. The team realised that by repurposing the content, they could use it for other clients.

The Business Creative therefore developed iDEA (Interactive Digital Entertainment Activities), a subscription platform to deliver the latest entertainment, fitness and dance activities to hotels and restaurants, schools, gyms and leisure centres through on-demand video content, presented by leading experts

www.thebusinesscreative.com

www.ideagetactive.com

Draw up an asset map

First of all – what is an asset map? It's a list of everything your business owns. But it needs to cover **everything** – from property/premises, to your tools, your software and your vehicles, as well as your intellectual assets and IP. Use the SPICK diagram on pages 55–59 to prompt you, but listing all the 'stuff' you own around you as well adds a different perspective to this.

Write it up big on the wall. And stand back.

Are there any surprising opportunities when you look at all of this together that you haven't spotted before or have overlooked?

case study

AN ASSET DURING DARK DAYS...

A friend of mine had a small consultancy business, which entailed her driving many miles round the south-west of England to visit and support her clients. It was fun getting out and about, meeting engaging company owners and their teams. And she loved what she did. But one day – out of the blue – she had a blackout at the junction of two motorways. It was momentary – three or four seconds, apparently. Luckily she was travelling slowly and came to a halt, bumping one other car lightly. No one was hurt.

But for eight months, she was off the road while they assessed the cause and ensured there would be no repeat.

But Rachel had to continue to earn her living. After three weeks, she started to work again. But using the train network around the south-west was tricky, time-consuming and it frequently didn't go where she needed. Taxis were useful, but costly.

So between us we drew Rachel's asset map to see what other ideas we could come up with. We included her small stone cottage.

As we stood back to take a long hard look at the diagram, we realised that instead of going out to some of the small businesses she worked with, she could invite them to attend away-weekends in her home. It would be cheaper than an away-weekend at a hotel and would give them two days

For example – if your office is shut at weekends, could you run a training programme for other local companies or start-ups there on a Saturday? If you have a kitchen, could you hire it out to other food producers on your non-production days? The ideas can be delivered by you or you can bring someone else in to run them. Or you could just offer your assets for hire.

of focused company development time in a delightful non-corporate environment.

Rachel ran six weekend events during her non-driving months, and still occasionally holds business events at her tiny home. Combining a unique mix of being a personal guest, focused work, home cooking, long walks in the fresh air and her own brand of real care for the success of their companies, it has allowed her to generate revenue from her home.

How to be inventive to drive growth

I realise, in writing that title, that I've probably damned myself from the outset! But there we go...

We are all inventive – in some way or other. But often we don't recognise it in ourselves. This is partly because we value creativity in such a variety of ways and sometimes do not rate our own individual creativity to be on a scale that means much to us.

What do I mean by this?

I am not a techie. I don't invent technology products and I can't code. So on that scale, I don't perceive myself as having much creativity. However, I do understand where there are interesting ways of using tech products, or parts of them, to do new, valuable things (which someone else would have to build). On that level of inventiveness and creativity, I'm really on solid ground and love it.

So what creativity and inventiveness can you tap into to help drive growth? What skills, what outside influences can you bring to the table? Can you work with another company to help 'swap' creativity and ideas?

Quick tip... Be ENDLESSLY inquisitive. About your customers, your competitors, your market, your company, your team.

WATCH, THEN MAP THE MARKET

That sounds pretty obvious. If you want to stay in business, you have to be selling products that the market wants, anticipating its needs, movements, and areas of growth and contraction. And it is likely that it won't just be one market you are going to be watching, but maybe two, three or four. So how do you know which to use as a guiding star for developing new products and services, or where other aspects of your business might drive new revenues?

If you've already done the 'How to draw a business plan' section of this book, find the list you developed for the market part of the 'External' half.

Using two or three different highlighter pens, identify two, three or more markets that are key to your business. List them at the tops of the columns across a table.

Using the diagram below as an example, down the left axis of the table list some of the key factors impacting your market now as well as those likely to have an influence in the future. These will really differ depending on the world you work in. They could include obvious things like market size, market growth and new entrants. There will be other things like market radius, new technologies, changes in the law, health and safety updates...

key factors		Market 1	Market 2	Market 3
Market size		x x		x x
Growth potential			Example	x
Market radius		Example		
New technologies		Example	Example	
etc				
etc				
Opportunities		Massive growth Tech key	Interesting new entrants	Service potential
Assessment factors		Expensive £££	Lots to sell	Easy £: but lower revenue

Quick tip... Make it everyone's responsibility to innovate. Don't feel you always have to come up with all the right answers. Your team are just as creative as you, so get them involved.

When you are thinking about what being inventive means around the products your business sells, accept that we all have different types of creativity. Harnessing your own creativity in conjunction with that of others around you can really help you come up with new ways to originate new ideas.

If your business is just you... grab a friend you trust, go out for a walk or a coffee, find a different environment in which to talk about innovating. She helps you, you help her. Win-win.

Complete all the rows for each of the markets you are in, inserting as many factors for each in the boxes as are relevant.

Once you've done this, at the bottom of each column list any new opportunities you feel your company could really go after in each market sector, and why. If you are working with a team, ask everyone to do this separately. Each will emerge with a different set of results.

Put these in order of 'easy wins' through to 'hard to achieve', 'financially doable' to 'requires new funds'. And so on for all the other factors that will come into play.

This chart may not produce good news in one or two of your markets – they could be contracting, swamped by over-supply or just old, with your product having come to the end of its life cycle. It's vital that you identify these quickly so you can adapt your offer accordingly.

Do this map every 4–6 months. Things move fast. Windows of opportunity come and go. Sometimes there is a short burst of activity in a market you can take advantage of. Grab it, then – when it's exhausted – let it go.

Understanding that you do or could work in a variety of different markets brings all sorts of new opportunities

case study

FURNITUBES

Since the end of the Second World War, Furnitubes has been making, supplying and fitting street furniture across the UK's public spaces. With a carefully structured marketing methodology, they map construction sites that are being redeveloped to ensure they are known to as many procurement officers as possible in their target companies.

But what was becoming increasingly clear to them was the change in the way we all use public spaces. The company could see this happening, whenever the team walked round any outdoor location.

Many of us are using technology – our laptops, mobiles, tablets and other devices – out of doors. On warmer days we sit working outside, heralding yet another behavioural shift of remote working, refusing to be tied to an office. And the growth in an ageing population means there is a rising need for more seating, with the walking distances in between reduced to cater for their decreased physical ability. Meanwhile, the popularity of outdoor gyms due to the escalation in numbers of fitness-minded citizens is also having an impact.

Ensuring that they had the products to fit this changing landscape was vital. Furnitubes mapped the trends and started to actively go out to talk about them at conferences, events, and to their existing clients.

They developed two new sectors in their product offer to cater for the marketplace changes. The first was called 'Outdoor Office'™. It groups existing product ranges together with new product ranges, allowing a highly adaptable modular system designed to accommodate seating with 'desk space' in an outside or atrium environment.

The second new sector they researched extensively was how to use space more efficiently across a range of ages and needs, and what added functionality would be useful – such as charging points, additional lighting and WiFi capability. The working title for this was 'Smart Space' and involved them collaborating with companies outside their normal partnership circle.

www.furnitubes.com

LISTEN FOR WHISPERS...

The really, really early stages of a new trend don't announce themselves... they emerge from one, two and then more people changing their behaviour in some way or other. It can be through technology, economics or any other factor shifting. You just don't know.

If you want to stay abreast of what is happening (or might happen), sign up to various trend-analysing mailing lists. Most industries have them. Lots of Pinterest and Instagram pages are also about trends.

But then there are those insights underpinning an emergent trend that come to you in whispers.

OK, in the real world that's going to sound a bit *Mork & Mindy*, but if you are really tapped in to your customers, your end users and audiences, if you talk to them, watch them, read their body language, go where they go – you will see clues and small triggers. Look everywhere, listen everywhere, read everywhere.

Make sure you collect these clues before you forget them. Talk about them with your team, to your clients, to your suppliers, to see if they're reflected in their experiences.

If it looks like there's something changing, even if it is at a very early stage, think through how you can capitalise on it. How can your business use this very-early-stage trend to devise a new product or service? Or perhaps it's about reframing your existing offer in a new way, to appeal to a new market, or initiate a new use...?

HARNESS ANY TRENDS YOU FIND HIDDEN IN YOUR DATA

While you might hear whispered trends from the world outside your company, remember to look for hidden trends in the data you already have.

There may be some simple pointers in your bookings system or in how people find you. You may identify that a tiny marketing initiative had a higher conversion rate... why? Is there a new product hidden in that data set? Or does it highlight a different way people are connecting with you?

The equation is simple – you can't spot your own internal business trends unless you have data to look at. Data can be really basic – don't let the contemporary penchant for 'big data' confound you. 'Small data' interpreted well can be just as valuable to you. Use what you have. And if you are bad at collecting it, improve your collection processes. Ensure you tag data properly and that this is done consistently, otherwise you will lose or misread its secrets!

If you find it hard to spot anything, get others from your team to help you look for new patterns and threads.

case study

MEDIA DATA COMPANY

Even companies who know they have lots of data apportioned to individual clients forget that by aggregating (pooling) all the data, there may be other services they can offer. In its own silo, the data is only valuable to that client, but when you have 10 or 20 clients' data anonymously pooled, you can see other interesting and informative patterns.

I was working with a media reporting company who had many, many clients across the globe. Each client's data was in its own discrete file. But as soon as it was completely anonymised, pooled and searched in a completely different way – perhaps by country, by city or by broadcaster – this huge amount of data threw up fascinating new patterns and opportunities. Yet at no point was any company's private information being compromised. Nor were future ambitions being compromised as all the data was 1–5 years old.

This refiling of the data threw up countless new service ideas the media company could potentially offer, allowing them to build even better relationships with their clients.

WATCH YOUR CUSTOMERS

Sometimes, just chatting to or watching your clients do what they do can help you spot gaps in the market or ways of helping them that neither you nor they had realised. It's a pretty easy win.

VISIT YOUR COMPETITORS

Their shops, their websites... Learn what you can from them but then offer your customers something different that outperforms them. Not necessarily on price (no point in a race to the bottom), but by adding a service, a discount for loyalty – some form of value your customers would welcome.

And ensure you are not telling the same story as your competitors, and have some real points of difference.

PROJECT KNOWLEDGE FUNNEL

Here's a really simple diagram that you can use to generate lots of knowledge-based ideas.

We've all heard about the 'learning curve' – that steep curve of new knowledge you learn, discover, take on board when you are faced with the start of a project. It could be a skill you are trying to master, a recipe involving ingredients you haven't used before, or exploring a new city. What the knowledge funnel does is help you map what happens in that learning curve to see if it could add value to your business in some way.

When you start a new project with a new client or have initiated something internally – no matter what area you are in – you have to do some research to find out more about it. This work can be really valuable. Note it down, list the useful websites you visited, people you met, knowledge you gleaned, stats you found, potential competitors you unearthed, apps or processes you spotted.

As you start work on your project, you'll automatically discard much of what you discovered as irrelevant to that project. But it isn't irrelevant to your business, so don't waste it!

Either pass the unused discoveries to a colleague, or come back to them when you've finished your project.

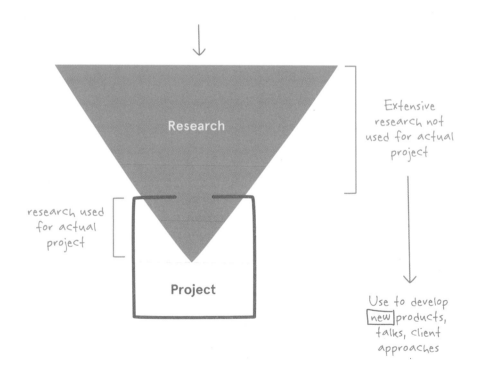

research used for actual project

Research

Extensive research not used for actual project

Project

Use to develop new products, talks, client approaches

Ask yourself where else or to whom this could have value. Could you do a talk using these findings? Could you instigate a new service at your premises? What else can you do with all this good work to increase awareness of you in the market, to allow you to approach a new market or benefit your business in some other way?

Quick tip... Be fearless. From time to time we all get one project, one client, that really pushes us. But I've learned that what matters is to just go for it. Try it out. It's good to be scared from time to time – to push your comfort zone. It stretches your capability and increases the world you could operate in. But keep it fun. Make it fast. Keep it challenging.

INNOVATION: EVOLUTION OR REVOLUTION?

Innovation is one of those words that gets bandied around so much today. We see it everywhere, hear it mentioned by organisations ranging from government departments and universities, to digital and science companies doing things way out at the cutting edge of human experience to new inventive concepts that will get us to Mars.

While those types of innovation are amazing, much of it is beyond the capability of most of us. And our businesses. But that doesn't mean that you can't innovate in your own way. Or making innovation part of your culture has many benefits in all sorts of interesting ways.

So how do you innovate? And what might this look like in your business?

First of all, let's start with the premise that innovation means you **have** to be open to new ideas, ways of doing things, seeing things. You have to have your radar switched on to the behavioural trends in your marketplace. You have to see, smell, sense or create change. There needs to be some form of new dynamic – whether instigated by you, your clients, the marketplace or what is happening in the world around you. Innovation can't happen in a static environment. It just can't. And it won't.

Most companies innovate through **evolution**. They look at existing services or products, then develop the next step from where they are now. Similar to Darwin's Theory of Evolution, there is a progression. Generally, this is the cheaper and easier way to innovate.

Use the 'How to draw a business plan' external trends (page 32) to see where there might be room for growth and trends you can take advantage of to innovate products and services. Then look at the SPICK diagram on page 55 to unpack some of the ingredients you have to work with.

What next steps could you take? Could you evolve what you're doing now to offer something different, with a competitive advantage? Where is your market going? Can you be one or two jumps ahead by evolving a product faster so that by the time the market has caught up, you have the right product in place to seize the opportunity?

You might be able to do this in-house, you might need to bring in someone to help short-term or you might need to partner with another company to help deliver. Look at all the options – weigh up the risk and the potential. Sometimes the 'not doing anything' risk can be higher than the 'do it, fail fast, redo it' if your competitors threaten to outperform you.

The other brilliant thing about evolutionary innovation is that everyone in the company can help. They all know what you do already. So encourage their imagination. Allow them time in their schedule to do some blue-sky thinking. Ask them what new ideas they could bring to the business.

And remember, innovation doesn't just have to be about new products, it could be a better way of delivering, neat shortcuts in production schedules, or reworking packaging.

Then there is **revolution**.

This is where your innovation isn't evolving from anything you are currently doing but is looking at something completely different. And it may be totally unrelated. It can mean the business does a total pivot. For example, Nokia was originally a pulp mill company, and in 1922 joined forces with a power industry company. It wasn't until the 1960s that it began to go into comms.

So here are some tools that will help you explore both evolution and revolution...

SCAMPER: A FRAMEWORK TO HELP BRAINSTORMING NEW IDEAS

Coming up with new revenue or product ideas can be a bit of a thankless task – until you hit the one you **know** will work.

Needless to say, there are all sorts of helpful tools out in the market, loads of books you can read, card games and other prompts you can buy. What

Quick tip... Beware of cannibalisation... If you extend your product range to align new merchandise or services alongside existing ones, be careful that the new really does grow your market and doesn't just cannibalise (eat) your existing one. It should bring in more customers, not just shift the existing ones across. (Unless, of course, that is the intention!)

matters more than anything is finding one suited to **you**.

And then to make a **habit** of initiating new ideas. Do it regularly and enjoy the process. The more fun, the more crazy the ideas you have, the better you get at it. Somewhere in that list of mad, bad and hilarious ideas will be the one that makes the difference.

SCAMPER is an acronym that always makes me smile. You can invent brilliantly alternative things when you do this, Professor Branestawm-style. So try it out on one of your existing products and then let it loose on some of your new concepts… (As ever, a big piece of paper up on the wall is best to pile up all those ideas!)

Substitute: What would happen if you substituted something else for this product? What would it be? What would you use? Or could you substitute a component? Or a material? Or could you substitute the person using it?

Combine: Could you combine any element of it with another product, service or knowledge/database to create something new?

Adapt: If you adapted it in any way, would it work for another market? Could you create something totally original?

Modify: Could you modify it and, if so, would it appeal to a different user?

Put to other use: If you put it to some other use, what might that be, and why? Is there a market gap there?

Eliminate: If you had to eliminate a part of it, which would you choose and why? Or a material? Or a function?

Reverse: What would happen if you could use it inside out? Upside down? Back to front? Any merit in anything there?

These are just a selection of questions, but you get my drift. Try asking the un-askable, thinking the unthinkable. Play, play, play with the ideas. Turn them on their heads and enjoy it.

Once you have the ideas collated, look at them with a cool, appraising eye. Talk them through either together or with a person outside of the meetings. They could spot the gold in the dross. They may also be aware of market gaps and audiences outside your experience.

You are looking for ideas to trigger growth in your company. To solve a problem. To effect a saving. To get rid of a bottleneck. To do something new.

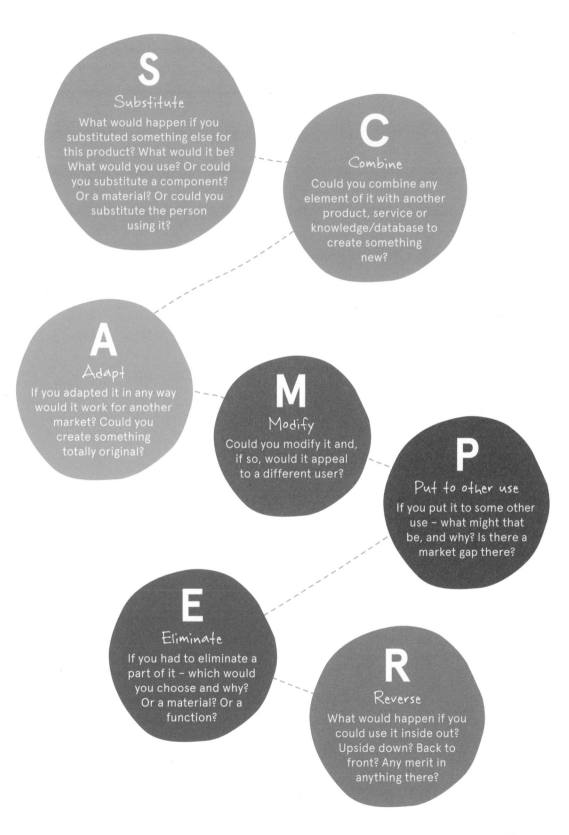

S

Substitute

What would happen if you substituted something else for this product? What would it be? What would you use? Or could you substitute a component? Or a material? Or could you substitute the person using it?

C

Combine

Could you combine any element of it with another product, service or knowledge/database to create something new?

A

Adapt

If you adapted it in any way would it work for another market? Could you create something totally original?

M

Modify

Could you modify it and, if so, would it appeal to a different user?

P

Put to other use

If you put it to some other use – what might that be, and why? Is there a market gap there?

E

Eliminate

If you had to eliminate a part of it – which would you choose and why? Or a material? Or a function?

R

Reverse

What would happen if you could use it inside out? Upside down? Back to front? Any merit in anything there?

OUTMANOEUVRING THE BIG BOYS: GET TO GRIPS WITH THE OODA LOOP

You are a small business – that's probably why you are reading this. To get some new ideas, and discover ways of looking at opportunities and problems differently. And perhaps one of your concerns is how you will position your business in a market that has lots of big fish, fish way bigger than you. Fish that can eat your company for lunch.

Well, rest assured, there will always be a special, unique place for you – because you have the ability to create it yourself.

Small companies have the ability to outmanoeuvre big companies and conglomerates **every single time**. Without exception. (Where they may fall down is in getting the market to hear about that new product, service or whatever... but that is a different issue.)

How is this capability possible? There's a really easy but effective system called the OODA loop...

It's not often that I bring a military strategist into a book about growth, but this is such a great idea. Developed by Colonel John Boyd of the US Air Force, the OODA loop is about making decisions and taking action quickly. It has been widely adapted and is used by organisations around the world who want to dynamically change how they respond to market situations. But it's also a brilliant method for small companies looking to outmanoeuvre big competitors.

Use this to create innovation momentum around a product, for your business, a market sector, a service, your career – it's highly adaptable. And if you do it fast, with a team, it can get very noisy too.

OODA stands for:
Observe, **O**rient, **D**ecide, **A**ct.

So how does it work?

OBSERVE

As a small player in the market, you need to have your antennae up and working continually. You will see, hear and smell behavioural trends in ways that bigger company players can't and won't. They can be small things or market changers.

When you are trading, you may be aware of a number of factors that are impacting or might impact your product/business/you. These comprise:
● outside information: such as the 'market', your competitors
● unfolding circumstances: such as new behavioural trends, new thinking
● unfolding interaction with the environment: you have identified outside changes that are actually increasing/decreasing sales
● anything else that might create an effect.

You corral all of this information, and feed it forward to...

ORIENT

Because you are smaller, you are more agile. You have a short decision-making process so can see how to map into this trend effectively, inventively modelling and positioning yourself to take maximum advantage.

At this point, using all of your previous experience and background 'heritage', you process the new information and reposition your thinking (reorienting yourself) in your market, which should lead you on to...

DECIDE

Once you've spotted the potential and have oriented yourself in the market, you now need to decide quickly whether you are going to respond to all the market factors, and, if so, you then...

ACT

This could be the launch of a new product or service. It could be a marketing initiative. Hiring a new member of staff with unique market sector knowledge. Or if **you** are the

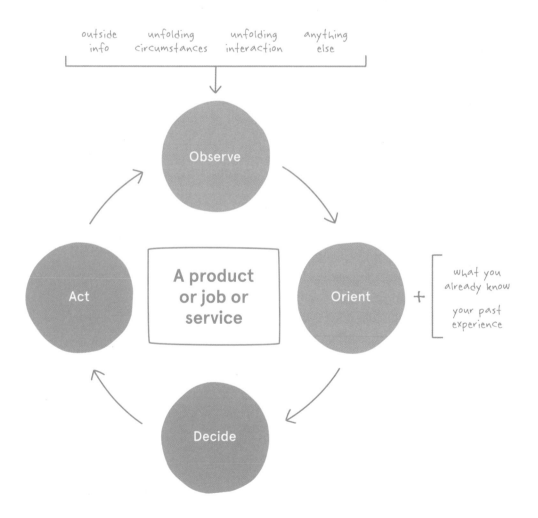

Quick tip... Create rapid prototypes. Don't get lost in endless decision-making, bogged down in getting it perfect. Do it quickly – fail, learn and do it again.

If you offer a service, try the idea out on your first client tomorrow morning. Or send out a survey to six people you know. Don't feel you have to build something new, just try out the idea.

subject of your OODA loop – it could mean looking for a new job!

Testing out the action in the market should then allow you to feed back into the 'unfolding interaction with the environment' part of the 'observe' activity and the loop starts all over again.

Going through this cycle more swiftly and more effectively than your competitors allows you to keep them guessing as to what you will be doing next. It keeps you on your toes. Lets you be both responsive and proactive. And it gives small companies a dynamism, with their short decision-making processes, that large companies find hard to match. It puts you in a really positive David vs Goliath position and we know what the outcome was of that. And remember – it's easier to pivot a small boat than a large tanker!

ROTATE AN INNOVATION TASK FORCE

Most people reading this book aren't likely to have a team whose sole job is to focus on innovation. And if you are self-employed, **you** are the innovation team... So how can you best manage to come up with new ideas and ways of innovating *and* still do the 'day job'? By keeping it simple, fast and fluid.

• Appoint an innovation task force from across your company, and split it into three cohorts. Each third can be just two people...
• Month 1: Get the the **first cohort** to identify a sector, product, service or whatever, and spend the first month researching it – as forensically as you can.
• Month 2: Pull the research together to see what's emerged, the target audiences and which ideas have potential for your company.
• Month 3: Trial them, mess about with them, then either a) agree to take one (or max two) further within a structured plan over months 4–9 or b) drop them all.

- Month 4: **Second cohort** starts and follows the same three-month plan and moves forward with any good ideas.
- Month 7: **Third cohort** starts, and so on, rotating the three cohorts every three months.

By the year end you should have several new products with the potential to bring in new revenue streams for your company.

OK, freelancers and self-employed – I recognise this is really hard for you to do on top of everything else. But in order to grow your offer or revenues, you **have** to make time – in some way or other.

Let's think about ways you could try this...

- Find an innovation collaborator – someone who understands your market but doesn't compete.
- Work with an individual where 1+1=3.
- Build a small hackathon with other freelancers from your network and agree at the end how to take all the ideas forward.
- Book in a two-hour or half-day session where all you are allowed to think about is having fun with new ideas.
- Treat yourself to a museum or gallery visit, or head out for a long beach walk – wherever you feel inventive – with the sole ambition of letting your mind wander but **having** to return with two new ideas.

Whichever of the above works best for you – do it regularly. And ensure **you act on what you've come up with!** No escaping.

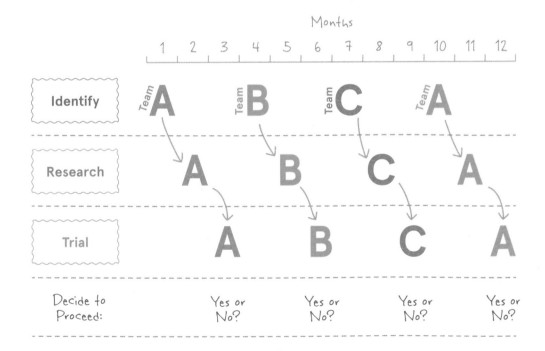

PESTLE: A USEFUL ANALYSIS TOOL TO HELP ASSESS NEW IDEAS

I'm sure you have times – just like the rest of us – when it's hard to see the wood for the trees. You question whether your 'inspired' idea is really going to drive growth, interesting company developments and revenues... or whether you are just wishing it would happen like that.

Here's a well-tested 'big picture' analysis model that can help you take some initial steps. It takes into account the **external factors** that may have a bearing on what you want to do.

PESTLE stands for:

Political: Is there anything in the political road map ahead that may impact on your new idea or product, either locally, nationally or internationally?

Economic: What economic factors may come into play – for example, will you be reliant on importing materials and on sterling's stability?

Quick tip... The PESTLE model can be used for your company and for other products and services. It's really useful to give you a quick update on things you need to factor in to any growth you are planning.

Social/cultural: Are you tapping into a particular social sweet spot that could grow or, indeed, contract? What other factors in this area could have an effect on you/your idea?

Technological: Are you reliant on technological advancements, or are you triggering them? Where does your product play in this space?

Legal: Will any particular legalities have any resonance in what you want to do? Do you need to license some other company's know-how?

Environmental: Does being environmentally responsible impact on your idea – if so, how and through what?

Write all the main factors that have an impact on your product or services beneath each of these main headings. Again, doing this list large and up on the wall allows other people to contribute while you are doing something else.

Other countries and organisations have added other aspects to the PESTLE acronym, such as:

Demographic/**R**egulatory/**E**thical/
Educational/**P**hysical/**R**eligious/
Security/**G**eographical/**H**istorical/
Intercultural.

Choose which elements apply to you and then create your own acronym!

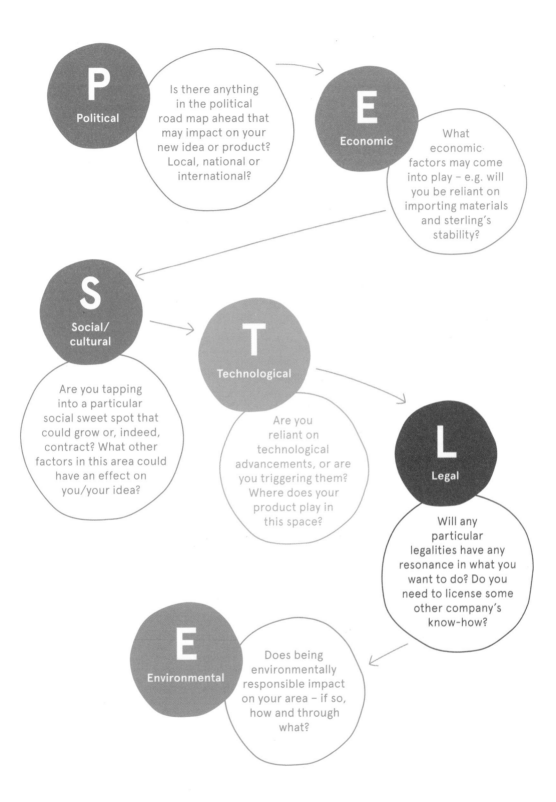

P Political — Is there anything in the political road map ahead that may impact on your new idea or product? Local, national or international?

E Economic — What economic factors may come into play – e.g. will you be reliant on importing materials and sterling's stability?

S Social/cultural — Are you tapping into a particular social sweet spot that could grow or, indeed, contract? What other factors in this area could have an effect on you/your idea?

T Technological — Are you reliant on technological advancements, or are you triggering them? Where does your product play in this space?

L Legal — Will any particular legalities have any resonance in what you want to do? Do you need to license some other company's know-how?

E Environmental — Does being environmentally responsible impact on your area – if so, how and through what?

DIGITAL + REAL WORLD COMPLEMENTARITY

It's a bit of a mouthful of a heading. But it's easy to understand and use.

So try asking yourself these questions:

Q. If your trade is largely done in the digital space, what can you do in the real world to complement it?

So if you run a blog, or your trade is solely e-commerce – can you run an 'on the ground' event that taps into your digital audience? It could be a pop-up, or a talk. It could be an adventure for your top clients. It might be a tasting session, or the chance to meet the team. But for those who only work online, doing something for real could bring all sorts of interesting benefits, not least the chance to get some ideas from those you sell to.

Q. If your business is really a 100% face-to-face, real-world experience, how can you earn digital revenues in ways you haven't thought of? Is there a useful idea you can crib from a similar business in a different sector?

My business is largely face-to-face, but I have written three e-books targeted at a particular market sector to generate digital revenues allied to my real-world revenues. What could you do in a similar way?

CUSTOMER NEEDS

If you are not offering what your customers need then you don't have a business – so ensuring you put their requirements at the centre of your business is critical.

WHAT CAN YOU OFFER EXISTING CLIENTS...

... that they haven't thought of but would love your help with?

---

case study

PRODUCTION COMPANY

A small video production company was working with a renowned brand making corporate videos for a hotel chain. However, they realised that the story behind the chain's original hotel was rich, political and socially pivotal in the region, and could form the central location in a documentary. So they asked the hotel chain if they'd be interested in working together on a broadcast-standard documentary, which could be offered to TV stations, as in-flight entertainment and on other platforms across the world.

Let's talk about...

Beyond the safety zone

It's scary out there – make no mistake...

Whether you are in the very early days of planning your start-up, or are looking to scale up big time, we all get daunted facing the unknown. Well, most of us do.

But what might be unknown for you or for me is someone else's normality. Their 'every day'.

If you are finding some of your next steps or your ideas for new products or ways of working or collaborating challenging, there are two things you need to do:

1 *Write a list of what the scary things are, and why you find them worrying.*

2 *Think through who you know, or is in your network, who has already faced these scary things, and ask them for advice and guidance. And if there isn't anyone – put it up on Facebook or LinkedIn. There truly is pretty much nothing that someone somewhere hasn't already faced.*

And go to every seminar, talk and networking opportunity that you can. Not just to meet people who can help; potential clients may be in attendance too. And there is nothing better than practising talking about what you are going to do – it makes it become real.

Growing your own community

Each and every company has a community pretty much from the get-go. While you may not have mapped it or harnessed it in any way, it's there, humming away in the background, growing quietly day by day.

But what you choose to do with that community depends on the business you're in. You may decide to do nothing. You may turn it into a mailing list of clients, potential clients, suppliers, etc. – each uniquely tagged so you can offer them new services or whatever else.

However, you may also recognise that you don't want to 'sell' to them, but just want them to be part of your 'outreach', part of your 'club'. This can have value in many ways – some of which you won't even spot now.

*Much of this can be developed across social media, but it may be that you want to use your community differently. How could **your** community help, inspire or drive new revenues for you? Think about it from all the different angles.*

My Lola 'community' is really wide and diverse. I did little or nothing to harness it at all – contrary to the advice above! Until four of them met each other...

I'd been asked to put together a panel of creative entrepreneurs for a discussion panel at a client's event. Four great people duly turned up to provide a stimulating discussion for the host. Afterwards they all congregated, fascinated by each other's contributions. And then they all rounded on me. Why had I not invited them all to meet up over a drink, so they could swap cards, stories, experiences, etc.? I was made to feel I'd seriously failed them! So that's what I'm now doing – getting Lola's community together every couple of months. It doesn't matter who comes, what the mix is. They all find great things to talk to each other about. And we have a blast in the process.

Running a strengths test

This is going to seem so obvious. You, your team and your clients all work best when you are in roles that play to your strengths. You know that, I know that. If you are good at something, invariably you are happier doing it, perform better, and reduce the stress you feel when you struggle.

Of course, we all have to take on things we don't necessarily enjoy, may not be good at or which involve us learning something new. That's life.

When was the last time you ran a

USING TEAM STRENGTHS

case study

A film production company was looking to build some new innovations out of its existing business, to take advantage of a client opportunity. But the board was feeling uncomfortable, disconcerted. It was only when we mapped the team's strengths that we understood why. Sam found the loose evolution of the new work hard to grasp. Meanwhile, Karim was struggling with the actual delivery. And the third board member, Mark, was trying to grow the company and hold it all together.

An engineer by training, with strengths in structure, process and delivery, we therefore left Sam running the original company in a way he knew and understood, giving him freedom to grow the business, tighten up processes and improve profitability. The supreme networker, ideas-driven, funding-oriented maverick Karim was allowed to follow up all leads and set interesting thoughts and connections in motion, but would bring in Mark when the actual deals needed to be nailed down. Which then, of course, Sam would deliver.

strengths test? Ask each of your team, your board or even yourself what strengths they/you have. Now ask other members of your team, or clients. Map this against each person's role to ensure these are aligned to best advantage. If not? Shift things around to ensure it works for them and you. The benefits to your business should emerge really quickly.

Appetite for risk

Running your own venture is a risky business. You know that, I know that. It would be much less risky to work for a large organisation where you can fit into the hierarchy, turn up every day, do the job and go home at the end of your contracted hours.

But that's not what you signed up for. You want to be master of your own destiny. You want to determine your own future. You want to have the flexibility and creativity that running your own company allows. And you were and still are prepared to take that risk. Well done.

But this can play havoc with you too. When you are running your own venture, how do you mitigate risk and keep it to a minimum?

There are some simple and effective ways you can do this:

• Ensure you have a really clear business plan for 2–3 years ahead, so you know where you are going.
• Switch on your company or team's radar for market trends that offer

opportunities for growth, but also signal threats that could come up and bite you in the bum.
• Don't rely on two or three really big clients in terms of value – have a mix of small, medium and large. It's safer.
• Build three or four revenue models that bring money into your business in different ways (see pages 151–174).
• Try to have 4–6 months' operating money in the bank. Yes, it can be hard to build, but it feels safer and allows you to face hard times.

Commerce and altruism: Not mutually exclusive...

The upsurge in altruism in many start-ups today is wonderful to see. The 'tech for good' movement harnessing the power of digitisation, VR and other new tools to help communities, the ill and the less privileged has brought cutting-edge thinking to new areas of society.

As with other organisations, these companies have to make money to survive too. Relying on government handouts is a risky place to find yourself, as election results bring new ministers, or procurement rules change.

So try to ensure you always have at least two, if not more, revenue models to generate income, but allow altruism alongside it. I commonly find myself saying 'you need to pay the electricity bill, then once that is done you can choose how to structure your earning models'.

case study

TESTIMONY
FILMS

Bristol-based, multi-award-winning documentary production company Testimony Films is a fine example of how commerce and altruism can go hand in hand. Owner and film-maker Steve Humphries has always been fascinated by the personal testimony of ordinary people caught up in extraordinary times. He first set out to record individuals' stories in the 1980s when he was producing radio shows. The stories also made their way into the social history books he was writing.

On moving to television production, Steve's passion for asking questions about individuals' life experiences continued to inform his work. Often he would meet someone who intrigued him, or follow up a lead to a contact's family member, interviewing them on camera. As his interests grew, so did his library of documented testimony. Steve and his team interviewed the last 100 survivors of the First World War – not just soldiers, sailors and airmen, but nurses and ambulance drivers. It is a unique archive of hidden gems. And while altruistic in that no one else was capturing these lost voices, Steve found threads that he could turn into history documentaries for the BBC. For example, the story of the horses on the First World War battlefields and of attitudes to sex during the war, among others.

But perhaps he is best known for the spoken testimonies he filmed following the 9/11 disaster. Steve spent days in New York in the years after the destruction of the Twin Towers, quietly asking questions that elicited powerful, unheard stories. No one else was doing this work, and he now holds the biggest filmed archive of survivors' stories from this tragedy. Many of the documentaries you've seen about it will have been made by Steve and his team, determined in their efforts to ensure those unknown voices are heard.

www.testimonyfilms.com

TESTIMONY
F·I·L·M·S

Changing behaviour

If you want new, different or improved results in your business, you can't expect it to happen without changing your behaviour and how you work. Just introducing a new set of tools is not enough. You have to really unpick what you are doing, see where the issues lie, reframe them, come up with new ideas and **change** to ensure you deliver these.

There is a well-known definition of insanity – repeating the same thing, but expecting different results – and businesses are no different.

Change is hard but crucial if you want to up your game, increase profitability or introduce new products and services. It also brings the chance to really refresh your offer, so should be welcomed.

The context of consumption

Do you ever think about how your customers are feeling when they buy from you? What they have done just before? How they got to making that decision? Think about it...

If a customer buys a guidebook about Morocco from Waterstones, there is every likelihood they are planning to visit. So, what else might they need or be interested in? You can apply this same 'context of consumption' thinking too.

I know that when companies reach out to me looking to start a dialogue, they have already made some decisions about their own growth. They are already in a very different place in their journey to those companies who might just hear one of my talks at a conference. They are very different contexts and allow me to structure my offer accordingly.

How best can you map the differing contexts customers will be in, in order to wrap a new product or service offer around their route to you?

Self-limiting or customer-limiting behaviours

Just like human beings, companies can be self-limiting in how they operate. Sometimes with good reasons, other times not.

In a company, self-limiting behaviour can originate with the board, from the team, from reliance on suppliers or a restrictive business model. Self-limitations can be found in all manner of places and can occur for a variety of different reasons.

If you hear yourself or anyone in your team starting to criticise inventiveness, new product development programmes or the hunt for business growth, ask whether there is a genuine reason, or is it being driven by self-limiting factors?

What can also happen is that you find yourself walked down a one-way street by clients. They have grown to expect you to behave in a certain way. In fact, they may have forced you to behave or trade in that way. And as you have been pushed to accede to this trading method, you can't get out of it.

It's easy to think: 'This is the way our client/supplier relationships have always worked, so by changing it I might risk losing customers...'

I hear this mostly from companies who are in long-term contracts with big clients. They are rightly worried that if they change the status quo, the client will go elsewhere. Yet the big client may well be behaving in a way many of us would consider unacceptable – demanding, bullying or driving down prices. We often read about supermarkets behaving to their suppliers in this way.

What can you do if you are a small

LOCAL MARKETING AGENCY

case study

A small local design and marketing agency was doing just fine. Work flowed in relatively consistently from a mix of big-name and smaller clients. Life also looked good from an outside-observer perspective.

But creative director Stuart felt restricted. He couldn't do some of the riskier work he wanted to do – not only for start-ups he was looking to collaborate with, but also, on looking at his company website, because wilder projects would be unlikely to flow his way due to the 'safe' feel it had. He was caught in a double bind – he needed the 'safe' big-name clients to pay the bills, but this also meant that he was unable to step outside his comfort zone and risk compromising the company income, endangering the security of the team and possibly endangering future work.

So, after some head-scratching, we came up with a novel solution to get beyond this joint self-limiting and client-limiting position. Stuart started a new small design company alongside his existing firm.

The new venture's website emphasised the wilder side of his design passions and introduced imaginative new working practices and different ways of charging and approaching projects – all were blown up large on this site. It was also given a contentious name to drive interesting and different traffic. And while it may not have generated a level of work to take over from his other company, it refreshed his attitude and brought much greater work satisfaction to him and the team.

company and find yourself in this position, either through self-limiting or customer-limiting factors? What are the changes you'd like to see but feel unable to make?

Recognising the situation and how it manifests itself is a great place to start; then talk about it with your team. And although you may not be able to change your current contracts until they end or come to a break clause, you can start working with **new** clients in fresh, different ways.

Putting your preferred ways of trading in your pitching documents, your draft terms of trade, sets your stall out in a new way. You will determine the agenda.

Broad or niche markets? (Horizontal or vertical scaling?)

Another term around growth that might seem confusing...

There are so many ways to look at the potential for new products in your market. One of the easiest is to consider whether you want to 'broaden' your audience or get more of the same people to spend more.

Horizontal scaling is about widening your market, your appeal, to other audiences that aren't in your existing niche. It might mean widening your offer, taking you into new worlds.

There are times when this means you need to adapt your product or services to attract that new audience, but it does broaden your base. It may mean you have to invest in your future rather differently from the vertical option, but it also spreads the risk. If your vertical market contracts for reasons outside your control, you have other irons in the fire.

Vertical scaling refers to ways of growing your business in the same niche that you are already in. So you are growing what you do, providing the same basic products to the same core audience. You are not widening your reach. It's more about trying to gain more revenues, more profit in a similar way. For smaller businesses who are tight on time and may be risk-averse, this can be a good move.

Have a think what this might mean to your company. How can you develop your existing niche? Are there ways you can grow it by offering incremental adaptations to what you do? What of selling a bit more to your existing customers? Or finding more customers wanting to buy what you sell already?

There is no right or wrong answer... except to bear in mind that you are trying to grow your business, so what will help you do that best? You might decide it is a combination of both!

Intuition as a business tool

At what point did intuition get cut out of the boardroom? Or your business? You use it in the other parts of your life, so why does it seem to have little or no value in companies?

Is it because intuition is seen as one of those indefinable 'soft' skills, and its quiet voice gets shouted down in the headlong rush towards profit and maximising output and other KPIs? It is one of the most powerful innate skills in a business armoury, yet your team may have to be encouraged to even talk about it.

Intuition will tell you when a deal feels wrong. It will help tell you when a hire is right. Overriding it can put you on a dangerous course. Intuition will also help spot trends and the upsurge of new behaviours that could open up advantageous opportunities for your company.

So from time to time, just ask what 'feels' right. And listen to your gut.

However, another way of looking at intuition was suggested to me by a really smart friend. Alex told me she didn't believe in intuition. It wasn't your gut talking at all. She said that what we often mistakenly call intuition is our minds reading the many, many, many tiny little data points we have collected over our years of experience – and making a fast decision based on those.

Whether you call it intuition or fast processing of your data/knowledge – use it to your advantage!

Integrity and core values

Name two or three small companies you really respect. Write them down here:

1

2

3

What is it about them that has earned your respect? It can be useful to list those factors too.

Now ask yourself whether people who trade **with you** might have you on their list. Yes? No? And why is that?

In the complicated business world we all operate in, whether at local or national level, all of us respond to companies with integrity, who state and live up to their core values, whether they manufacture, have a retail outlet or are a local tiler. Integrity and core values are or can be the essence of who you are and how you trade. They can set you apart from the competition. And they can also help ensure that someone's money is spent with you, rather than with another company in a totally different industry.

Establishing these core values is critical at the start of a business, or when you pivot. You either have integrity or you don't. And you need to live by them as well as stating them, with your

Quick tip... Don't just offer your customers what they want; try to offer them what they haven't yet realised they need.

case study

TOUCH PRODUCTIONS

Malcolm Brinkworth was an award-winning film-maker at the BBC. He left to set up an independent documentary production company, Touch Productions, which he ran for over 25 years. When asked – as he frequently was – why it was called 'Touch', he replied that it stood for all his core values around programme-making. He believed that television programmes had a responsibility to touch people's lives, to communicate experiences and stories that changed thinking, attitudes, practice... He had a philosophy for the company that he practised, and expected his team to adhere to.

This integrity of approach became core to the company, and the programmes it produced. At times, this approach went out of fashion – it became harder to get work – but then it would swing back into popularity. But he knew where he stood and what mattered to him.

Malcolm made many of the films about Simon Weston, the ex-Welsh Guardsman who was so severely injured on RFA *Sir Galahad* when it was bombed during the Falklands War. He still has a production company today – Brinkworth Films – making TV programmes with the same integrity, telling stories with the core values of truth and belief that he has espoused in his work since the beginning.

team, with every customer touchpoint. Companies like howies® and Patagonia live and breathe their core values. You know they have integrity. Do you?

Curiosity

Who is the most curious, inquisitive person in your business? You? Your assistant? The newest hire?

Curiosity seems to get a bit of a bad rap – it is linked to being nosy, something no one liked being labelled as a child. But profound curiosity – about life, the universe, clients, potential clients – is a real driver for growth. You can never know too much about how the market around your business is working... and people **love** being asked about what they think, what works for them, what advice they would give. So allow all your people to be curious – encourage it. And then use it to solve the bottlenecks it identifies, to create the new product or service it has illuminated.

Or how about, just one day a month, asking all your company connections one question when you see them, speak to them or email them – not only will you gain valuable insight, but you will show you care about what they do, who they are, their opinions.

Necessity – the mother of invention

You don't need money to innovate. To come up with new ideas. To look at your business closely to see where there are opportunities.

Take a real up-close look to see what is there already that is underused. What are your clients telling you that you can build on? Where are there small but interesting gaps in the market?

If you need to find new revenues because your market is tough, you really can do it without spending much. Go through your business with a fine-tooth comb to see what you're overlooking. Use as many of the tips and pointers given here as you can.

But the key rule is not to let your business get to the point where you are so up against it that inventive thinking becomes impossible.

Play your own game

One of the overused buzzwords around in business at the moment is 'authenticity' – the notion of being true to your values and ensuring they underpin your commercial transactions.

To me, this is the 'wrapping' around really understanding what your core values are and ensuring that these form the DNA of your business.

One of the reasons it is really important to draw up your business plan' (see page 16) is to dig deep into what matters to you and what your business is about, and to give you that unique edge. Once you have this insight, it is vital to use this to play your own game – to use the knowledge as a springboard to working with customers and delivering a service in alignment with all your values and what you stand for.

It will not only build on your competitive advantage and USP, but will also allow you to build your business on your terms.

Think big, think small...

If you are looking to do new things in your business, to come up with new services or invent new products, don't always feel that it has to be a **big idea**. Sometimes the smallest of details can be that grain of sand from which a pearl grows.

We can all let information that might give us the edge – a competitive advantage – slip through the cracks. Just sitting down talking with the team, shooting the breeze, can produce insights that could fuel an innovation.

In his book The Signal and the Noise: The Art and Science of Prediction, Nate Silver writes:

> **'Good innovators typically think very big *and* they think very small. New ideas are sometimes found in the most granular details of a problem where few others bother to look.'** Nate Silver

Ensure you are looking at the small as well as the bigger picture.

Work *on* the business, not just in the business

Most of us don't spend enough of our time developing our own businesses. Fact. I certainly don't. I suspect you don't (which is why you are reading this). Most of my clients don't.

*But time spent working **on** the business is so incredibly valuable – giving you perspective, time to research, plan,*

Quick tip... If you're finding it hard to set time aside to work on your business, take your computer or notebook – even your colleague – and find another space to work in. Maybe just for two hours. A café, your home, a friend's kitchen table. Somewhere quiet, but outside your 'normal'. It's amazing how a new, set of surroundings or view can unlock your ability to stand back from the every day.

innovate, market. All those things you know you need to do. There isn't really any excuse for not doing it, although you will come up with hundreds of them. And I've already heard most of those, believe me.

If you are finding it hard to extricate yourself from the day-to-day to do this, bring in an outside coach, mentor or whatever to support you. Then turn to pages 16–40 and draw the business plan leading to your SWOT analysis, vision and goals as your first steps.

By having that person mapped into your diary, by agreeing to work on areas you discuss together against a delivery plan, you have already started working on your future.

Table-top problem solving

In our fast-paced worlds, we're all driven to come up with new ideas or answers to problems quickly and correctly. But that pace can lead to poor decision-making because we're not allowing ourselves sufficient time to really digest the issue, bring our unconscious into play and develop a mulled-over solution. This 'need for speed' affects big and small companies alike.

Many decisions are made in a hurry that could really benefit from a little more time. If you are forcing the pace on an issue but feel it's still not clear enough – stop. In most cases, no one will be hurt or die. Put the issue 'on the table' – either your own or your team's – and 'walk' round it in your mind. Look at it from all sides, at whatever time of day suits, retrieving all of your intuition, knowledge and relevant past experience, without pressure. Invariably the outcome will be better and more considered – even if that's a 'no – let's not do it'.

Say it out loud
We all know people who 'talk the talk', but noticeably fail to 'walk the walk'. 'Saying it out loud' is not talking about a subject for the sake of impressing an audience. It is actually professing that you **will** be doing something, then hearing yourself saying it and moving firmly to make it happen. It doesn't matter whether you intend to do it quickly, or get there rather more slowly. It is setting the agenda and actioning it that matters.

When I decided to write this book, I told lots of contacts, clients, colleagues, family and friends that I was going to do it. By saying it out loud, I could hear my reasons, my motivations and also what I wanted to incorporate. My actions and their responses edged me into doing it… and here you are reading it. We forget how powerful this affirmation process is in business, say it with intent. It will shift your thinking into 'action'.

Your goals

What you sell
By dipping in and out of this section of the book, you should now be able to start setting yourself some clear goals in terms of what you want to achieve through product development and innovation.

Write them down here. You can have big, ambitious headline goals for the next 5 years – but to achieve these you will need to have smaller, closer goals for the next 6–18 months.

BIG GOALS

1
2
3

6–18 MONTH GOALS

1
2
3

Carry these forward to the GOALS section at the end of the book, when we will look at how to make a plan.

SECTION 2

YOUR VALUE AND YOUR FINANCES

Hah! When I told people I was writing this book, pretty much everyone asked if I was going to include the work I do with clients around value, money and finances. It wasn't so much a request, more a demand.

So many of us seem to find it tricky to talk about value, ask for money or understand our finances, whether freelance, or running our own domestic money or a small company budget.

But there is a flow to it... If you've mapped the factors determining your marketplace, such as your competitors, any price sensitivity, exclusive products and so on, you are likely to feel more at ease asking to be paid what you're

worth. You will also have gained a better understanding of the financial environment within and around your business. This in turn will lead you to feel more in control of your financial position. Having that strong financial basis will allow you to develop some of the ideas triggered by this book around growth and a wider range of business models and new revenue streams.

If you feel comfortable with all of

this, great! Just pick and choose the paragraphs in this section you might find useful.

However, there are also some basics worth reiterating for those who have less confidence around money and value.

But first, some disclosure...

I have been taught little or nothing about money, yet I became the financial director of the small documentary production company I owned with my ex-husband. I stepped into the role because we couldn't find someone locally who understood the complexities of our business. With some welcome guidance from a friendly accounting software developer, I learned to manage all the book-keeping as well as the financial planning. Our turnover was in the low millions. We operated in the UK and the US with international filming happening in the Middle East and Africa. There were some tricky things to get my head round, so I had to keep it as simple as possible.

I'd only run the basic accounts of my other ventures and our household – all in an Excel spreadsheet – before I took on that role. If I can do it, you can too.

And while it may not have been the most enjoyable part of my career, it taught me the critical importance of being in control of the money, instead of money being in control of me. And it really isn't complicated.

Quick tip... The homily 'A fool and his money are soon parted' is just as pertinent in business as in your private finances.

You have to understand your money.

You cannot abrogate all responsibility for your money to another – whether that is a book-keeper or an accountant. They are there to help you – sure. But you have to know how to brief them, what you want from your finances, how to see warning signals, how to ramp things up.

If you find it tricky to get a grasp of where you are, draw up a list of what you want to see in a report every week, or fortnight or month. Ensure it gives you a clear picture, then ask your book-keeper to provide it, regular as clockwork. If you do your own books, you should be doing the same reporting back to yourself. A little bit of careful analysis goes a long way!

YOUR ATTITUDE TOWARDS MONEY

It's also worth taking time to think about what money means to you, because this will fundamentally impact how you launch, build and run your business. And each one of us has a different perspectives and outlook.

Money could be about security, flexibility, opportunity, an exit with millions in the bank, lifestyle, fulfilment...

So just take a moment to list the top three things money means to you...

1

2

3

And remember to ask each person in a senior position in your company to do the same. How can you use this to set the financial framework for what you do?

While there are lots of business books, amazing amounts of online support as well as easy-to-learn programmes out there about book-keeping and accountancy, I'm going to keep this to the minimum so you get a handle on:

a. Understanding your value
b. How different products and services make money
c. Simple financial planning diagrams
d. A range of useful ways to make money through different revenue models.

Anyone who can run and control their household or personal finances has already got most of the skills needed to run a small company's finances

If you are already comfortable with one point, just move on to the next. Dip in and out as you want. Everyone reading this will have different experiences and needs from this book.

Understanding your value

Assessing your 'value' or your worth is at the heart of what you offer as a business and how you should be paid. But there can be so many different aspects.

We're not going to be able to cover all of them here, so let's just look at some of the ways that we can assess what we're worth and how to charge for what we do or sell.

Looking at the two pictures overleaf, we have several values we can attach to each of them:

1. Diamond necklace

High-price item

Rarity of materials

Rarity of skill to create

Will increase in value during lifetime

Long lifetime

Small market as relatively few can afford

Can only be owned by a single person/small group in its lifetime

Little brand engagement

2. Loo rolls

Low-value item

Recycled/new materials not rare

Made by machines everywhere in the world

Many millions made each day

A commodity, so new ones sold with great frequency

Sold in every corner shop

Massive market that most can afford

We will all 'own' many throughout our lives

No reuse or secondary value

Branding adds value

What the above lists show are two completely different products with vastly differing values, but each has its own value set by a range of factors. While the diamond necklace is obviously the higher-value item, globally the loo roll has a bigger market, with a huge customer base.

DIFFERENT SPECTRUMS:

Of course I've chosen these as they are really poles apart in every way, but your business will also have a range of different metrics or spectrums to help you understand your value in the various markets you supply. For example - is your service simple, more complex or very complex? Can anyone offer it or does it require greater amounts of training? Do you require no machinery, some machinery, or expensive machinery? Look at where you sit on a range, as it will help you better understand your value.

Quick tip... Sometimes, the more expensive end of the spectrum in your market can be a good place to be, **provided** what you deliver backs this up. It could winnow out 'time-wasters' from getting you to quote. It will certainly mean that those who haven't thought through their budgets think twice about contacting you. It will mean you have somewhere to negotiate down from, if that is part of the pricing model used in your industry. Try tweaking your pricing over 3–6 months, to test out whether slightly higher pricing could make you more profitable. Does your market have the capacity to allow you to earn a bit more?

DIFFERENT REVENUES ACROSS THE SPICK MODELS

(SPICK is my acronym for Services, Products, Intel/data, Client/Customers and Knowledge – the five basic things customers pay for – see pages 55–59 for more details.)

Each of the five SPICK categories will have several alternative potential revenue models, so let's unpick them one by one...

A SERVICE

Companies who offer a service to their customers are generally selling their time. They are paid depending on the amount of time spent delivering their service. This is how a hairdresser, a mechanic, a designer or a software developer is paid. Payment will be charged by the hour, by the day or by what they have delivered (predicated on the time it took).

The level of what they charge will depend on:
- their skill level
- the complexity of the project
- additional pricing metrics set by experience, reputation and other market factors.

Other elements that also need to be taken into account include what competitors are charging – other organisations offering this service. The skill in setting your rate is **not** to get involved in a race to be the cheapest (see page 184).

case study

One of my nicest clients charges 30% more than similar companies in their marketplace. Their clients know it. Their competitors probably know it. Their potential clients know it. And they've been at that level for years.

In the process of the work we did together, I was asked to hold one-to-one interviews with some of their clients and ex-clients to see if – in this free exchange of information – there were any extra pointers about servicing their clients better.

During these conversations, the subject of pricing came up several times. While the clients knew they were paying more, **not one** single company moaned. They openly explained they were prepared to take the hit, pay the 'premium', because they knew they would get unbelievable service, above and beyond what they would ever expect from anyone similar in the market. And what's more, because they were paying for it, they could ask for a level of capability and attention to detail they were unlikely to find elsewhere.

So if you want to ask for higher fees – you have to be able to deliver!

How to charge

When charging for a service, your day rate needs to cover your overheads + paying you + profit.

If you are just starting to charge a day rate for your work, it can be useful to work out your annual salary from your day rate to give you some idea of where you stand in the market. To do this:

• multiply your day rate by 4 to give you how much you are likely to be earning per week. (Most small companies and freelancers don't charge 100% of their working hours.)

• now multiply the weekly rate by 3 weeks per month. This is to allow for some downtime, time to win business, do marketing, etc. This will give your monthly rate.

• finally, multiply your monthly rate by 10 months to give your annual rate. 'Why not 12', you ask? Because you have to allow time for vacations and bank holidays, etc.

If you are already charging for your time, it can be a good idea to run a mapping exercise to find out what you are spending your time on. How much is chargeable? What are your team

$$\boxed{\text{Day}} \times 4 = \underline{\text{Weekly}}$$

$$\boxed{\text{Weekly}} \times 3 = \underline{\text{Monthly}}$$

$$\boxed{\text{Monthly}} \times 10 = \underline{\text{Annual}}$$

A simple way to calculate salary if you are selling your time

Quick tip 1... Ensure you really know how much it costs to open your door every morning. If you don't know this, you have no reliable way of working out your fees.

Quick tip 2... If a client can't afford to pay you for all the work you do for them, is there any way you can license the work to them for a given period, with you retaining ownership? The work then reverts to you when the licence period is over and you can resell. Or – if appropriate – can you sell it to several companies in tandem, allowing each of them to use it, and split the revenues with your original client once the original outstanding price is paid back?

Quick tip 3... Are you charging enough for your or your team's time, and charging out their time appropriately?
   An extra £5 per hour on your individual staff member charge-out rate x 5 working hours every day = £25 extra a day. Multiply this extra £25 by 4 days a week = £100. Then apply this to your 5 employees = £500 per week across the company. 48 working weeks in a year multiplied by this extra £500 = £24,000 additional profit – or perhaps a new employee...

spending their time on and how much of that is chargeable?

It's important that you regularly ask yourself questions around how much of your/their time is being billed. Can you bill for more things? Can you charge new clients differently? Have you mapped in inflation? What 'value add' would allow you to charge more?

A PRODUCT

We're all probably fairly familiar with the model behind selling a product. The company or person creating the product generally carries the cost of production before a customer purchases it. So the bulk of the risk is taken by the producer. Unless, of course, something is made bespoke...

How to charge

When you sell an item for a price, the basic equation works like this:

Materials + overheads + your time + staff time = Cost price

Cost price + %* of profit = Wholesale price

Cost price x 200%** = Retail price (subject to VAT sales tax if you are registered)

*the % of profit you incorporate to create your wholesale price will depend on the value of what you are selling
**The multiplier to get you from cost price to retail price can vary depending on your market. Some companies have a 300/400% mark-up, others only 40% or less.

A range of different business models can flow from this basic principle, whether you sell cabbages, designer shoes or documentaries.

INTEL/DATA MODELS

The charging models around intelligence and data are less easy to generalise. These models are based on behaviours, patterns, flows, and how these can be changed and influenced.

For example, Tesco's Clubcard gives the company who owns it a huge amount of data about Tesco customers' spending patterns. By analysing the data, whether it is aggregated across towns, products, your shopping lifetime or whatever, they can gain huge insights into who will buy what, and what will sell when and where. This behavioural information can then be used to do deals with suppliers or be sold to those looking for predictive models.

While you may not think you have anything of value in your data because there isn't that much of it, it is surprising

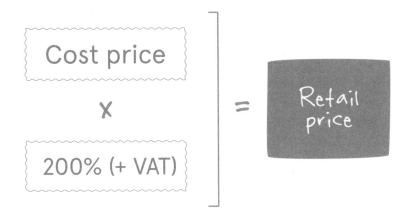

Quick tip... It is really important to understand your profit margins on different customers and sales routes. If selling to a trade buyer/wholesale mechanism isn't working for you as well as it could, how can you develop a direct-to-customer market? You may be able to offer a different range or a rebranded selection that could go straight to their door, without cannibalising your wholesale market. Or you could decide to pull out of trade altogether – while this might impact your turnover, it could really increase your profitability.

once you have done the SPICK + Span model where you might be able to find unexpected data and possible revenue streams.

CUSTOMERS/CLIENTS

Earning revenues from information around this is more obvious. If you have a big list of clients engaged with you, say on something like a blog, you can charge retailers or other product brands for access to them. You can sell a mailing list. You can earn affiliate revenues from promoting other sites.

You can host other businesses in your store and use your client mailing list to invite your own audience in. There are a range of ways you can work this.

The value you look to earn is based around a whole set of determining factors, such as the 'quality' or size of your list. If you have a customer list spending high sums of money regularly, this potentially could be of greater value than a huge list where the spend is very low and with a low conversion rate. But

for other companies, the bigger the list, the better.

If you are going to think about monetising your business in this way, obviously you have to ensure you capture the details consistently, otherwise you won't be able to manipulate and gain the value you want from it. That process needs to be carefully thought through, with expertise brought in as needed. There are some good CRM (customer relationship management) tools on the market, available via the internet.

The other factor to bear in mind here is what is legal and what you have permission for...

If you are collecting customer data, you need to ensure you protect it securely and that you have the client's permission to store it, use it, sell it or whatever you are doing. You also may have to register with the Information Commissioner's Office (the ICO) – see www.ico.org.uk – you must be compliant with all of the General Data Protection Regulation (GDPR) requirements.

KNOWLEDGE

Most people and companies have a large raft of knowledge about their market sector. The knowledge can be around materials, processes, skills, markets – it really is extensive. Some companies focus on gathering knowledge, researching and studying, in order to sell that knowledge in some way or other.

Newspapers and digital news services are 'selling' knowledge in some way or other. A market report is knowledge packaged up for a specific sector.

How you set your pricing around selling your knowledge depends on a range of factors, such as:

● How complex is the knowledge you are offering?
● Is it exclusive, or quite rare?
● Does it come from a unique perspective that few other organisations offer?
● How is the knowledge offer made available? Through one-to-one support? Online download? In a university lecture hall?

- What is the market dynamic around this knowledge – does it have contemporary currency due to a particular trend?
- Who is competing to sell knowledge in this market?

It's useful to draw yourself some spectrums to map where your knowledge lake/strands sit, to see what value you may be able to extract from the knowledge you have within your business. It never fails to amaze me not only how we all overlook the value of our own knowledge, but also how we underestimate the potential audience interested in paying to have access to what we know!

LOCAL? REGIONAL? NATIONAL?

When you are thinking about value, one of the most useful things you can consider is where a new business idea could have traction.

Time for another big sheet of paper, divided into three or four columns...

Head the three columns 'Local', 'Regional' and 'National'. Now write in each column what you and your colleagues buy locally. Do the same for regional and national purchases. (You could add a fourth column for international purchases if you are in that market, but Amazon and Apple slightly muddy the water on this.)

Really encourage your team to think this through.

- **Local** items will include coffee, gym membership, fuel, food, and so on.
- The things you purchase **regionally** will probably include your household rates, furniture, car purchase, maybe clothing and shoes.
- Then at **national** level we pay taxes and buy flights or a big-ticket holiday.

Review all your lists and some key insights should leap out at you...

Local spend is small in value, but really frequent, often daily. **Regional spend** is generally a bit higher in value, but a little less frequent – perhaps weekly, definitely monthly. What you spend at **national level** can be quite large sums, but with greater infrequency.

Now, if I asked you where on this diagram you'd put Uber, or Airbnb – what would your response be?

Most people put both of these unicorn companies in the international column. But in fact the bulk of your transactions with Uber will be *local* spend. Small amounts spent getting you home. The money stays in the local economy.

Airbnb is different – you don't usually spend money on accommodation locally, because you are at home.

However, you do spend with Airbnb when you're planning a city break, catching a quick beach holiday or going for the trip of a lifetime. The value will be higher, the spend far less regular. So it is really a regional or national spend.

The fascinating thing about this diagram is that creating a new product/service for an ultra-local market could be infinitely more valuable to your business than creating for a national or international market. After all, there are only 196 countries in the world – but there are thousands of regional markets and potentially millions of hyper-local markets.

LIFETIME VALUE

Lifetime value is so easily overlooked in the everyday process of running a business – but it can have such rich aspects to it, no matter the size of your business, freelance or small company.

Let's look at what I mean by lifetime value…

Ask yourself which brands or companies you use or visit regularly.

How much do you spend with them over the course of a week? A month? A year? Several years? Only when you do this easy calculation do you realise how it all adds up.

Yes, there are the obvious ones like coffee in the same café, but there are also the less obvious.

My sons all support Chelsea FC. It started way back when our company made a documentary following their youth team. My then-husband and my eldest son were invited to a match, with my son ending up playing football with Gianfranco Zola's son before kick-off.

Although they haven't been to many actual matches, they've had endless football shirts, posters and footballs, all emblazoned with Chelsea colours. And they've watched countless matches on TV and played online games in support of the club.

Now, Chelsea FC is big business, and, in truth, I have no idea even how to start calculating my sons' lifetime value to the club. I know there is no direct relationship (other than through

Quick tip… One of the key metrics you can work with is how to increase the value of each order, rather than just going after more and more orders. When you shop online, you get offered free postage and packing when you spend more than £50 or £75. This promotion is trying to push you to a higher order value, as the companies know it is easier/cheaper for them to get their existing customers to spend more than it is finding new customers.

How can your business try to develop this thinking in its own way?

Chelsea FC radio), yet some part of their 'support' through their spend will have made it back to the club's coffers, whether through a licence product, a payment to Sky or BT Vision to watch matches on television, or whatever else.

Trying to build just some of this thinking into your own company is a great way of building long-term profitable relationships with your clients.

You could start offering your clients a retainer – a regular monthly fee they pay you for regular work. It could be through licensing something from you that means you earn some royalty payment. It could be through the simple use of a 'buy 6 coffees, get the 7th free' discount card.

There are lots of different mechanisms to try to build this all-important lifetime value from your clients – what can you put in place?

Don't hesitate to borrow ideas or ways of approaching this from big companies. Then apply the right ones to your business.

INCREMENTAL OR REPLACEMENT REVENUE

When you are looking to add different revenue streams to your business, you have to ask yourself whether these will lead to incremental (i.e. additional or new) revenues or whether they will be replacement revenues (i.e. a client will be spending the same money with you but in a different way). Obviously, it's the former you are after!!

CUSTOMER'S NETWORK LIFETIME VALUE

Just as understanding and building on a client's lifetime value can bring benefits to you, remember that each long-term client also has a network. Many of these people may be potential clients as well. So how can you access these one-step-removed networks to generate new customers?

SUPPLY CHAIN VALUE

Sometimes just looking up and down your supply chain can help you spot interesting ways to keep more of the 'pie'...

If you regularly pay other companies, freelancers or individuals to supply your business with a product or service, or buy knowledge from them, ask yourself whether it would make sense and prove more profitable if your business did this and it was brought in-house.

When you are buying from an outside source, you are paying for their costs but also their profit margin. Having this on tap within your own business could prove cheaper, but *only* if you would use it sufficiently for it to generate a profit within your own company, of course.

PRICING THOUGHTS

There are lots of books and tracts written about how to price what you sell. Inventive thinking around this whole question can help small companies find extra pots of money or revenue streams in alternative ways:

• If you offer a service (i.e. you are paid by a time-based model), can you offer one or two 'packages' that mean clients buy an 'all-in' deal? This can be very profitable for you, as you can fit these 'package' deals around other work. It takes the clients' thinking away from buying your services by the day, which can feel restrictive.
• If you offer a product, you may have noticed that your best seller isn't your cheapest item, but is somewhere in the mid-range of prices. Could you shift all your pricing up slightly, without damaging sales? And occasionally you get lucky – if your best seller is tapping into a trend, is unique and of the moment, you can push the price up to take advantage of that interest.
• Buy a host of magazines to flick through – both from your industry and others'. What ways of charging do all the different companies on each page have? Do a quick analysis – can you borrow any of these?

Target: An easy-to-follow financial planning diagram

Most of us do a financial plan in some way or other to help understand where we are with our business figures.

It gives perspective and allows us to make decisions about where we've been, where we're going and how the numbers stack up – usually in some form of computer spreadsheet, or perhaps using an online programme accompanying our book-keeping tools.

But just as drawing a business plan large on the wall (see pages 16–40) gives a fresh, unique picture of all the elements contributing to your business, drawing up a financial plan as an image can help you to see the big overall picture. It stops us getting too embroiled in the small details.

I first used this diagram several years ago, and have consistently used it ever since. It's great to help set the agenda about how to structure your business as it grows.

You can use it for your whole business, for a division, or for an

Quick tip... If you have already set some goals or established some KPIs, have these to hand to ensure you map them clearly. However, if you haven't yet worked out what these might be, this diagram can certainly help you to set some.

individual product or service. Or, if you are freelance, use it for your way of working.

The basic diagram has four concentric circles. Each circle is labelled with a year. The inside circle is 'This Year', the circle next to it is Year 1, the next is Year 2, with the outside circle labelled Year 3.

By drawing radial lines, like the spokes on a bicycle wheel, out from the innermost circle, you can start to develop a three-year plan. So let's see how it works....

RADIUS A: TURNOVER

This is generally the first line drawn by pretty much everyone. Label it as shown. Where it touches the innermost circle, write your turnover for this year.

Now move to the outermost circle – Year 3. If all the growth you want happens to your business, what do you envisage your turnover to be in three years? Be optimistic but not too imaginative!

Working your way back to Year 2 and then Year 1, write in the turnover steps you need to make to get you from this year's turnover to Year 3's.

Bear in mind it will be a smaller financial jump from this year to Year 1 than from Year 1 to Year 2. Year 2 to Year 3 will be bigger still. This is because between now and next year (Year 1), you will be setting lots of activities in place that will start to generate new or increased revenues, but which are unlikely to have contributed to turnover – yet.

Stand back and see how it looks. Realistic? Achievable? Scary? 'Just about achievable, approaching scary' is where I try to position most companies. This means you really need to start thinking inventively about growth. 'Business as usual' won't cut it. And if you're not looking for growth of some sort – why are you working through this book?

RADIUS B: PROFIT

To run a successful business you have to ensure you make sufficient **profit** (the difference between all the costs of your business and your turnover). For the purpose of this, let's calculate 'profit' as a percentage of turnover using your gross profit (i.e. the profit

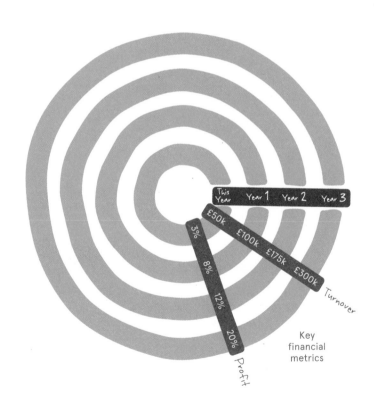

Key financial metrics

you make before you have paid corporation or any other tax).

You should be able to work out approximately the <u>percentage profit</u> for this year, so add it to the line. If you aren't sure, put a low figure or 0%.

Now go to Year 3... on the turnover you've envisioned, what's your ambition for your percentage profit? It could be 50%, or 25–30%. If you've been in business for a while, you'll be aware of what a reasonable profit on your turnover in your industry should be. Push it a bit. (If nothing else – this book should help you generate some growth, so let's see that on the diagram.)

Do the same calculation for Year 2 and Year 1. The profits may be less for each of these years, particularly if you are investing in the business through increased staff, new premises or machinery.

SUBSEQUENT RADII

Once you've done turnover and profit, you can then work out which other lines you need on your diagram. Some useful lines or small groups of lines include:

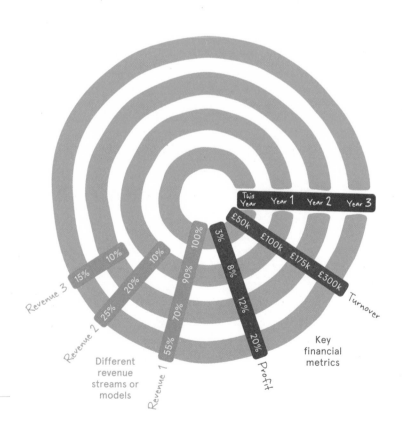

i. Revenue streams

Doing a radial line for **each** of your different revenue streams is incredibly useful. You may have several ways of earning money, or, if you have just one or two, be looking to add more to ensure greater resilience.

Put a line in for each of these, as well as the new streams you are planning between now and Year 3.

On each of the lines, put the percentage and the actual financial figure as a share of total turnover for that revenue stream. If you haven't

started earning revenues from that stream yet, don't put a figure until the year it's planned to start. (And a low, more pessimistic figure is best!)

If you add together all the revenue stream percentages on each circle, they should add up to 100%.

ii. Market sectors

Again, doing a radial line for each of your current or anticipated market sectors is a really informative way of looking at how you will achieve your growth.

If you are looking to venture into a new sector in Year 2, by adding it to the diagram you will start to see more clearly when and what you need to be planning in advance.

iii. Project or client values

Another good set of radial lines to have on your plan is around project values, or spend per client. For example, you could break down project values into a set of ranges such as:

a. £1,000–£5,000
b. £5,000–£15,000
c. £15,000 upwards;

or the value of the average customer spend on your website, together with the percentage of visitors purchasing.

This year, 80% of your projects might be valued in the £1,000–£5,000 bracket, with 10% between £5,000 and £15,000 and 10% £15,000 upwards. But as you look to achieve the growth in turnover

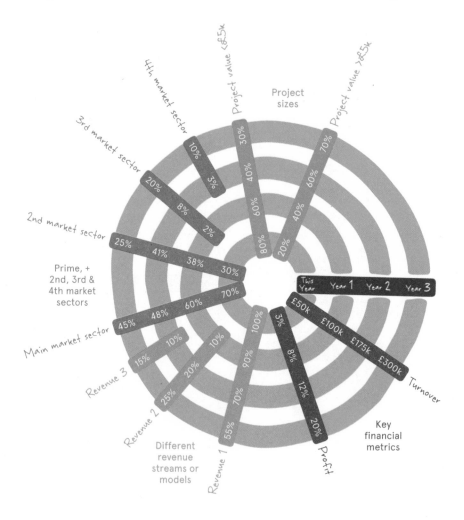

and profitability, in Years 1, 2 and 3 you will need to work to move project values up so there are more in the higher brackets; or, on your website, you work to raise average basket value/spend per visit, with a higher percentage of visitors actually purchasing.

All of these things can be mapped on this diagram.

OTHER USEFUL RADIAL LINES TO HELP SHAPE YOUR FUTURE...

So we've looked at some of the basic financial building blocks – but what about staff and the working space your growing team will need? This diagram is just as good at shaping the future picture around these.

Once you've got some of the basics up on the diagram, the best thing to focus on next is who you need to deliver your visionary plan.

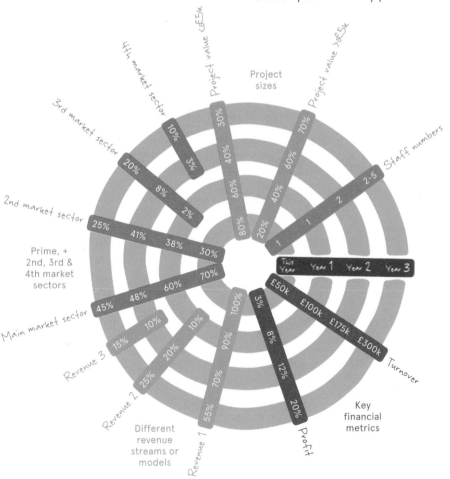

There is a range of different radials you can put here. They include:

Staff numbers: To deliver the growth, whether in a store, in the office, in the sales team. It's up to you to list who you will need and to map on the diagram *when* you will need them.

Revenue per head: This is a really useful calculation to do. If you divide your current turnover by the number of staff, the resulting figure is your revenue per head. As your turnover grows, you should aim to increase the amount of turnover per head, but you are also, most probably, going to have to increase the number of staff. When this is all likely to happen can be clearly marked on the diagram.

Staff and freelancers: Some companies use a mixture of staff and freelancers – either to bring in additional skills or to help even out trading peaks and troughs (such as around Christmas). You can plot this, too – looking at your desired increase in turnover to see who you will need and when.

Space requirements: As your team, your turnover and your product range grows – perhaps alongside your manufacturing capability – you will have varying working space needs. You may want to open subsequent shops, or need more storage. Or perhaps with

the envisioned growth you are planning, to outsource your manufacturing or franchise your business – meaning that day-to-day space requirements can go down. All of these can be mapped on your diagram.

Key equipment or tech purchases: Plot these on the diagram too, whether it is buying a CNC machine or investing in improved tech capabilities for the business. These big purchasing decisions will have an impact on your productivity as well as your profitability for that period before the upswing revenue benefits come into play.

Marketing spend/impact: You can add several different radial lines to add marketing to the diagram. It could be the percentage of spend – perhaps it is high in the earlier years, say 12–15% of turnover, then falls back to 7% as the higher spend helps deliver the anticipated growth in Years 2 and 3. Or you could look to tweak your ROI levels (see page 188).

ADAPTING THE TARGET PLAN

The target plan is really easy to adapt for a whole range of different uses.

You could map just one product on it, with all your ambitions for three years of growth. Or maybe you want to get a clearer picture of how best to structure your sales team. Or as a freelancer for planning different projects, or working out when you can start to employ others.

Or perhaps you could analyse year on year how much it costs you to open the door and get just ONE client... All of these different metrics can be mapped on here and will provide incredibly good insight.

Whatever your needs, flex the diagram to suit your ambitions.

Quick tip... When you are looking at market sectors, don't worry if your business sits in just one niche. Niche markets can be very deep and profitable, and with the access to global markets via the web, you can reach that niche around the world. So if this is how your business is structured, ensure you are really driving value and maximising that niche.

50+ revenue models and ways to earn money

When I work with companies, I am always intrigued by how they earn money. What revenue models do they use to charge customers or clients? Is it a straight over-the-counter cash sale transaction in exchange for a cup of coffee, a slab of cheese, or is it a payment for their time and skill – such as a beauty treatment or a graphic design service? Or are you paying for an audience – for example, putting your ad on Google?

This also begs the question: 'Where does the value arise?'

What do I mean by this? Well, think it through a bit further... If you are selling a beauty treatment – let's say a facial – you are effectively charging clients for your time and expertise, but through the treatment you are actually offering them a service.

Your client, of course, expects you to have warm, welcoming surroundings, to be proficient in what you do, to know the preparations you use. But they are also 'buying' how they will feel about themselves when they emerge – nourishing their health and well-being. So if this is the attitude they have about your service, are there other things you can offer them that align with this, but which mean you are not wholly reliant on selling your time?

Why does this matter? As you will be aware, if you are ill, or urgently need to pick up a sick child from school, you will earn no money for that time you have missed. But by developing additional ways of earning revenue, those breaks in your time will matter less.

This type of thinking can be applied across every industry, large or small. Being too reliant on one revenue model can be so limiting. I try to find three or four ways of earning revenue and being paid in different ways for the clients I work with.

This notion of a mixed economy will help you to build resilience into your business. Earning fees, being paid retainers, having some subscriptions coming in and selling a product allows each one to ebb and flow with the

case study

FIRM OF ACCOUNTANTS

A really clear example of what I'm trying to convey to you arose when I went to visit an accountancy firm. They are quite well known in the UK, with a range of creative companies as clients. The head of their small business team and I were chatting about this book, when I mentioned I was including a list of different revenue models and ways of charging.

I then asked if they had a list, a glossary, of all the different ways their clients earned money or charged for services. I thought it must be something that young accountants were given in 'accountancy school'. By the look of surprise in his eyes, I already knew the answer. 'No – I've never thought about researching it', came his reply. I was slightly stunned. By reviewing even a small selection of different clients' models, anonymising and analysing the information, here was a proactive service of real proven value they could offer their other clients – at pretty much no cost to themselves.

It would add a data analysis/benchmarking report to the service they could give or sell to their clients, and they could springboard some great PR stories in the press and on social media. And if you have to use an accountant, wouldn't you prefer to work with one that is coming up with both new and proven ways to help grow your business rather than just someone who reports back? I know I would.

rises and falls in the market.

Another way of looking at some of these ways of earning revenue is that they could add small, incremental amounts of money to what you are doing. But this can make a real difference to your profitability. For example, if your turnover is £60,000 a year, and you are making 15% profit (£9,000), finding an extra revenue that brings in an extra £3,000 through rethinking how you charge and finding an additional way to charge, or a new audience, could up your profit to £12,000, or 20%.

BUSINESS AND REVENUE MODELS

First and foremost, let's just clarify what we mean by the terms 'business model' and 'revenue model'.

A business model is the financial transaction you or your company uses to create, deliver and capture value and is recorded in your accounts. A business model will include what you offer, your customers, all the financial aspects, your organisation and how it works, your relationship with suppliers, your systems and your processes.

A revenue model is really just the structure and mechanism used to earn money – i.e., you sell a product for a fixed price in a shop.

B2B: Business to Business Model: This is when a company sells its products or services directly to another business.

A good example of this is 37signals, who created the project management tool Basecamp. They are a B2B service, as they don't sell to the man/woman in the street.

B2C: Business to Consumer Model: This is where you sell your products or services directly to the end customer.

Some companies can be both B2C and B2B by offering a product that you and I might buy, but also selling it wholesale/trade to another business.

Sky TV is both a B2C and B2B business. It offers its subscription service direct to the public, but sells commercial advertising space online and in the programme breaks to other companies (B2B).

D2C: Direct to Consumer Model: This is similar to B2C, but an example is if you are a very small producer who is making bespoke items and selling those you make via Etsy or your own website.

HOW TO GET STARTED

The revenue model list below is one that I have compiled from all sorts of different areas. Because I mostly work with companies in the creative industries, it does reflect that market; however, there are ways you can apply these to your business – it's about understanding the model and then being inventive.

It's not exhaustive, so if there is something I've missed, please add it in.

Before you work your way down the list, you need to unpack what it is you are actually paid to do.

If you've compiled the list for the 'What you have been paid to do' section of your business plan (page 27), have it to hand. Also, if you have done the breakdown under the SPICK matrix on page 55, then have that somewhere nearby to refer to.

It is always easiest to start with the way(s) that you currently earn money, so you clear these from your mind early on. Write these down on a sheet of paper.

Then read down the following list below of over 50 different revenue models to see if you can find answers to these three questions:

1 Is there an **additional** way(s) that you can earn from via your existing clients, for new work or a new service?

2 If you think about your existing clients, are you 'giving away' something to them that you could and should be charging for?

3 Have you identified something of value in your business that you can offer a different audience, but perhaps using a different revenue model?

The list has been drawn up alphabetically for ease. Some models are referred to by different names in different industries. If a model is called two names but is basically the same, I have cross-referenced the names. And some are very similar to each other too, such as licensing and franchising.

I have also added in examples and case studies to help illustrate the opportunities thrown up by some of the models on the list.

Please do bear in mind that these are just bullet points. If there is a revenue model you think could be right for you, do some more research and ask other companies you know if anyone uses it – they could already be aware of its opportunities and pitfalls.

By adding different revenue models to the way you work, your business becomes much more resilient

Revenue models

....

Access fee

If you work with a hard-to-reach market or audience, have a membership or are regularly in touch with a unique group of people, you could charge an access fee to other companies looking to market to them.

This could be through sponsored events, special offers, etc. But do remember – the value sits in your relationship with them, so do *not* give away their details. Get the other company to prepare an e-blast, newsletter or other materials for you to send out – in that way you are protecting your relationship with your customers.

You also need to ensure you don't fall foul of the Data Protection Act or any other personal data protection legislation.

Affiliate revenue

This is revenue made from a 'click through' from one website to a second website, as a percentage of any purchases made on that second website.

If you have a blog/website that has a high level of traffic and audience engagement, you can set up 'affiliates' that promote their products/websites on yours. Any sales generated from the individual that clicked through on that link will be recorded and you could receive a percentage of that sale.

Attendance fee

Many people have extensive knowledge that is of value to a particular audience. Rather than just offer to speak at an event or be a panel guest for free, ask for an attendance fee.

Most conferences are charging their delegates substantial fees to attend, so why should you not receive some of that fee? They will, of course, say that it is raising your profile – yes, perhaps, but it also means you are not earning revenue while you are there...

Back-end share

A back-end share is similar to a royalty or other participatory revenue.

In the creative industries, client companies will often do a rights' 'land grab' because they want to *own* everything they have commissioned or bought from you. However, there could be all sorts of interesting values in selling or promoting that work to other audiences, or on other platforms that may be outside their core business.

Suggesting that you and your client develop something and participate in it together, with one of you as the lead and the other earning a back-end share in the project's profitability, can create a real shift in their thinking. Yes, it can bring in additional revenue (and who does not want that) but it can also position you as a **partner** at the table rather than a supplier.

Beneficial equity

This is a really useful mechanism that benefits both a lender to a company and the company. We often talk about this with the companies we work with as it can be a good solution when you want to retain your equity.

So how does this work?

Let's say you run a small company and a family, friend or other associate offers to lend you money to achieve a company ambition. You would like to take up their offer, but don't want to give them shares (equity) in the company. But they would like to be able to benefit from their loan as it helps the company grow, rather than a pure repayment with interest.

By offering them beneficial equity, you can allocate them 'notional'

OLIVER HEATH DESIGN

case study

Oliver Heath is a global expert on biophilic design – the practice of bringing natural elements into our living/working spaces to improve well-being in the built environment, leading to more focused learning, greater productivity and other proven benefits.

He was approached by a well-known high-street brand who invited him to talk and share his knowledge with 50 of their interior designers.

Oliver had done this frequently before with other companies. He commented that, despite the regularity of talking invitations, remarkably little work had arisen from these in-house gatherings. We discussed why. And he realised that what he was doing was effectively giving away his know-how for them to use themselves.

So, on this occasion, Oliver put in an attendance fee quote to cover some unique targeted research into their particular market, valuing both his time and expertise. His quote was turned down, which was disappointing. However, he recognises that his knowledge has value – as an 'attraction' to events and to companies for in-house training – and he is not prepared to just give it away for someone else to exploit and earn revenue from. Unless he chooses to.

So it is important to ensure you fully consider the potential for return when participating in an event. www.oliverheathdesign.com

---

shares in return for their financing. So if a dividend is paid to you and other shareholders, they too would get a dividend to the value of their 'notional' shares. If you sold – they would get paid the profit value of their 'notional' shares too. In other words, they get the **benefits** as if they owned equity.

Bootstrapping

This model is one with which we are all familiar, even if you don't know the term.

Bootstrapping is where a start-up or early-stage company uses its own resources to launch itself or build a product without resorting to any form of outside funding or loan. Many companies start like this because they may not be able to raise loans or capital until their idea is further down the line.

Often, redundancy money, savings or inheritance cash will go into bootstrapping, but it is critical to have a well-thought-through business and financial plan and to look at the viability of your idea before you commit to throwing yourself and your capital into it.

Buyout fee

There are certain ways of working where a client or customer might pay only for the **use** of a specific design, photograph or other item – this is called a 'usage fee' (see later), but they may decide that, rather than just getting the benefit of an item's use, they want to own it. The fee they would pay its creator is called a buyout fee, and gives them total ownership and all the rights around it.

case study

ARTS ORGANISATION

When working with an arts development and production company, we were mapping out the flow of their project development and production processes. I was really concerned that each project only saw them earning revenue in one or two ways, and always at the very tail end of the process. This could mean they were not seeing any revenue until 18+ months after starting – an unsustainable model for a small company.

As we drew up a big diagram of their way of working, it became clear that part of their offer was to access/bring in funding for the arts programmes they were developing on behalf of their commissioning clients. These funds could be to pay the artists, to do a feasibility study for the event, as sponsorship, etc. And they were very good at it. But they were only charging a production fee when the event actually happened.

So we initiated a new charging structure in their revised terms and conditions, saying that any funds they helped to source and bring to the table would incur an agreed percentage commission, payable on receipt of the agreed funds.

As some money was paid upfront or in tranches, it not only brought in additional revenue but also gave the company much-needed cash flow.

Click-through revenues (also known as affiliate revenue)

If you have a website that has a fair bit of traffic, you can host either other companies' products on your site or advertising banners. If a visitor to your site clicks on the link to their site and then goes on to purchase from them, you can set up a commission deal with that site to pay you a percentage of that sale. (Remember to ensure that any clicked-on site opens in a new window, as they might not be able to get back to your website...)

Commission

Commission is an agreed fee paid by one person or business when another person or organisation introduces work or brings finance to the table. It can be based on a flat fee (e.g. £250 per introduction) or a percentage (e.g. 1 or 5% of the value of the new business or funding).

Content sponsorship fee

In the online world, content sponsorship fees are a familiar revenue generation mechanism.

If you have a blog, vlog or large online audience, brands will pay you to feature their products in your content. Or they will pay you to use their content.

You need to have audience figures in the tens of thousands, with regular engagement in an area aligned to the brand's business.

If you are going down this route, do bear in mind that legally you need to state clearly somewhere on your site that you have been paid to feature these products or this content.

This content 'sponsorship' mechanism is also used in places like supermarkets or upmarket stores. For example, the aisle-ends in supermarkets are 'sold' to brands, as they attract higher rates of sale than somewhere in the middle of the aisle. Another example is an airport's duty-free lounge – perfume brands will have paid to position their stores close to the central walkway.

Can you use this concept to earn additional revenue for your business?

Concept fee

A concept fee is often used in the world of creativity.

If you are a business known for your good ideas – whether a product or a show or an event – a client company might approach you to ask you to come up with a totally new product or concept for them. Sometimes they don't want you to go any further than that. It's just about generation of ideas.

Or an agency might come up with concepts (such as a creative pitch for business), thinking that it will help them win business from the client, or that they will be paid to develop the project when it moves forward.

However, a client will sometimes

expect not to pay for this idea generation, as they want to see how you perform and whether they want to work with you – so what you are effectively doing is giving your work away for nothing.

By charging a concept fee, you are putting a value on your ideas, your time and your expertise – which is why they came to you in the first place. And even if you don't win the business, or they choose to take the idea and just mull it over themselves, at least you have been paid for your time.

Contributor's fee

If you are asked to contribute content, comment, creativity or whatever else to someone else's blog, event, documentary, etc., for which they are receiving funding or some form of payment, then it is perfectly acceptable for you to ask for a contributor's fee to cover your input. After all, they are profiting from your work.

Convertible loan note

OK – this one is slightly outside my comfort zone, as it's a business model used in financing and the venture capital world. But I think it has interesting potential for smaller companies to use – hence its inclusion here.

Normally when a company receives money from an investor or 'angel', they sell some equity (shares) in return for the money. Let's say they sell 10%

of the company's equity in return for investment of £100,000. This would effectively 'value' the company at £1 million – because if 10% is worth £100,000, it follows that 100% is worth £1,000,000.

However, start-ups or very early-stage companies or products may need money to get them off the starting blocks, from 'seed' investors or angels who *don't* want their money to set the valuation for the company. They don't want equity in exchange for their loan – at that very early point in time.

Instead, their invested money is structured as a *loan*, which then converts to equity as and when there is a Series A funding round. This is once the company is more established, has started to earn revenues, etc. The mechanism for this is called a convertible loan note and is legally accepted.

Corporate venturing

Corporate venturing is an approach as well as a business model. Large corporations and companies recognise they are often slower to respond, develop new ideas, etc., than smaller companies or start-ups.

By supporting a range of smaller businesses, perhaps sharing resources, technology, some knowledge or a market, they can gain from the new product development, materials or whatever the smaller venture is developing. Meanwhile, the smaller company benefits from the experience, advice and capabilities of the large company.

Corporate venturing can take the form of just providing something simple like premises, or it can include technologies and investment for mutual gain.

If you are looking to find a larger company to work with, you need to ensure your ambitions are aligned, you agree what you are both putting in, and also, if possible, what you would both like to emerge from the venture. And whether any money or IP will be exchanged at any point.

Cost per thousand/million

If you own a database of names, email addresses or other data, you can charge other companies to access this through a fee per thousand or million names.

The more targeted and detailed the list is, the higher the value. So a list of UK millionaires would be far more valuable than a list of everyday supermarket shoppers.

Organisations and charities derive value from their lists in all sorts of different ways – by selling to competitors, to marketing organisations or to research companies.

If you have a list that you are considering selling, you need to ensure you have the permission of those on the list to pass it onto third parties, and ensure you comply with all the GDPR regulations in force at the time.

Creative debt

This was an idea we developed to help our clients turn a 'debt' into an opportunity. It can be applied in all sorts of different ways across different industries.

Many types of companies are approached by potential customers requesting a quote on a given package of work, whether you are a plumber or a design company.

On your submission of a quote for the actual cost of the briefed work, plus the profit you need to earn, the potential customer may find that the price exceeds their budget. Through your experience, you know that for the complexity and volume of work they want undertaken, the figure given is the proper price for the job. So how do you

Quick tip... You don't just have to stay with the financial structures you know or that are familiar to your industry... Borrow some from other sectors, adapt them to suit you. It's fun and relatively easy to do! And could also give you the lead over your competition.

case study

PR COMPANY

A PR company we work with had extensive experience in a particular sector.

A new start-up in this sector approached them to ask if they would help them promote and launch their new company. The PR company knew exactly how to structure the campaign to ensure good results. They also knew how much time and effort it would take, and therefore what their quote should be. However, the start-up only had just over half of the budget required. By limiting the launch promotion, the start-up was unlikely to achieve the social media and press coverage it needed to attract its audience and trade successfully.

This is where creative debt can help.

The PR company indicated that if the start-up could contribute at least 60% of the fee, they would do the job. They settled for 60% cash payment and 40% 'creative debt'. To settle the creative debt, the start-up had to 'give' the PR company **unique** opportunities in its business area to the value of the 40%. This package was a mix of different elements.

The PR company then took these unique opportunities, repackaged them and offered them to some of their other clients as prizes. But they were paid the proper value for the prizes (plus a profit and organisational fee).

This turned the 40% creative debt into actual cash, and, in fact, brought in a higher return than the original value. But also they were seen to be offering something different and unusual to their other clients.

bridge that divide? By using creative debt...

Creative debt allows the client to give you, the initiator, something original and different to offset the balance they can't afford, which you can raise funds against or 'sell' to someone else to monetise the balance.

Design fee

A design fee is payment for the development of a graphic design, an interior or a product, from initial concept through to actual oversight of the final drawings or artwork.

The ownership of the design rests with the designer unless this is passed over to the client in a contract or on payment of a separate copyright fee.

It effectively pays for the designer's thinking and research time, their knowledge and ability to understand the client's audience and market, and their originality in coming up with something that meets the brief and is not copied from elsewhere.

Development fee

A development fee is the next step along from a concept.

A client may ask you to look at the development of an idea or concept, to push it further along, see the pros and cons, the up sides and down – to see whether it has real legs.

Commissioning editors for broadcasting companies will often give independent production companies a development fee if they like one or more of their ideas, but are not sure of the storytelling arc, or whether they can get access to the location/contributors needed.

It is a useful 'next steps' fee, which can set a limit on scope, time, etc., but allow further exploration of an idea.

Distribution fee

If you produce digital content for a platform or broadcaster such as a drama or documentary, you will probably be paid an agreed budget fee for its creation, which will include your permission for them to show it a given number of times on their platform.

If the content is good and really original, it is likely to have value to other platforms and broadcasters around the world.

Distribution companies will be interested in taking your programmes to TV markets to sell under licence to other broadcasters. The fee paid to secure your programming in their catalogue, redeemable against any licence sales, is a distribution fee.

With the exponential rise in mobile, tablet and TV screens all hungry for content, companies outside the normal agency/broadcast production orbit may find it possible to earn distribution fees for good-quality shorts and programming they have produced.

Event activation fee

This fee is paid by a brand who would like to invite another brand's audience or online community to an event. The first brand pays for access to that audience.

This is frequently used on social media, in advertising or for big events and occasions. However, it can work well for smaller companies who have a unique, interesting community that it has worked hard to build.

Exclusivity fee

There are certain times when a company sees an opportunity that it would like some time to assess in greater depth, without fearing it will lose out to a competitor. It can ask for a period of exclusivity to allow it some breathing space. If the organisation offering the opportunity – whether a product or service – agrees, it can ask for a fee to ensure exclusivity, as it will not be able to market its product or service while the 'lock out' agreement is in place.

It is similar to you going into a shop, trying on a garment and asking them to put it aside for you for a few hours, but for a fee. During that period, no one else will be able to buy it.

Feature sponsorship fee

This is a fee charged for the sponsorship of content – whether in a newspaper, on a website or blog, or on television. It is a payment to have a brand's name featured in a prominent position within or around the content named as a sponsor.

Unlike an advertisement fee, which just pays for the space, a sponsorship fee links the brand more deeply to the content, which is generally aligned in some way with its values. For example, Volvo has sponsored much of the ground-breaking drama on Channel 4.

If you have a sizeable audience/community for whom you provide a newsletter, blog or other content, you may well be able to find a sponsor for it, who is keen to have their name seen in association with your brand.

First-look deal

A first-look-deal is particularly suitable for companies who create original ideas – for products, services and the like.

What a first look deal fee would cover is a regular meeting at which you would show all of your new ideas and thinking to the client to whom you had given this opportunity.

If there was an idea they liked and with which they wanted to proceed, you could then map out further stages of working together for appropriate fees.

You should only go into this deal with an organisation you trust. And do ensure that in the deal terms, you set out clearly that all of the copyright rests with you and not them.

Format fee

A 'format' is the name given to a television show that is developed, produced and screened by one production company/broadcaster, and then the concept (or format) is sold to production companies/broadcasters in other countries, who produce it with some simple local adaptations to appeal to their own audiences. The format will follow strict guidelines as laid out in the format 'bible', which must be adhered to, ensuring it does not stray too far from the original.

The BBC show *The Voice* is a format, and once bought by ITV only certain elements could be changed as the 'format' itself had to stay relatively close to the original format set out by the creators. *The Apprentice* and *Big Brother* are also formats.

The format fee is paid by the purchasing TV production company, who may be asked to pay a new format fee for every subsequent year this series is produced.

Although widely used in the TV and content industries, a format can be developed for pretty much anything. *See* Franchise fee (in principle this is pretty similar to a format fee).

Franchise fee

We are all familiar with franchises – most of us use them on a regular basis. Fast-food chain McDonalds is a franchise, so too is The Body Shop, and many Costa coffee outlets are franchises, with companies owning three or more outlets.

Franchises bring benefits to both parties – the franchisor (or owner) and the franchisee (the purchaser).

If you have a small successful business offering a unique service to a relatively local audience, you can choose to develop it into a franchise, whereby you can package together all of your products, knowledge, branding, marketing and support services to offer to others looking to start exactly the same business in another geographic location.

As a franchisee, if you choose the right franchise for your area, you may well cut down on risk compared to starting an untried business from scratch.

A franchise fee is paid by the franchisee to the franchisor under a set of agreed contractual terms for using the brand name, collateral, products, etc., to open a business under their 'umbrella'.

If you think you have a business you could franchise, do get professional advice to help you investigate the process. It can be a highly profitable way of building a business without too much capital exposure.

Freemium model

A freemium model is widely used by software companies. You are encouraged to download an app or some other software for free to try it out for a period, or use its limited capability. Then, once you understand its benefits, you are asked to purchase or pay a regular fee. This model can be adapted in a whole variety of ways across different industries, so it's a good one to try out.

Future contract income

If your business involves helping other companies win business, new contracts or sign-up participants, don't just ask for a one-off fee. Link your success in developing their business to the ongoing future value of that new relationship for your client. This is similar to the idea of lifetime value (see pages 141–142).

Impact investing

This is investing with the intention of generating a measurable, beneficial, social or environmental impact **alongside** the financial return that you make.

Investors put funds into the business to allow them to harness the positive power of the enterprise and do the good work they have set out to achieve, but they are also keen to ensure there is a measurable return on their investment.

Licence fee

A licence is effectively an agreed set of permissions to allow someone else to use and profit from something you own.

Both the format fee and the franchise fee are different forms of licence fee.

A good example would be if you manufacture a product – let's say you make a unique, healthy type of chocolate bar in the UK, which you export to Europe. Due to the restrictions on food imports, the high cost of shipping, distribution, etc., you decide not to export to the US, despite recognising it would be a good market for your goods. A way of tapping into the US market would be to work with a manufacturer based out there who would buy a licence from you to make and sell your product in the States.

A licence can have a variety of deal restrictions, and payment can be made

in several ways. It offers the licensee a geographical area, a particular market segment, a time span of one, two or whatever years; it can be platform-based, market-segment-based and so on. As the licensor, you can set the parameters in the negotiations.

Mark-up

If you buy in goods and services on behalf of someone else as part of your working practice, you can agree to charge an additional percentage on top when you invoice your client for these, effectively 'marking up' the cost.

It is commonly between 5% and 15%, and is justifiable because you are managing the money and the purchase and carrying their financial 'risk' – albeit for a short time before you bill it through to them.

Music publishing fee

The world of music publishing rights is really complex, with a whole variety of different rights being available, which allow the composer, the arrangers, the performers and the publishers to earn revenue from their work.

If you are a composer or musician, you need to understand the rights that you own and how best to bring in revenues from them.

However, if you **regularly** commission music from composers – let's say for use in documentaries you make – then by registering as a music publisher you can share in publishing revenues.

Because it is such a complex area, it is best to get advice from a music rights expert.

Overhead recovery

As you are doubtless aware, your overheads represent the cost of 'opening the door' and trading every day. They are the costs you pretty much **have** to pay, whether your company is busy or not.

For many companies, their overheads will be recovered within the cost of what they sell. If you run a café, the price of your coffee, food and beverages will incorporate the ingredients, a proportion of the overheads and some profit. You can't charge an overhead recovery fee on top.

However, if you are running the type of company for which taking on a project involves bringing in extra staff to your workplace, new computers, new software licences, uses extra electricity and so on, it makes sense to calculate the cost of your overheads and add them to the project budget. After all, if you were not working on the project, you would not be using them.

Passive income

If I earned a tenner for every time a company or person asked me how they could make money while they slept, I would be much better off than I am now! Earning money for seemingly no

effort – or passive income – is what lots of us would like to do.

It is the income you earn by having an online marketplace, by having a licensable product, by having a resource that extensive numbers of people pay for without you having to put in any more heavy lifting.

A good example of this is if you develop an online training programme. Once it is up and running, its efficacy proven, and it gains a reputation for excellence, people can find it, engage with it, pay for it, download it, etc., without you really having to do anything other than to ensure there is continued access, and perhaps add a little more content or tweak it to keep it up to date.

Pay-per-click

Whether we are searching for something or just generally roaming around the internet, our browser serves us a variety of ads for goods and services their algorithm has identified we might be interested in. Pay-per-click is the fee charged to the advertiser when you click on the ad you see.

If you have a very popular platform or exclusive audience, you can earn a proportion of the revenue charged to that advertiser.

Pay-per-view

This business model is simply paying for a viewing of some form of content. Instead of offering it for free, you are charging the individual to watch it.

A cinema or theatre uses this model, but so too does a paywall around certain newspaper content on the internet.

Performance-based fee

A performance-based fee is a really interesting way of charging that can be applied to many different industries.

What it does is to combine the cost of buying an item with the cost of servicing and maintaining it, powering it and operating it into one big figure, which is then divided by how many hours it will be used during its life (plus some profit). And that is the hourly price you pay. Or you can structure it as a daily, monthly or annual fee.

It is an interesting model, as it shifts risk for big capital expenditure back to the manufacturer, so the end user is just paying for time-based use. Rolls-Royce use this in their 'Power by the Hour' model.

Aim to find around 4-5 revenue models that can work for you and your business. This will help you in the down times

Production fee

This revenue stream is commonplace in the TV production industry. When a programme is commissioned by a broadcaster, a production fee is an agreed percentage paid on top of the programme-making budget, generally around 10%, as the company's 'profit'. It is therefore similar to a mark-up – however, a number of 'rights' can be exchanged for variations in this fee.

If you are undertaking a project for another company of any sort, with them expecting delivery of a finished item, product, website or whatever, you are effectively carrying the risk of the project as it progresses. Therefore, asking for a production fee in addition to overheads and team fees is perfectly acceptable.

Promoted post fee

This is the fee paid for a single cross-social media post for a brand/company wanting to attract the audience of a blogger/vlogger or other company.

Publication fee

If you have built a brand that has a particular audience attractive to another company, they may approach you to ask if you would consider various ways of working with them to bring their company to the attention of your clients. This could be through advertising on your newsletter or website, or sponsoring an event you are holding. They could ask you to work with them to pull together a recipe book, a guidebook, or any useful publication that uses your skills and their money or products. This can be digital or actual.

If you do this for someone else, you will obviously charge them costs and your time fees, but you can also ask them for a publication fee to cover its development and management through to its distribution.

A publication fee can also work the other way round. Published authors are charged a publication fee to cover the costs of having their work peer reviewed and published in respected trade journals and the like.

R&D fee

An R&D (research and development) fee is a cost found in a wide variety of industries – from engineering and product design to chemicals and tech – across the board. As its name suggests, it is the fee paid for your team undertaking the research into a new product, service or whatever, and then, once agreed, developing it along an approved path.

Although this fee may sound well outside the scope of your operation, think about your own business and how you develop projects for yourself, and whether this could also be done for clients. Is there a chargeable R&D fee for what you do for them, to cover the cost of your investment?

Retail sale

Everyone is familiar with this business model. You make something and sell it direct to the public via either a website or your own shop.

But perhaps you don't think you are in the world of retail – you don't produce a product, you sell your time, your skill.... So why read about this topic?

During the course of their work, most companies create and use their knowledge on a regular basis. But if you map and look at that knowledge more widely, could it be turned into a book or a product that the general public (or a section of it) might pay for, thereby expanding your market and revenue?

Now, I am definitely not advocating you branching away from your core business, but in looking at it more closely, you might be able to see if there is something that could usefully be repackaged or repurposed to generate direct-to-an-audience retail sales.

Retainer

A retainer is an agreed fee a regular client pays you to 'retain' your services on an ongoing basis. It can be paid monthly, quarterly or annually.

A retainer has several benefits. It can help you even out your cash flow so you are less reliant on continually bringing in new business. It can also help because they know how much they will be spending in a given month and even out **their** cash flow too. So it should work for everyone.

But do bear in mind the pitfalls surrounding retainers. Sometimes clients can become really demanding, asking that their projects are always put before those of other clients; sometimes they may feel they are receiving less value because you know their money is coming in; sometimes you can end up doing way more work than they are actually paying for.

Royalty

A royalty is the payment made when someone else produces a product or makes money from a service that you have designed or contributed to, but for which they have agreed to pay you a fee for every item sold.

When a book is published, the author will be paid a royalty fee by their publisher for every book sold on Amazon, in Waterstones or anywhere else. The royalty is generally a percentage of the profit made once all

Quick tip... One of the best ways I've come across of running a retained client was at a design company I worked with.

They had a well-known brand who paid them a good retainer each month. In the first year of the retainer payment system, they had been overburdened with work from that client – ostensibly all paid for by the retainer. The demands went well beyond the level they were being paid for, impacting badly on their other clients and their profitability. They knew something had to change, otherwise their business would slump. They came up with a simple mechanism that worked for everyone.

As each project came in from the retained client, they quoted for it and ran it exactly as they would for any other project, ensuring the client signed everything off as they went along, from budget to outside costs, to approvals, amends, etc. But they did not send out any invoice, as payment was covered by the retainer.

At the end of each six months, their book-keeper drew up a balancing account with all the backup paperwork to send to the client. In this way, both parties knew where they stood and any adjustments could be made.

GROWING YOUR BUSINESS

the costs of producing and marketing the book have been accounted for.

If you work with a client to help them produce something to offer their target market that is your original idea, as part of your contract with them you could negotiate a royalty to ensure you gain ongoing benefit from your work.

Social media revenue models

Most of us use social media in some way or other, whether privately or for our business. Facebook, Instagram, Pinterest and others offer huge opportunities for revenue generation in many, many ways. If you are using social media to promote your business, ensure you maximise the revenues you can gain from interest in what you do, whether that's on the simple 'click to buy' button on a featured product, or highlighting the service you've just completed.

Slate development fee

I first came across this business model in the television production world, but have subsequently applied it to several other companies in other industries.

When you have a good, exciting reputation for your creativity, client companies will be approaching you asking you to work for them. Mostly this will be done on a project-by-project basis, or perhaps on a retainer. However, in the broadcast world, broadcasters and platforms will ask inventive production companies to come up with

a range (or 'slate') of ideas exclusively for them, giving them time to look at the ideas thoroughly and develop them a bit further before deciding which they would like to commission.

This idea of an exclusive raft of ideas is similar to an R&D fee.

Subscription fee

This is a regular fee – either monthly, annually or whatever – for access to or delivery of a product, service, newspaper, app or whatever.

Building up a subscription income can really help a business to thrive, as the consistent, predictable payments allow you to plan better.

If you have not investigated this business model, it is really worth asking yourself if there is something you could offer that customers would pay for on a regular basis through a standing order.

Success fee

I love the idea of success fees. It means that everyone involved in a project or enterprise has achieved or exceeded what they set out to do!

If you have a team working for you, you can incentivise them with a success fee for certain tasks – perhaps helping raise turnover, bringing in more clients or achieving a deadline.

Or if you work for a client developing a project or running a service, set some targets, and if you reach or exceed them, ask to share in the profitability through a success fee. It helps make everyone feel part of a bigger venture.

Syndication fee

Syndication is the reuse of existing content or assets by a third party for which they pay you a fee.

An example might be that you produce regular content such as sudoko or crossword puzzles for a client or publication. These are only available in the UK. You know that people around the world like doing crosswords, and, although many are available for free, and also you want to earn some money from them.

You approach a syndication agency – similar to a distributor – to sell your weekly puzzles on your behalf into local newspapers and other platforms across the US and Canada, in Africa, or wherever. While the weekly fee per publication may not be high, what you are aiming for is a payment **every** week for a lengthy time, across lots of local papers.

Synthetic or ghost equity (see Beneficial equity)

Trunk sale

A trunk sale is really a way of asking customers to place advance orders for merchandise to minimise wastage. It is particularly useful for those with a large social media following but who may not be known for offering a direct-to-customer product. In many ways, it is

---

case study

SELLING OFF SOCIAL MEDIA

With a small team of talented designers creating inventive social media imagery and campaigns for brands, this studio's images are witty, delight-filled and inventive.

Not only are they crowd-pleasers for their clients, but they have now acquired their own avid followers.

When posting an image, animation or whatever for a client, the studio also offers a 'click to order' connection to the post for those who might like this unique image on a T-shirt, a cap or an agreed range of merchandise. Only available for two weeks following the post, the studio takes the advance order and works with a fast-turnaround printing house, dispatching orders through a fulfilment house. Revenues are then shared between the studio and the client.

---

similar to a publisher's 'print on demand' model.

Turnaround/options

Turnaround is not quite a business model, but is a useful tool to use with a slate development fee or R&D fee.

When a client company pays you for the development of one or a range of ideas, they may choose, for their own reasons, not to take any of them forward. This can be immensely frustrating when you have really invested your creativity, energy and time into producing the best work you can.

For this reason, it makes sense for you to include a turnaround clause in your contract with them, which states that if they do not choose to use them or do anything more with the ideas in a given period of time (the turnaround period), these ideas will revert to you to develop as you see fit.

This model is particularly prevalent in the TV production industry.

Usage fee

This can be very similar to a licence. Effectively, this is a fee paid for the usage of a piece of content, an image, your logo or something similar for a given period of time, for a certain audience or geographic territory.

The fee will depend on both the size and value of the audience it is being used for, as well as the length of time, and so on. It will also depend on whether or not the client company is using the image for commercial purposes.

White label fee

'White labelling' is often used on the web and in software development, but it's a particularly useful approach and can be used in all sorts of other ways.

If you have developed a software programme for a client, Bloggs Ltd, that is sold to *their* clients with the Bloggs name on it, you could sell the same programme to another client, Smith Ltd, for them to sell to **their** clients with the Smith name on it. This is white labelling.

You have developed the product, and sell it several times for a fee to your clients, who then sell it as theirs.

This always reminds me of own-label product ranges in supermarkets. Each supermarket has its own range of white sliced bread, but they are probably all made by the same manufacturer – who is likely to also make their own branded range, which is probably in the same supermarkets!

Wholesale (or trade) price

Most people are familiar with this model. If you manufacture goods, you will either sell them direct to the end user at a retail price or you will sell them to another business – who in turn will sell them to the end user – at a wholesale price.

There is greater potential for you to

keep a higher profit if you sell it direct to the end user, but you will get your products sold more widely if you offer it to other retailers. You therefore have to set a wholesale price that allows you to make a profit on your goods, but allows them to make a profit too.

This model also shares the risk.

★ ★ ★

I hope this has given you some ideas – now it is up to you to work out how best to implement them in your business!

MIXED ECONOMY

When you are looking at the various revenue models that might be right, it's a really good idea, if you can manage it, to give yourself a mixed economy of models and income streams. By sorting the different revenue models into different brackets, you can start to look at how you can adapt what you already do to take advantage of other ways of earning.

A. SINGLE-SALE MODELS

This is where you are selling a bespoke product or your time, which you can only sell once.

B. REPEATED-USE MODELS

This is where you have created something at the outset that can be sold again and again. Publishing a book, white labelling an app, charging membership fees, starting a franchise, selling a podcast or earning distribution income from a documentary are just a few of the models that can fit into this category.

C. SUCCESS MODELS

When you have achieved something additional through the work or input that you've provided a business, you can earn revenue this way too. Payment by results, access fee, commission, share of underspend and early delivery bonuses could all tuck under this heading, as could equity and other forms of shareholding.

D. PASSIVE INCOME

Is there any product or service that can earn you revenue without requiring regular attention? An app that you can sell online, an e-book that could be available from your website or Amazon?

It is really this mix of revenue streams, methods of earning and different markets that can help you to grow and build greater resilience into your business. And this thinking works whether you are a one-man band or a company.

Investment: Equity or debt?

....

If you need some money invested in your business to generate growth – whether that is for new products, to help with marketing spend, to bring in new people – you need to consider whether you are looking to **borrow** money, which you will have to pay back (debt), or to gain **investment** in the business in return for shares (equity).

One of the important things to bear in mind is that if you are bringing an investment into your business, there will be a partnership bond between you and the investor. Both of you need to add value to the transaction, otherwise there will be an imbalance and the relationship won't work.

Another disclosure about me...

Although I have worked with countless companies, most of them have used debt (borrowing) to build their business. Some have already raised equity investment but I have largely not been involved with this. Raising equity investment is hard work, make no mistake. When companies want to trigger fast growth that they are unable to fund themselves, this is the route they often take.

It can have many upsides, but there are also downsides.

However, the basic principles that govern debt and equity are easy to understand.

BUSINESS-GROWTH FLOW

First of all, we need to think where you are in the growth of your business. Pretty much all companies follow this flow:

a) An idea or concept leads to...
b) A small business starting to trade, which then leads to...
c) A growing trading business that turns into...
d) Regular repeat business, growing revenues, an expanding team with a proven concept and...
e) A fast-growing business with owned IP.

Each step along the way has very different needs in terms of cash, as well as different revenues it can generate. However, it is also true that each step will be able to access different financial support or investment, depending on a range of factors.

So let's look at each in turn.

a) An idea or concept; and, b) A small business starting to trade

When you are in this situation, there are generally only two ways you can source funding. They are:

1. bootstrapping
2. borrowing from family and friends

1. Bootstrapping

Bootstrapping effectively means that you are funding your venture entirely yourself. All the growth, the investment, the work is being done and paid for by you.

All the risk is yours. **All** the rewards are yours.

Positives	Negatives
Own boss	Potentially slower growth
Can maintain control	Can limit vision and opportunity
Own drive	Tendency to do it all in-house, not out-source
100% retained ownership	

2. Family and friends

This is borrowing from your family and friends, who are supportive of your ambitions and believe in your company.

'Borrowing' from family and friends is still a **debt**. The risk is **shared**. They need to be **rewarded**.

How?

a. Repayment – no interest

b. Repayment with interest – commercial or favourable rate

c. Equity or beneficial equity (see page 156)

Positives	Negatives
Can be interest-free or negotiable on private terms	Sometimes lack contracts
Can often be a cheap loan	Fund recall can be inconvenient
Easier to retain/share equity	Can rupture relationships
	Potentially limited experience from both parties
	Equity giveaway could be high

Quick tip 1...

Start-ups and small businesses often give away equity way too early. **Retain 100%** of your equity for as long as you can.

Quick tip 2...

Use a different type of repayment mechanism such as a royalty-type payment out of sales, or use some form of beneficial equity model.

c) A growing trading business; and,

d) A business with repeat customers, growing revenues, expanding team, proven concept

If you are in either of these situations, there are more options open to you. With money coming into the business regularly and a trading history, anyone you approach to lend you money will have a much better picture about the risk they are taking and be able to draw better conclusions from any analysis. So you can use:

1. **Debt**, by raising money from:
- the bank
- government loans or grants that may be available to your industry, sector, geographical locality or whatever
- peer-to-peer: lending through funding circles or similar

2. **Equity**, by raising money through:
- crowdfunding
- SEIS/EIS funds
- family offices/high net worth individuals
- angel investors
- venture capital

Bank borrowing

There needs to be some reasonable cash flow in your business before you go to the bank, as most are increasingly risk-averse. Remember that they are in business to make profits for their shareholders – they are not your 'friends' and will ensure you fulfil the agreed terms of your deal.

Government loans and grants

There are various loans and grants available if you search for them.

For most of them there is no equity swap, although certain govenment

Positives	Negatives
Secure contractual relationship	Solid past trading accounts needed
Fixed term with fixed repayment plan	Generally only want to lend when you don't need the money
You retain all equity	May not understand your particular industry
	Easy to lose their confidence if you don't match your plan

Quick tip... If your business is starting to grow, funding this growth yourself can be hard as you have to really manage the cash flow, which could be under pressure – you have a growing team whose wages you have to pay and you have to settle suppliers' invoices before your clients have paid you. There are various ways to help manage this, such as factoring your invoices or asking your bank for an overdraft allowance. However, it is always best to ask your bank for money at a time when you *don't* actually need it, so that you have that allowance ready for a rainy day.

Look at other bank options away from the high street, such as British Business Bank.

agencies are starting to look for this.

There are a variety of application models, which can be very advantageous from grants to loans – each are looking for different results, e.g. new IP with potential to export, increase in employment, skills training.

You will be able to access differing financial help for your business depending on its trading history. Keep detailed records!

d) A business with repeat customers, growing revenues, expanding team, proven concept; and,

e) A fast-growing business with owned IP

You are trading well and have good potential for fast growth, so this is the time you may start looking for investment. There are a variety of sources including:

- crowdfunding
- SEIS/EIS funds
- family offices/high net worth individuals
- angel investors
- venture capital

But remember – those who offer you money to invest in your business will want a *return* in some way or other.

This could be through selling your business on to other investors, once

Quick tip... Try **corporate venturing** – this is where a large company becomes a 'sponsor' to a smaller one.

It provides an umbrella supporting the smaller company's ambitions and growth.

You could negotiate a deal to asset-share, as your sponsor company will understand the opportunity, see what you need and may well also put up some cash.

Ensure you work out what you want from the deal and know what they want. Their horizons are likely to be very different from yours – but you may have some tech or an idea that gives them a competitive advantage.

they have made the growth they wanted on their investment. Or it could be they believe your company has such potential for big growth it could go for a listing.

I know little about this side of the market, as most of these companies are larger than those I normally work with. However, some key points to bear in mind are:

CROWDFUNDING
• Disintermediation model – you don't know the people who are investing in you
• Variety of ways of raising crowdfunding money in the market – check them all out carefully
• Broad scope of investors – all looking for different things, not just financial returns
• Crowdfunding is particularly useful for:
  –product improvement
  –buying kit
  –starting manufacturing to fulfil orders
  –hiring team members
  –grant match-funding
  –marketing and advertising

Your proposal will need to be professionally produced and many of the crowdfunding organisations will give you good advice and support.

It's generally quicker than a venture capital raise – around four months from the start to money in.

SEIS/EIS
This stands for Seed Enterprise Investment Scheme and Enterprise Investment Scheme. It is a government mechanism allowing investors to gain tax benefits for investing in smaller companies. The maximum you can raise under SEIS is £150,000 and under EIS is £1 million.

Look online for further information, or talk to your accountant.

VENTURE CAPITAL

Venture capital funds come from seasoned investors who have experience in identifying companies they believe have exceptional growth potential. Venture capitalists invest anything from £150,000 upwards and will expect a return of **at least** three times their investment.

Quick tip... Remember

– you don't have to say 'yes' to an investor if you don't feel they are right for you. You have just as much negotiating power as them... You have:

- Ideas
- Potential in addition to a thriving business
- Customers and growing markets
- IP
- Tech, perhaps
- All the equity

The investor has:
- Money
- Some know-how, but this will depend on their investment strategy
- Experience in investing and driving deals

When they invest in a more risky early-stage company, they may be looking for between three and five times their money back after five years.

Most venture capitalists are tough dealers, with money and return being their drivers. They lose their money on average six out of ten times, so need to drive the hardest bargain they can.

How to talk about money with confidence

Some of us find talking about money tricky. If asked what we charge, we, 'um', and 'er'. Some are useless at negotiating. Or talking about a price rise. Or telling an employee that they are not quite worth the pay packet they're angling for.

So what contributes to this? Why are some people so much better at talking money, negotiating, being comfortable in this space? Here are some useful tips.

TALKING MONEY WITH CLIENTS AND CUSTOMERS

I think that most of these issues sit with your perception of value. Your value, the value of what you sell, the value of 'you' to someone else. It's not about the actual figure – more about the woolly soft-focus area around it.

Think about it – if you walk into a shop to buy a book or a magazine, the price is printed on the cover. You choose whether it is worth forking out your hard-earned cash for that magazine. You look at the cover headlines. If none appeal, you might return it to the shelf. If you like all the writers, the content or are attracted by the cover shot, you will choose with your wallet.

The value is sitting in an actual 'thing' – a product. It's easier to set a price for an item with its 'cost plus profit' price structure than a service, where you could be selling 'you', your time or your creativity.

But really understanding your capability, your offer, your place in the market is crucial to talking confidently about money.

If you are practised and skilled at what you do, that's worth more than someone who has just started, or has not taken time to learn their trade thoroughly.

If you work quickly, rarely make errors and deliver the results the client wants – that too is worth more.

If you are just as competent as your competitors, but have smaller overheads, then explain why you represent better value.

If you deliver an incredible service beyond others in your market, show proof in your case studies, and be confident in charging higher prices.

Do your research – don't just take a stab at pricing. Ensure you know why you are priced fairly and well.

And you don't have to charge one price for the same thing, so have a range.

If I am working for smaller- and medium-sized organisations, I have one fee. But if I am asked to work for large corporations, I will ask for a higher fee. This is partly because yes, they have the money, but also because I know the decision-making process is longer and I am going to have to spend more time on the management of the project.

TALKING TO THE BANK

While I was writing this, I thought: 'Why don't I ask my bank what they would like to see when people come to talk to them?' So I emailed Michele, Emma and Sarah with some of my points, asking them to add theirs. Our combined list is as follows:

• Understand the 'story' behind your accounts and money. If you don't know, how can you expect the bank to understand and be helpful? Knowing your way round your accounts and plans will give you confidence – and them.

• Ensure you touch base regularly with your bank team, if you know them. Twice a year is great. They want to see your business grow, too.

• If you feel an overdraft would be a good safety net to have when growing, or if invoices are being paid slowly, ask for it at a time you don't need it, when your bank account and trading is looking healthy.

- Banks have to make a profit. You need to be realistic about the movements they can make during any negotiation.
- Don't expect the bank to know all about your industry. Show them that *you* know it, and why you believe your business is able to grow in this space.
- Be honest – if they know exactly where you are, they are way more likely to be supportive.

TALKING TO YOUR TEAM

When you are talking to either a single member of staff or your team – again, be honest about money. Keep the information you share simple and clear. And be simple and clear too when they are asking you about 'their money' - a payrise or bonus they may have earned. Don't fudge.

If you were in their shoes, you'd want to know:

- Is the company stable?
- Will I be paid what I am owed on time?
- Will I be paid fairly for what I do?
- Will I be offered a pay rise regularly, or if I do something well, or if I take on additional responsibilities?
- What are the opportunities for shares, profit share or other benefits?

It's much easier to sort out the answers to all of these in your mind **before** you meet with them. Make sure you know where you stand, what your position is.

As with all things money, no one likes to be caught unawares – either an employee or an employer – so it can be useful to put all the above in their contract or staff handbook. Good contracts should be fair to both parties, then everyone is happy.

PRACTISE, PRACTISE, PRACTISE...

Talking about money takes practice. Just like anything else.

When you have decided what and how you are going to charge, practise talking about it. To a friend, to a local business friend, to whoever you can get to listen. The reason is that you need to feel confident about what you are charging, just as practice makes you confident and more experienced about the service you are offering.

I once interviewed a leading designer in New York who had started up her own design studio in her late 20s, after several years of employment. Her tiny design business was being asked to pitch against other, well-established studios. They knew they could do the work as their meteoric talent was obvious, and they thought as they were cheaper than the big studios, they'd get the gigs. But they lost one pitch after another to the established, more expensive outfits. They were dumbfounded – until someone told them that when starting to discuss fees, they became nervous, apologetic and suddenly seemed really inexperienced. This was losing them work.

So the solution? Every morning the designer stood for five minutes in front of the mirror talking about money until her face stayed the same and her gaze didn't falter. She got friends to interview her about money, rates and work packages until she felt really at ease. As a result, her confidence with clients around her business management flowered and work started to flow in.

So really, this is about unpicking those areas in which you lack confidence, ensuring you know your market, your expertise and how it should be fairly valued, then understanding how to talk about it in a way that works.

Simple management accounts – minimum effort, maximum control

If you are managing a business, you need an easy-to-read, simple-to-understand, **regular** picture of where you stand **today**.

Lots of accountancy firms can supply management accounts. There are plenty of reports you can interrogate your book-keeper for, and if this is where you are already – well done you.

However, there is a fundamental issue that I have with most management accounts – they don't tell you where you are today in conjunction with your budget for the months ahead, so you can't really know where you will be in two months' time or six months' time.

When I first had to run a company's finances, this lack of knowledge terrified me. How on earth was I to know whether I could bring in new staff, buy a computer, know what would be in the bank on a daily basis? There wasn't anything that integrated:

a. what I'd spent over the last few months (from my nominal accounts), with...

b. all the money I knew was coming in from signed contracts (confirmed future income), together with...

c. my **budget** for all the planned spend for the year ahead.

So I wrote an Excel spreadsheet to do just that. It gave me so much more control than anything else. It didn't replace doing regular book-keeping or ensuring all my contracts were signed, but it let me know where I stood, so if I needed to tweak how I was planning to spend money – I could. Secure in my knowledge.

If you want a copy of this spreadsheet, go to my website and download it from there, together with instructions on how to use it: **www.lola-media.co.uk/shop**.

Let's talk about...

Adding value

Adding value is a particularly useful way of both winning and retaining business. It can really create a difference between your company and the competition.

So what do we mean by 'adding value'?

When a client or customer comes to you wanting to buy something or to give you a project, they are likely to have both the rough cost of their purchase and some form of budget in mind. They know what they are expecting for their money, whether it be a cup of coffee, a room to be decorated, a new front door or the development of an app.

However, you are not the only business in the market they can approach to fulfil their needs. There

case study

SET-BUILDING AND PHOTOGRAPHIC STUDIO

A set-building and photographic studio was attracting many high-profile clients looking to shoot catalogues, merchandise and other products there. The management had created a welcoming environment with a can-do attitude. But this is a tough, competitive market, with price being a key determining factor in winning work.

Following their first successful year of trading, the team listened carefully to why clients came to them, but were realistic that other prospective clients went elsewhere because they could 'buy cheaper'.

They were aware that if they dropped their prices, it would effectively become a 'race to the bottom', with them earning less profit and finding it harder to cover their overheads. So the team looked at how best they could 'add value' to their offer to win more business and remove price from being the determining factor.

They identified that the addition of a small food preparation kitchen and a stylish polished concrete floor to their studio would both broaden the types of clients coming to them and ensure that their existing clients felt they were getting greater value for their studio hire fee.

are myriad other cafés, decorators, hardware supply stores or app developers from which to choose. And invariably one or more will be cheaper than you.

But instead of always thinking that you have to be the cheapest, understand what motivates their purchase and add something to your offer, without dropping your price, that sets you apart and gives your product or service greater **perceived** value.

It could be a free small biscuit with that coffee, a bunch of flowers in the repainted room, free out-of-hours delivery or three months' additional support once the app is live.

Effective, inventive ideas needn't cost much money
Truly.

There are many times we think we haven't got the cash to kick-start an idea, whether to generate new

---

INTER- NATIONAL AMBITIONS, LIMITED BUDGET

case study

One of the ambitions for a UK-based design company was to have international offices. But they knew any second or third office would be expensive and would dilute their current office set-up. So we came up with a different plan. Rather than open a permanent office in another city – they opened a pop-up office.

We set some criteria as to why it would be in the places suggested, how long it would be open for, who would staff it, what the company would gain from the experience, how it would benefit the staff, and also what opportunities they could develop in the city they visited. The latter varied from winning new business to giving talks about design and mentoring students.

The first one took place in an East Coast USA city over an eight-week period one autumn. The city was picked because the company had a major client based nearby and they had also been asked to pitch against local US companies for another client. They based themselves in a temporarily empty office space, renting computers, and threw themselves into the city's design and marketing community. All the directors visited at some point during those weeks. A number of their staff travelled out there too.

The cost was kept as low as possible, but the experience was fantastic, giving the company a real insight into a different work culture and way of life.

revenues or develop the business in some new way.

Changing this thinking is really crucial. You can be infinitely inventive within your current constraints. It just needs a different approach.

Inventive marketing across social media channels is cost-effective but can achieve lots. Appointing an advisory board doesn't cost much. Thinking through an idea a day from this book is free.

Turnover growth doesn't matter – happiness and profitability do...

If you are running a happy company that allows you to live the life you want, lets you do what you enjoy, allows you to spend time with your friends and children – don't feel you have to chase growth and turnover. It's a lie that every company needs to keep on growing to ensure we feel fulfilled. It's just not true.

However, what does matter is that the business you have is profitable and pays you and your team satisfactorily for the work you do.

I've acknowledged to myself that I won't be heading up a multinational media business any time in this life. But my business pays me, I make a profit, pay my taxes, work with great clients and do something I love.

Sometimes this attitude is pejoratively referred to as a 'lifestyle' business by City pundits or investors whose key driver is money focused. Of the approximately 5 million companies in the UK with under 20 employees, many of these would fit that description. Some find it hard to understand that these can be deeply satisfying, very profitable and allow people to work in fulfilling ways. So go for it... it's a fine achievement.

Loss leaders

The term 'loss leader' refers to a client or project that you take on for little or no money, in the belief that it will lead to more full-paying work in that area, or from that client.

In all my years of working with companies, I don't think I have ever come across even one of these projects leading to more work.

Loss leaders mostly just become losses for you, and don't lead to anything.

Rather than undertaking a project for little or no recompense, think about how you can charge your normal fee for this, but offer to **add** more value to it in some way.

Money management – the myth

That old chestnut!

If I had a fiver for every time people, start-ups, trading companies told me that they were bad at running the money – I'd be really rich.

There is a great myth around money and how hard it is to manage it. To be quite frank – **if you can run your personal or household finances competently then you can certainly run the money of a small company.** Simple as that.

Read the pages about money carefully – it isn't hard. But it is vital that you understand the basics yourself, because if you don't, you are effectively abrogating responsibility for your business.

Yes, as a self-employed person, partnership or company you will have a different set of legal obligations around reporting, VAT, etc. However, lots of online support and advice is available, and there are plenty of online tools – so do use them.

Profit centres

Most of us will probably view our business as one main entity – with a single turnover generating one profit.

But by splitting your business into smaller notional entities, you can create several 'profit centres', setting turnover targets, revenue streams and profits for each. Often this can really up the money you make, as you are trying to ensure every corner of your business is profitable.

Let's take the example of a small garden centre...

We could break the total overall turnover down into several profit centres, such as:

- outdoor plants
- bulbs, seeds and other packed goods
- compost and other plant nutrients
- planters and other garden hardware
- garden design service
- garden landscaping and planting
- seasonal merchandise (e.g. barbecues, Christmas trees, etc.)

I'm sure there are many other ways we can look at this type of business, but we will go with that list for the moment.

Each particular segment of the business will have different requirements in terms of outlay and facilities, but also times of year that customers purchase and the value of that purchase. The discrete areas are also likely to use varying business models, adding resilience to the whole.

Understanding each area really well, tweaking the offer, pricing, marketing and so on, allows you to set clear targets or KPIs (see page 272) for these. By focusing on **each** area individually to make sure it makes a profit, the central profit will benefit, as the weaker elements or non-profit-making strands are easily identified. These can then be adjusted accordingly.

Even if you are a sole trader, you can divide your business into small profit centres, each with its own trading characteristics, charging models and profitability. Write a list of how you could set different centres...

The big gains to be found in tiny tweaks

I've always loved the story about the British cycling team's long-term preparation for the 2012 Olympics... and its approach to all subsequent championships.

When Dave Brailsford was made British Cycling's performance director, he implemented a 1% improvement policy. In order to gain maximum advantage in every single way possible, every aspect of the team's performance was taken apart to look for any potential area for improvement – no matter how small or unimportant it seemed. If he could squeeze 1% improvement from everything, the aggregation of all those tiny improvements would make a huge difference.

The bikes were taken to bits, with each part tested to see where marginal gains could be made, in weight, performance and improved aerodynamics. Each athlete's performance was broken down to see how tweaks here and there could gain extra power, mobility or seconds. And the improvements were not just limited to the machines and the performance, but applied to every aspect of the athletes' lives too.

Put together with the incredible hard work of the athletes themselves and the team support, we've all seen the startling medal-winning shower that resulted from this policy.

You can implement this in your company too. Yup, you may not be on for a gold medal performance, but try taking every aspect of your offer and organisation apart to see where you can improve by 1% – or even 10%.

Can you do something a little faster – and get the invoice out for payment more speedily? Can you get clients to pay you 10% faster? Can you use your space 10% more efficiently, thereby adding a new workstation? Where are the incremental tweaks you can make to improve what you do, so that you work smarter, better, more efficiently, more profitably?

Return on investment (ROI) and how to calculate it

This is one of the basic measurements used in marketing and business growth. Simply put, it is a calculation you can make to understand whether the money you've used to develop a new product, or added to your marketing spend, has generated the returns you hoped for.

And this is how you calculate it:

$$((\text{Payback} - \text{investment}) \div \text{investment}) \times 100 = \text{ROI}$$

Hmm, equations weren't my strongest suit at school either – so let's turn this into real numbers to show how it works.

Payback = the figure you have made from a new service or initiative. In the calculation below, we have set that at £5,000.

Investment = the total sum you spent on generating that initiative or idea. Let's call this £500.

So: $((£5,000 - £500) \div £500) \times 100 = 900\%$

a. The first step is to subtract the investment from the payback, i.e. £5,000 - £500 = £4,500
In this instance, the £4,500 is the total profit having removed the money you spent (invested) to generate it.

b. The second step is to divide that new figure (£4,500) by the original investment, i.e. £4,500 ÷ £500 = 9

c. The third step is to multiply 9 by 100 to give the percentage return on your investment – in this case, 900%. A good investment in most people's eyes!

Turnover is vanity, profit is sanity
It's really concerning how many small- and medium-sized companies I come across don't have control of their figures.

If you recognise yourself as you read this, you are not alone. It is a scary place.

As I've said elsewhere in this book – if you can run your household accounts, believe you me, you can run the accounts of a small company. It isn't difficult. If I can teach myself from scratch, so can most other people.

Regular attention to and control of the numbers allows you to do so many things, including:

- planning ahead for growth
- overcoming downturns
- seeing off the competition
- seizing opportunities
- better understanding of your market and your value within it.

I also have very little sympathy for anyone who says they 'don't do numbers'. That's a load of tosh. Anyone who learned how to add, subtract, multiply and divide at school – which is most of us by around the age of eight – can do simple accounts for their business. Otherwise, they don't deserve to run a business or have customers or staff...

The basic principles are very simple – you have to sell your goods and services for more than it costs you to make them. The greater the difference between the total cost to you and the sale price, the greater your profit.

Of course, there are complexities as a company grows – there are more staff, product ranges, export markets, etc. – but the same basic principle applies, whether you are Rolls-Royce, sell second-hand cars or are a mechanic.

One of the key sayings in this area is 'turnover is vanity, profit is sanity'. In other words, no matter how high the turnover you can boast, if you are not making a profit you will be on a downward spiral.

Have a look at the different product pages to see different ways of charging, depending on what you are selling.

Non-routine problem-solving

As creatures of habit, when we need to solve a problem we largely turn to our regular 'toolbox' of processes and ways of thinking. That's all well and good, but this time try shaking things up... After all, as a misattributed Einstein saying goes: 'Insanity is doing the same thing over and over again, but expecting different results.'

If you are finding yourself stuck with one particular problem, what other approaches can you use to try to solve it?

Add in the emotive, the emotional. Look at all the impractical positively. Turn things on their heads. Go against the grain. Look for solutions in unexpected places. How do totally unconnected worlds and industries do it?

The difference between book-keeping and accountancy

This is a question that comes up continually with all the freelancers, micro, small and medium companies I help. And having been both a creative head and a financial director, it's one that I have perspective on.

Most vital of everything is that **you** as a business owner need to understand **your** money. That is mission critical. No one will look after it and care about it like you do.

Then there are two other layers:

- Book-keeping is about the day-to-day (and you need some form of programme like Xero, unless you want to do it on a spreadsheet!)
- Accounting is about the profit and loss, the legal compliance, etc. – you may need to bring in an accountant to help you with this, depending on the size and complexity of what you do.

Keeping the mantra 'turnover is vanity, profit is sanity' at the forefront of your mind means you will always be focused on making more than you pay out

If you get the book-keeping right and invest time in it, the accounting can be done with less frequency.

Book-keeping is about money in/out, paying people/suppliers, keeping on top of the bank account, etc. There are lots of online products that can help you or your book-keepers do this.

You will be able to pull out a variety of reports, such as profit and loss, from all of the online systems, but it is advisable that this is still looked over by an accountant, who will include accountancy elements like depreciation, etc.

I insist that all the companies I work with have a money session once a week. It matters that you always know where you are. My book-keeping is done every week, so as the year end gets closer, I know where I am.

You can do your books yourself, use a freelance or in-house book-keeper, or use a bureau. The former is best so you can talk to them, work with them, and you're all on the same page. Remember – it's your money, so why wouldn't you want to look after it?

Your goals

Your value and finances

By dipping in and out of this section of the book, you should now be able to start setting yourself some clear goals around what you want to achieve in terms of value, managing your money and finding new revenue streams.

Write them down here. You can have big, ambitious headline goals for the next 5 years – but to achieve these you will need to have smaller, closer goals for the next 6–18 months.

BIG GOALS

1 --

2 --

3 --

6–18 MONTH GOALS

1 --

2 --

3 --

Carry these forward to the GOALS section at the end of the book, when we will look at how to make a plan.

SECTION

3

YOUR PEOPLE

People make your business happen.
If you are a sole trader, that person is you.
Or if you are involved in running a company,
your 'people' may include another founder
and/or a board, as well as your employees.

Whichever you are, the other people who also have a major influence on your business growth are those just beyond your direct employ, such as your suppliers, collaborators and the like. Then there are your wider networks that sit beyond, which you tap into to foster new relationships and markets.

Harnessing the undoubted and often underused talents in both closer and wider networks can make your business thrive in ways you may not expect.

This section is full of ideas around thinking about the people in your 'world' in a different way, and tapping into their skills and connections to help generate growth in some shape or form. It is *not* an HR guide!

I think it is really key to enjoy the bit of your life you spend working. So many people feel unfulfilled in what they do – which is so sad.

How much better, more productive, interesting and engaging would it be – for you, those you work with, the town you work in, the city and the country – if as many of us as possible enjoyed what we do? One of the keys to this is to ensure – as far as is humanly possible – that you work with people you like and value and who like and value you. This may sound like some utopian dream, but one of the key tenets when I set up my business was that I didn't want to work with any arseholes. I haven't since.

So, let's see how we can generate growth from the people in – or soon to be in – your orbit.

People map

Another ridiculously easy diagram – but one we all forget to do...

Most companies forget how big the map of **who** they know is. Not necessarily as clients but as a network, as interesting connections, or just as good people.

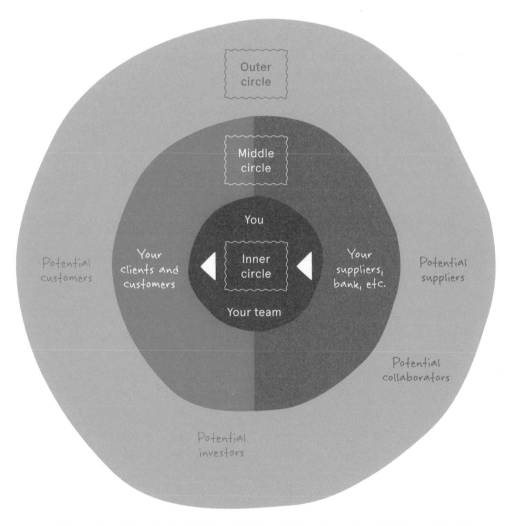

A MAP OF WHO IS IN YOUR INNER, MIDDLE AND OUTER CIRCLES

In the inner circle – name all the people critical to your business. They will be your team, you, maybe your family or friends if you are reliant on them in some way to support you.

Next circle out – in the right half, list all those with an input in your business who help your business trade, e.g. suppliers, your bank, your landlord... On the left side, list those who benefit from the 'output' of your business, such as customers....

The ring beyond this comprises the networks you are part of, the markets you operate in, the trade bodies you engage with.

The **inner** circle is the one you need to care for and ensure you look after most. If they are not happy, your business won't thrive. And that includes **you**. What do you need to do to ensure that everyone in this circle is feeling valued, working to their best ability and is able to contribute?

The **middle** circle is the one that you need to nurture and engage with regularly. Without these people, your business can't operate and do what it does. Yes, there will always be others who can replace them, but you need to get the very best you can from everyone in this circle. If you don't like some of them, go find others you do like. These are the people who can make your daily work feel fabulous or awful. I know which I'd rather!

The **outer** circle is your hunting ground, full of opportunities to find people, ideas, companies and clients to bring into the middle circle. You have to roam out here to keep that middle circle humming.

It should include the networks you are part of, the markets you operate in, the trade bodies you engage with.

Get your team to keep this diagram up to date, adding their thoughts to both the middle and outer circles.

But first, remember this...

EVERYONE WANTS YOU TO SUCCEED!

It's really important to bear this in mind when you run a business. There isn't a single person or company you engage with that doesn't want you to succeed...

You want to be a success. So, too, do your staff.

Your suppliers want you to do well, as that will mean their business grows as yours does.

Your support services, such as the bank – they too want you to do well and to swell your bank balance.

Your clients want you to do well, as that will help their business and they can have some of that reflected glory.

I would even suggest that your competitors could also want you to succeed – particularly if it grows the market for what you both do, rather than eating their business!

The Inner Circle

Using the people map you've just drawn up, we are going to look at some useful tips around the people, the team, in the different circles.

But first – let's talk about...

You

This whole book is about growing your business. You are the pivotal person in this space. It's really worth checking in with 'you' every so often to ensure you are happy, feel motivated and are enjoying what you do.

If you didn't complete them when you first picked up this book, then find a quiet moment to write down your hopes and dreams. Finding and nurturing that inner motivation to realise your potential, your deepest wishes, is really important to who you are.

Knowing that will give a really sound basis for building your business – take some time out to reflect and look ahead to what you want. Then go after it.

BANISH IMPOSTER SYNDROME

Have you ever felt that one day someone is going to 'call' you out, tell you that you don't really know what you're doing, and pull the plug on your

career or your business? Despite your 2/5/35 years of experience?

That is imposter syndrome.

It's that little voice inside our own heads telling us we're not good enough. And it imposes self-limiting behaviours on you, your business and its capabilities. It affects most of us at some time or other, but is particularly prevalent among women of all ages, even hugely successful women.

So how can you silence that voice, acknowledge your value and build on it?

One of the best ways is to turn to page 21 and go through the 'How to draw a business plan' process, but do it for you as an **individual**, rather than for your business. Be really thorough, working with a friend, mentor or coach who can question you and draw it up. Once you are finished, stand back and look at it clearly. Understand those strengths – they can silence that voice in your head. And if you have weaknesses you feel you need to address, enrol in some training or get support.

Just as you created the questioning

voice in your head, you can silence it too – never to return.

But also do bear in mind that if you have experienced this, so too may some of your team. It can be just as debilitating for them as it is for you. Ask them and support them through their own route out of this particularly self-deprecating rut! Your business can only benefit...

THOUGHT LEADERSHIP

Have a look at the section on marketing (starting on page 232) on why it's a good idea for you to be a thought leader in your field...

What is a thought leader? It's the go-to person who is an expert or an innovator in any given area. In your industry – could it be you? Do you have the interest, the knowledge, the skills to push forward with new thinking that other people want to listen to?

Your team

....

ARE THE RIGHT PEOPLE IN THE RIGHT ROLES?

This sounds blindingly obvious...

As an employer, you determine who you need to do what, the roles you need them to fill and how they will shape the business. You bring in people to do a certain job and fulfil that role. But people change. Their circumstances alter. They grow interested in different areas of work. They might be studying in the evening to develop their own potential.

Recognising all of this and keeping an open mind about who does what allows you to keep flexibility in how you use your team. Don't narrow your view of people because they've always been in that role. Allowing them to flower and fly will help them feel enriched in the business.

But it's equally vital to recognise when someone is struggling in a role. Yes, we all need to feel fulfilled, challenged and to widen our

Quick tip... Remember to remind yourself of what your team can do or have done in the past... Revisit their CVs. It always surprises me how rarely companies of all sizes review their team's CVs once they've been employed. But these carefully produced documents hold a wealth of useful capabilities, not currently part of their job roles, that can help you deliver your growth plans.

case study

PICTURE-FRAMING BUSINESS

I was working with a small art print and picture-framing business. Work came through an impressive online portal and word of mouth. During their business development process, they recognised that the addition of a small shop to the front of their premises could bring in useful passer-by trade, as well as providing a marketing asset. They had the funds to create the shop and the frontage, but were concerned about the additional staffing cost while revenues from this new resource grew.

I suggested they review their team's CVs – many of us have retail experience gained at earlier points in our careers. I know I do – a three-month pre-Christmas stint in a jewellers, and 18 months of being the 'Saturday girl' in a store on London's South Molton Street to augment my weekly income at the time (and get me a staff discount!).

They worked their way through the ten CVs – and struck gold. One of their staff had run a considerable family retail venture before moving away. Having retrained as a framer, she was tucked away in the back room of their workshop.

When she was asked if she'd like to take on the shop challenge, she leaped at the opportunity, delighted to be able to marry her retail and framing capabilities.

capabilities... For some, being outside their comfort zone is a painful place – it's important to recognise when individuals are struggling and unhappy. And why. Is it more support they need, or a different role?

Ensuring the right people are in the roles best-suited to their capabilities and talents can make a business go from good to great – without taking on anyone new.

JOB/ROLE CLARITY

Does everyone who works with you really know what their job role is? Has it changed since they took the position or started working with you? Job-creep happens the whole time as organisations flex and change. This then allows all sorts of overlapping to happen, and time and money to be wasted without maximising everyone's contribution.

It makes sense to revisit everyone's

job roles every six months if you can, but certainly annually. If you need to, rewrite their job description, adding in new capabilities and activities, with revised KPIs and targets (if they have them).

MAPPING LIFE CHANGES INTO YOUR GROWTH PLAN

When you run your own company or work for a small company, factoring in life changes can be tricky. And occasionally embarrassing. However, what I can assure you is that *not* facing them can be even harder.

For example, many individuals in their 20s, 30s, 40s and beyond may want children. Others will have caring responsibilities. Men as well as women face major attitudinal and physiological shifts around their early 50s. Relationships and marriages will happen, while others break down. These are just signs

Quick tip... If you ask everyone in your team to map their working patterns, what they do, where they are, etc., over a fortnight twice a year, you get a much richer insight into their actual function and value. Then you can use this to reframe their role or write a better job description.

of lives being lived.

Not incorporating them and what they can mean into your growth plan is a major mistake. After all, companies are made up of people, all leading rich, diverse lives. But equally, how can you predict what might happen, and when?

If you run a small company, you have the benefit of knowing your team pretty

Quick tip... Your formative years will have made you the person that you are. And the same goes for your team. There will be positive and negative parts to your own and everyone else's stories. These will often crop up when you are looking to grow your business – particularly when you are drawing a map like this. These are likely to impact on your business in different ways. Just as positive elements from childhood can have a significant impact on company growth, so too can negative aspects. In fact, they might be the barrier to faster growth. You need to be aware of everyone's personal challenges. Lending an ear, giving them a role that better suits their personality traits, or helping them access professional help, can be rewarding for them and the business.

well – so ask them. What would they like included in the growth plan around their possible life changes in the next year or two? Of course, some may be planning to leave and not want to tell you, while others will welcome the chance to put their hopes and dreams on the table.

Ask them how, as a company, a team, you feel you can best support other team members going through difficult times? Have some form of outline plan in place. Do it because you care, and because a company that recognises these sorts of issues will attract and retain the type of staff you want. And when you are going through tough times, they will be there to support you too.

MATERNITY/PATERNITY LEAVE AND HOW IT CAN BENEFIT YOUR COMPANY

Have you ever fallen into the trap of wondering when any of your staff might take leave to have a baby and how on earth you would cope?

I know I did. Until I looked back at how I felt when I had each of my four children.

Becoming a parent is – possibly – one of the most creative things you can do. You have brought a child into the world, a new person who didn't exist before and who has the capacity to develop into a unique individual. So why rail against this in the workplace – purely because we have to fund their maternity leave? So let's not feel cross because we have to fund their maternity/paternity

leave and their unavailability for a while, but embrace it for the creative process it really is.

How about we revisit this negative attitude and turn it into something amazingly positive. I can't be the only mum who felt so creative... Tired at times, absolutely, but it unleashed an overwhelming belief in my ability to do so much more.

By embracing those in your team who might be going to have babies soon, or are already parents, by making them feel welcome as active contributors beyond just their role, you can help your company grow in so many ways.

This type of attitude brings loyalty. It adds a sense of camaraderie, of recognition of people's lives outside of the company. It can harness that creativity, allowing it to feed into different areas of the business, helping evolve new ways of working, of engaging with other staff and with clients.

PARENTHOOD PLANNING

As a business coach, I work with many women running their own companies. Dynamic, engaged, profitable, growing... But I'm also aware that part of their trajectory may involve motherhood – with pregnancy and the few months after the birth demanding their time and attention.

I am also aware of men running companies who are expectant fathers or have children, with the consequent impact this can have on their commitment and time.

If you run a company, you just can't afford to ignore children and their impact. In fact, I believe you should really embrace them as part of your company's modus operandi, just as you should other caring responsibilities.

But equally, if you are running a company, with responsibilities for other people's livelihoods, you have to plan and prepare well in advance for welcoming your own children into the world. Because you cannot take your eye off the ball. You need to map into any growth plan you make where parenthood is going to fit. Will it require promoting a team member to manage the company while you are on maternity/paternity leave? Do you need to recruit additional staff? How are you going to support your clients, fulfil your role? What will the financial impact be on the company?

This type of plan needs to be in place for all key staff – particularly in small, owner-run companies – to ensure disruption is minimised and the opportunities that this new creativity and approach brings are maximised.

DIVERSITY OF THOUGHT

Look around your office, or place of work. Men and women? All ages? Range of different backgrounds? People of other ethnicities? LGBT?

If not – you are totally missing a rich slice of opportunity. The greater the diversity of your organisation, the greater the likelihood of sustained growth and profitability.

In our wonderfully rich, multicultural society, the breadth of people's experience, creativity and innovation can help companies grow by tapping into ways of thinking that widen the resources and pools of experience to draw on. It's obvious, really. If you only work with people similar to you, you will all be reflecting the same set of experiences. Nothing new will be brought to the table.

Consider how you can widen your team and the influences they can share – it could make a huge difference, and need cost little if you replace people when they leave with a more diverse team member.

Quick tip... If you are pulling together a team to solve an issue or develop a new product or service, mix it up a bit. Don't always go for the same faces. Bring someone in from accounts, from your creative team, a person who could be a good strategic thinker. The different attributes each person will bring different strengths and attributes.

HARNESS COLLECTIVE WISDOM

Let's make one thing abundantly clear. You *don't* have to have all the answers. No one has all the answers.

Running your own business, no matter what area, can be a lonely place. You think that you have to permanently come up with solutions to everything. You get asked all sorts of questions by clients, your suppliers, your team...

And yes, of course there are times when you know the answers – but when you are faced with a question you don't know how to reply to, don't fudge it. Recognise you don't know the answer and then turn to your biggest resource: other people's experience. That store of collective wisdom.

If you add up all the years that you, any partners, your board or team have behind them in your area of work, it can be mind-blowing.

Let's say there are four of you and you've all been in roughly the same working world for maybe five or six years. That's already 20 years' worth of experience from just you four alone! That's a fabulous resource. Now draw that circle a little wider... Who else can you add – how much more wisdom, knowledge and support can you access?

Now *use it* to help you solve the sticking points, the problems you are uncertain of.

And it can also help you to search out untapped opportunities, to hear

Quick tip... Some people are fab at ideas and creativity. Others are good at ideas, creativity and delivery. And then there are others best at delivering against someone else's creativity. Recognise which type you are, and get support in the area where you are weak. And understand where each member of your team stands too.

stories of other companies and their growth, of new plans and ways of working. It's a rich bank of amazing free stuff to draw on to help you.

OPEN VS CLOSED ATTITUDES

Working with the variety of companies that I do, you soon begin to realise that some individuals – no matter what – are naysayers.

They can be lowly, doing something process-driven and mundane, or they can be at the top in some form of leading role. No matter what rising trend, set of great figures or opportunities you offer them, their only response is 'no' or some form of 'no' couched in the nicest terms. Their attitude is closed and they are certainly not going to change just for you.

While I understand that you have to protect a business, and not changing

case study

Jo runs a multi-award-winning film and video production company that particularly focuses on making films around social issues across the globe. She is delightful, passionate and very good at what she does.

When we started working together to develop the company, she was in her mid-30s. We drew up an ambitious growth plan, knowing the trajectory would require new premises, new team members and more clients, bigger projects. As we were coming to the end of a lively meeting, I asked her very quietly where she was going to add having a baby to the plan...

She gave me a startled look before telling me firmly that 'no one has ever asked me that question – business coach or not', adding that perhaps I was the only person who she'd take it from. Stating that she had no boyfriend, no partner or husband, she said that the likelihood of her working life incorporating a small person was a long way off. Then she asked me why I'd asked the question.

Work and home lives are always seen as separate. But, of course, they are not. They should be seen as a continuum of one feeding the other, not opposite ends of a see-saw (see page 206). What you do in one will have an

can be a safe option, these risk-averse attitudes can also limit growth and mean opportunities are missed.

For these types, lifting their heads above the parapet is too risky and frightening. Or it might mean a loss of control or show them up in ways that are uncomfortable. Fear often underpins this approach. But the brake mechanism they operate can damage a company's potential.

Understanding, acknowledging and mapping the closed attitudes is a useful way of getting to the bottom of this. If they are a barrier to company growth, you need to deal with this. And it's about talking, talking, talking.

If they are a senior figure, do the 'How to draw a business plan' exercise, explore their background to see where this closed attitude comes from. See what you can learn to help understand their position, work out how to mitigate their fears and encourage a more open, effect on the other. Good companies and employers understand this and work with it, giving rise to happy teams. Having babies is part of this.

But as she was responsible for the employment of a growing team, if Jo did want a baby she needed to prepare the company for this. Did she have a senior producer in place who could run film shoots in out-of-the-way places? Who was going to manage clients? And how was the business admin going to be overseen? These were all critical to the growth of the company.

As we sat chatting, Jo's next move was to pick up a red pencil to draw in a tiny red heart about 30 months into the plan. 'That's when I'll have a baby,' she added.

Over the next months of working together, the plans for the company progressed. They expanded the team, after much searching found fabulous new premises, continued to work in the social enterprise area they loved. One day, Jo said she'd got a delightful new boyfriend, who also came to help her grow the company. They got engaged, and four weeks before their wedding, Jo told me their baby was due in November, remarkably close to where Jo had drawn that small red heart.

Whether it was cause or effect doesn't really matter. Jo had incorporated the possibility of parenthood into the company plan to ensure that it was robust and flexible enough to adapt to the changes this would mean – whether for her or her team.

growth-focused approach.

If they are part of the delivery team, take time to listen to their concerns, but explain their impact on colleagues and the business delivery. Supporting them through change can help open their eyes to new ways of working. Alternatively, finding them a new role better suited to them that lessens their concerns can increase productivity.

PAY AND REWARDS

In exactly the same way, your company doesn't work for no pay or reward, neither does your team.

Sure, in the early days of a start-up, everyone may get paid very little or be paid with shares as 'sweat equity', but rewarding your staff fairly for the work they do is vital. It makes for a happier, thriving company with a team who feel valued.

But if cash is tight, remember there are other ways to reward your team that can 'add' to their sense of being valued over and above what they earn. These can be really simple, but effective. Of course, they don't replace a wage, but they do show your employees you care about them. And this caring attitude is important in building the right culture in your company where growth can thrive. After all – in order to grow, you are going to be asking more of them, so treating them well to help on this road is vital.

Rewards can be inventive and fun, short-term or longer-term; for everyone to share, or to quietly reward an outstanding piece of work or contribution. What matters is that everyone is seen to be treated equitably without any form of favouritism, which is divisive and hurtful.

I've seen some really good ideas over the years:

- Every company should offer familiar 'treats' like afternoon cakes, office lunches, or ice creams on hot days. It generates a sense of being cared for. Other companies encourage baking days, where teams take it in turns to bring in home cooking.
- Evenings out together for a meal or a show are some more usual events, but away-days to the beach or a local festival are just as popular. Then, if the budget allows, weekend camping with outdoor cooking in the woods or trips to Morocco, the Med or Scandinavia are fun.
- Family days out or summer barbecues encourage everyone to feel part of a bigger team and let partners meet each other and children play. It really brings home that all your futures are interlinked, in a positive way.
- Store vouchers are great, but perhaps a little dull, so put some inventive thinking behind them, such as home decorating/furnishing stores pending a home move, or a year's magazine subscription.
- Skill-learning workshops such as calligraphy, quad biking or jewellery design are lovely. Ensure there is something that appeals to all levels, capabilities and diversities.
- Celebratory rewards on winning new clients, on achieving work milestones or KPIs are important to plan in, too. As the business owner, you will benefit financially from a growing, profitable business. But you can't do it without a good team alongside you – so acknowledge this in some imaginative form of 'well done, us' treat.

Rewards can also come in what you introduce to the workplace on a regular basis. A weekly yoga or Pilates class can benefit everyone. Friday afternoon working on a pet project. Talks to inspire new skills, allowing all to contribute to the company growth.

And then there are the opportunities as the company grows, to share in profits, to earn shares, become partners.

If you work alone or are freelance,

it's just as important to take time out to treat and reward yourself. It's incredibly easy to overlook this, letting the flow of work take over. If you win a new contract, allow yourself some time out to enjoy the feeling and celebrate with another freelancer, or friends.

PLAYTIME

'All work and no play makes Jack a dull boy' – a saying we've all heard many times over and mostly applied to our lives outside work. But playtime is vitally important within work as well.

We've all seen photos of offices complete with table-tennis tables, snooker tables, children's slide shoots, and all manner of other seemingly non-work furnishings. Perhaps you've sneered at them, wondering whether these added extras really do offer any commercial benefits?

But downtime, a hanging-out space, a non-work room to talk, can be invaluable in every single workplace. It allows everyone to get away from their desk and normality, bat ideas around, discover what others are up to both in and out of work. Providing opportunities for playtime can be the real differentiator between an average- and a fast-growth company.

It enables interaction between people who don't work together, or don't really know each other. And you can make playtime happen in the office in simple ways, or take everyone out to do something fun together, whether it's a pizza one evening, a quiz or a weekend outing.

Occasionally, an individual in the team needs an extra boost, which a bit of play can inspire...

At the first meeting of a new year, a long-standing client of mine, Al, just looked really blue. On asking about the problem, he said he felt down and bored. As the co-owner of a manufacturing company with 30 people reliant on him for their livelihoods, this was not what I needed to hear. On probing further, I realised how in the previous months he had been carrying the business while his partner understandably took paternity leave following the birth of a baby. Al needed some playtime, as work had become all-consuming.

Having just bought himself a new motorbike, I suggested Al took an extended road trip to visit potential clients, a trade show or two, and similar companies right the way across Europe, for three weeks in April/early May. Both directors looked askance at my suggestion – 'What?' But that time out to go play, permission to engage but differently, galvanised Al to plan and the rest of the company to think about how they could support him/the company in his absence. They all got involved in some way or other.

And on his return from his amazing trip, he was fired up with new ways to evolve the company, as well as potential projects and ideas for clients.

BIN THE CONCEPT OF WORK VS LIFE

One of the **saddest** things I hear in companies is people saying they want to improve their work-life balance. It's as if 'work' is competing with 'life' and vice versa. It feels as if they are in an un-winnable race, they never get it right, and everyone – them, their family and their friends – is suffering. It's so self-damning and defeating.

The main issue seems to be that work and life are put at the opposite ends of a see-saw. When one is up, the other is down. This is totally and utterly **wrong**.

Work is part of your life. And it should be a rich and satisfying part of your life.

So how do you ensure that the balance between time spent at work/ working and time spent doing home/ family stuff leads to a fulfilling life?

One of the ways is not to compartmentalise them – let them bleed into each other, feed each other, overlap in a positive way. The diagram opposite shows it as a continuum, feeding positivity through the process.

If you can, take your children to work on odd days. Talk to them about ideas – they've got bright minds, they can bring you added insights. When you're out with your partner and you spot something that triggers a work thought – talk about it. Do the same for their work. Allow the textures of the different parts of you to blend richly and informatively.

Your business will benefit so positively from this. And so too will your home life, your relationships... I know it sounds counter intuitive, but try it.

One afternoon, sitting at my desk, totally absorbed in what I was doing, the phone rang.

It was my eldest child, asking if I was coming to pick her up from school. Flustered, realising I'd totally overlooked pick-up time, I stammered yes, I was on my way. Then I asked whose phone she was calling from – it being in the days before she had her own phone. She mentioned a rather trad mother, Maeve (who always seemed to view me with forebearance). Then she added: 'I've

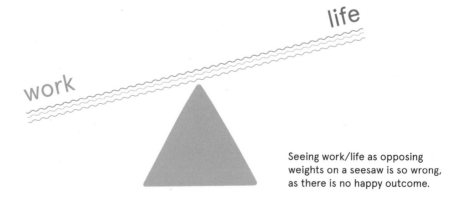

Seeing work/life as opposing weights on a seesaw is so wrong, as there is no happy outcome.

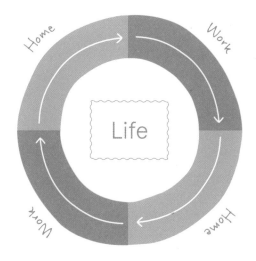

Home Work

Life

Work Home

told her you're probably just so happy in what you're designing or drawing that you'll collect me when you've finished.'

What this one sentence from my eight-year old told me was that – for her – my work, and how it absorbed me, was part of our lives. It wasn't a threat, it was something they were party to, they understood, it was just one of the many layers that made up our family life.

And not having work vs life as a battleground is just such a relief. It removes a burden that we simply don't need.

WHEN YOU PROMOTE FROM WITHIN – SUPPORT, SUPPORT, SUPPORT

If you have a hungry, ambitious team who want to help you grow the company, promoting from within can be highly cost-effective and unlock growth for little extra investment. It can also

give them, and others in the company, confidence that they can do/be what they've always dreamed of being. So if you can do this and it's the right move for you – great, but remember they will need extra support, in ways and means you might not have thought of.

Help them to understand leadership if they are now heading a team. Get them to see the world from the client's perspective if they are moving into selling. There are lots of courses, books and online tools they can use. Ask them what they feel they would like.

Not only will they grow as individuals, but the company and your other staff will benefit too.

GROW YOUR OWN TEAM

As company owners, I have no doubt you all have career development programmes for your staff in place. Of course you do.

But have you thought of developing a 'grow your own' programme to attract young talent, whether through an apprenticeship or a graduate or young persons' training programme? You don't need to be a big company to do this, but simply have a willingness to give people at the start of their careers an opportunity to work, to learn, to develop. It doesn't need to be complicated and needs no government funding if you don't choose to engage with external funding or support, but it can bring you huge rewards.

I've been involved with several versions of these, and they can be so simple to set up.

First, you have to write a job description just as you would for any normal role. But add into this how you will be training them, how there is a set programme to allow them to see the different parts of your company and the industry it operates in. Give them details of the programme and who will be managing them as they move around.

Set a pay scale that gives them a liveable wage but reflects their lack of experience and inability – for a short while – to contribute to the company.

It often helps to have a cohort of two or three at the same time (if you can afford them), so they can support and help each other.

But remember – they are not there as dogsbodies, but as young trainees who you want to develop as high-flyers within your company. Give them the respect you would like in their situation.

If you feel you are too small a venture to take two or three, join forces with a similar company to you locally, and devise the programme together. You can only benefit.

IS YOUR BOARD PULLING IN THE SAME DIRECTION?

Whether your board is two, three or more, it's a team of people who are all meant to have the company's interests at heart.

But they are people too...

Just as I suggested that you sit down and appraise your personal hopes and dreams at the start of this section of the book, it's also a good idea to ask your board to do it. Personally and professionally.

It may be that their hopes and dreams are very different to yours. That's fine. What matters is to ensure you understand theirs and they understand yours. This gives you a much better perspective on each other's visions.

This allows you to agree company goals together, but recognise that each of you will have different reasons and – most likely – different ways of getting there. That's fine too. But what it prevents is you all pulling in conflicting directions – which would not be fine!

Now ask the same questions of your team – do they have the same vision as you do?

HARNESSING YOUR OWN AND YOUR TEAM'S INNATE CAPABILITIES

One of the most delightful and surprising things about the human race is how very different we all are, how everyone is intriguing, interesting and possesses such a wide range of abilities. Yet rarely do we spend time unearthing these in the team we work with.

Going into new companies, with fantastic teams, on a regular basis is like an extraordinary voyage of discovery –

for me, but also for those I'm working with. They often know little about those with whom they share office space. Their passions, hobbies, skills, the books they are reading. Yet these are the very people capable of taking the organisation from good to great – of bringing a wide range of elements to the business, allowing it to develop a unique offering.

These people are part of your team already, so you need to ensure you aren't letting any of their hidden talents go to waste. Build some 'listening' sessions into the week...

- Hold a Monday lunchtime catch-up over a sandwich to discover what everyone did at the weekend.
- Find out what evening classes anyone's ever attended, or what they might like to do.
- Ask everyone for a surprising fact about themselves, or something they know...

Think about how these could lead to developments within your business.

case study

HEY HUMAN

Mick is an unassuming, hard-working art worker at experiential and marketing agency Hey Human. But every other weekend for the last seven years, he has taken his camera to photograph the striking street art in East London. Applying his own artistic sensibilities to the material he shoots, the images tell wider stories about the surrounding street life than just the paintings on decaying walls. Some of the artworks he's shot have only been visible for two or three hours before being overpainted, such is the transience of this medium. Mick's image may be the only record that exists of many hours of painstaking work.

But the agency he works for values and encourages his passion. They know that it is this type of creativity that feeds the work they do every day for clients.

The agency is about to move offices to new premises with big communal spaces, and is hoping that at some time in the future they will hold an exhibition featuring Mick's images of London's transient art, called *Blink: Did You Miss It?*

www.heyhuman.com

HeyHuman

The Middle Circle

The next circle out from you and your team are your suppliers, who feed into your company, and your clients, who your company in turn supplies. Having good, solid relationships with both halves of this circle is vital for the health of your business and your long-term growth. I'm stating the obvious, really.

DON'T JUST ENGAGE – ENCHANT

Do you really love what you do?

If so – how often do you tell your suppliers and clients how happy you are in your work, how much you enjoy working with them, for them? And why? These can be big reasons, or just small touch points. But hearing that someone really enjoys what they do, brings their whole self to their work, their commitment, their purpose, is wonderful. And it can have such a positive impact.

It makes people want to become clients, to join your team, to be your suppliers. There is an air of attraction around you that pulls them towards you.

No, of course we can't do it every day, and some are working in places that are tough and unrelenting, but bringing that personal passion, that enchantment to the table can be hugely rewarding.

You are probably reading this going 'yeah, right, what does she know?' – a world-weary cynicism to the fore. But you'll be surprised at how spinning this into a determination to enjoy and enchant your working engagements will make a real difference.

YOUR SUPPLIERS

Please treat your suppliers kindly.

They are doing their best, just like you. And they can be some of your biggest supporters, can help you out when things get tough, and – just like your clients – they want you to succeed too. That's what keeps them in business.

Talk to them, invite them to events, parties, coffee. Welcome them into your life. Ask their advice, what trends they are seeing... they will have valuable market knowledge that could trigger new service or product ideas.

case study

Benjamin Pollock's Toyshop can be found in Covent Garden, its home for the last 25+ years. Originally established in Hoxton, it has now been trading pretty much continually since 1856. Selling Pollock's toy theatres as well as a rich assortment of creative paper-play goods for adults and children alike, it is a magnet for artists, designers, actors and theatre/film directors, as well as Londoners and tourists, from within the UK and overseas. But in today's deeply competitive high street, and with tough online trading eating away at brick-and-mortar store revenues, how can a unique business like Benjamin Pollock's Toyshop thrive?

The team at the toyshop know that by keeping focused on their history, their archive and their product range, but bringing new contemporary artists and designers to illustrate them, they can keep their customers coming back for more. And rather than just building an ever-larger mailing list, they are launching a fan club, with both free and subscription memberships. Each level will receive exclusive offers, products, event invitations and the like. The intention is to ensure the toyshop really values, cares for and enchants its most engaged customers, providing them with an experience they cannot find elsewhere.

pollocks-coventgarden.co.uk

BENJAMIN
POLLOCK'S
TOYSHOP

SUPPLY CHAIN SAFETY

Your supply chain is critical to your business. If you can't trust your suppliers to deliver what you want, when you want, to the standard you want, it will endanger your trade and could mean you lose your customers.

Protecting your supply chain is vital. But looked at from their perspective, your suppliers also want you to succeed – because that gives them even more business.

case study

A YOUNG ATHLEISURE CLOTHING COMPANY

When you run a small, organic, ethically sourced fitness clothing business with a unique product range, your suppliers are even more critical to you, as there is not a wide range to choose from that echo your principles. Not only do you want a confirmed ethical supply chain, you need to ensure you use organic-based cotton and eco-friendly dyes. And because you are a small business, your supplier has to be happy with you placing smaller orders as you build your customer base.

But the team has been determined from the outset to ensure the highest codes are adhered to. Receiving their new range from their supplier just hours before an important high-profile direct-to-consumer fitness fair, they put the garments straight onto their stand's rails – then watched them fly off as their customers took to them in delight.

Just hours later, the first complaint was texted in... Unable to test the products themselves due to the tight delivery, they didn't realise their new printed logo was not wash-safe. Something had gone wrong with their supplier's dye batch.

Without a moment's hesitation, Lorna and Alice contacted *all* of the customers who had bought garments, offering them a refund or a replacement, and took the unsold items off the shelf.

It took the team several months to get the supplier to accept responsibility, and get free replacement batches and resupply their customers.

It knocked a hole in the year's profitability – but it also taught the team how vitally linked they were to their suppliers and how key it was to have a supplier contract *and* insurance in place.

Your upstream suppliers need to agree a code of trading with you in the same way as your clients do. Putting a supplier contract in place is a really wise thing to do, particularly if you rely on a limited range of key suppliers. It should cover quality control, delivery times and payment terms, but also what happens if they mess up, with the consequent impact/losses that will occur in your business. Who is responsible for this trading loss?

Some companies won't ever need to consider this if they are in a buyer's market, but if you are working with a very limited pool of suppliers – you need to protect yourself.

Advisory board

A great way to get help into your business as and when you need it is to appoint an advisory board.

Unlike a board of directors, who have legal and fiduciary duties, an advisory board can meet whenever it chooses and you can work out its role yourselves, and also choose how best you need it to support your company and team.

It can be a great way to bring different perspectives and experience to your business. You can choose people who have industry knowledge, can introduce you to other markets or who have already undertaken projects

you are about to embark on. Their involvement can be merely as a sounding board or with a bigger remit. They can be incredibly helpful – particularly if you run the company yourself or just with one or two partners. They can operate as 'friends to the business', or, if you choose, you can ask them to monitor your delivery of your goals.

When I float advisory board advantages to clients, many of them really like the idea. Others realise they already have a series of people they regularly turn to for advice. By bringing them together into an advisory board, they meet each other and provide an even better support network.

The other question that then arises is one of payment. Some want paying, others are happy to help for free, or be paid 'in kind'. What matters is that both sides feel they benefit and are not being taken advantage of.

Professional outsider

An odd title perhaps, but having a professional outsider for your business can give rise to fascinating insights leading to wide opportunities.

What do we mean by a 'professional outsider'? This will depend on your industry. We are all familiar with the notion of a 'second opinion' – needing someone else to take a look at a problem, whether in dentistry, legal affairs or whatever, in the hope they will either confirm/deny, or interpret a situation differently.

But sometimes bringing in someone who is unfamiliar with your industry, your way of working, can add value in unexpected ways. This can be through knowing how other companies or industries work and applying it to yours, or by interpreting what you do differently.

You can have differing levels of professional outsider – from a company 'friend' type of relationship to one who can fulfil a similar role to a non-executive director or participate on an advisory board.

Have you ever thought that this could be of use to your business? Who would you ask? And what areas would you like to explore with them?

My own dilemma…

My own business was going through a period of change. One of my team was leaving to further her own career. I was feeling a bit uncertain about our offer. I was changing my working methodology. Lots was happening and I started to feel a bit lost in the middle.

So I rang an ex-client to invite him to breakfast – urgently, tomorrow morning. I needed his perspective, his long-term view, his experience, his years….

He arrived wondering why I'd insisted on meeting so speedily. I had one question for him. He agreed to answer it honestly.

I looked him straight in the eye and asked: 'What do I do?'

Without missing a beat, he answered straightforwardly, in two words. It was a moment of clarity I needed to take the next steps. He had understood exactly where I was, what I needed to hear. But his outsider's knowledge of who I was and what I did gave a really clear focus.

Simple.

Your clients

I have some of the nicest clients of any business I know. I really enjoy spending time with them. I love hearing their news, what they are up to, what they love doing away from work, about their families. I genuinely care about them. And there is no doubt that, with some, that care is reciprocated.

Just as I treat my suppliers kindly, you want to be treated well by those you supply – your clients. If your business is growing and offering more services, these new services could benefit them. So staying in touch and keeping them informed is important.

But you also have to be aware that, as you grow, some of your clients will start being a drain on your business rather than being an asset to help your profitability. Knowing when to move away from some clients is as important as looking after them...

And I have another simple rule around clients: I refuse to work for arseholes. I've come across enough in my life to know that some clients just won't get what I do, how I work, and how we can grow their business together. They sap your energy – if you are freelance, you're spinning enough plates as it is. Having clients who are eating your soul is no fun. Of course, we may be reliant on them for income – and if this is the case, try to replace them as soon as you can.

Then there are others who employ you to do something, but then spend their time telling you how to do your job. It's back to that old adage of 'why keep a dog and bark yourself'... If they're draining your limited time and resources – move on. Look for clients who *want* to work with you, respect you and understand the value you bring.

CLIENT PARTNERSHIP – NOT PARENT/CHILD

One of the very dispiriting aspects of business can be the inequality you see in a client-customer relationship. This can have such a negative effect on how we all work – when the relationship should be the opposite.

When you are buying something from someone – whether a service such as a taxi ride, a part for a car, a website framework – the purchaser values what

Quick tip... Try to ensure you spread your clients across different markets, business practices and sizes. This will allow you fairer terms of business, and will allow you to have different contract terms with them.

Position yourself as their equal partner, rather than in a parent-child relationship. Neither of your businesses can thrive without the other, so a positive, well-written contract should reflect this parity of approach.

the seller is offering. And by setting the price, the seller is asking for a fair payment from the customer. This is the underpinning process of commerce. It is a contract – you give me *x* item, for which I will pay you *y* price.

But too often a hierarchy falls into place where one side feels they can treat the other less fairly or fail to respect the other's side of the deal. This leads to poor working partnerships.

If you can establish a balanced relationship with both sides effectively having 'a seat at the table', understanding both have roles to play, that both are stakeholders with an alignment in achieving a common goal, it produces a much healthier way of working, with fairer values ascribed to both sides. And provides a route to both parties achieving better results.

Try to aim for this in all your workings. It can take time to shift perceptions towards this balanced relationship but it is really worth striving for. If you know you are a valued part of a team, you provide a better service, you are happier doing what you do and it impacts the whole of the business.

CONTRACT FAIRNESS

You know when you are downloading software, have to agree terms with a remote supplier or some big conglomerate and you are asked to tick that box saying you have read their T&Cs – how does it make you feel?

I always get a sense of unfairness. Of me being the pawn in their big commercial game. Of allowing myself to be exploited for their needs, not mine. I feel the contract is not fair but is

case study

FACTORY SETTINGS

A fabrication company based in East London, Factory Settings is a small, fast-growing company building displays, exhibitions and fittings for visitor attractions, galleries and museums. Winning business frequently involves a competitive tender.

Talking through the tendering process, it became obvious that this took up a lot of their time, with unpredictable outcomes. They would be given a set of outline designs with suggested materials, but no budget to work to or really any room for discussion.

Despite the client organisations regularly needing Factory Settings' skills to stage their exhibitions, the company and others like them were firmly put at the bottom of the contract hierarchy, with four or five similar companies competing for the same project – all of whom were also investing time, money and skill for the same uncertain outcome.

The key to making the process simpler, less wasteful and better for everyone involved was to help the clients and their specifying and procurement teams to 'buy smarter'. If everyone had a valued seat at the same table with improved understanding of each other's processes, skills and costs, then everyone could benefit, cutting out task overlap and unnecessary wastage.

So Factory Settings approached two or three of their clients, asking for the always weighted in their favour, written by corporate lawyers.

So when I work with smaller companies and we discuss contracts with their clients or their suppliers, be they large or small, I always stress that contracts *must* be fair to both parties. Contracts are not about control of one party by the other, but about fair terms – an agreed supply of a product/service in return for fair payment in reasonable time.

Often you see big companies abuse small suppliers by tying them to a 90-day payment term. Yet these small suppliers will have to pay their suppliers in 30 days or less. This means that the small companies have to focus their energies on building resilient cash-flow management, rather than their core business – with the big company and their shareholders benefitting from this corporate bully-boy tactic.

tender process to be re-evaluated. They asked for a two-stage tender process – the first stage a simple response to the brief, following which the client could select a couple of companies to move forward with to a more detailed tender document. For those companies not on the shortlist, this saved time and money in not having to produce a detailed tender document.

The second request was to know what budget the client had, to ensure the tender fitted the brief more closely. If there were insufficient funds for marble or other expensive materials, other suggestions could be made early on in the process rather than just submitting a tender way beyond expectations.

And finally, they asked for a much more democratic way of working together – valuing their contribution to the process, as part of the team getting the exhibition staged. This included recognition for much of the work they had to do as part of their process, but which their clients had just automatically expected in previous tenders.

www.factorysettings.co.uk

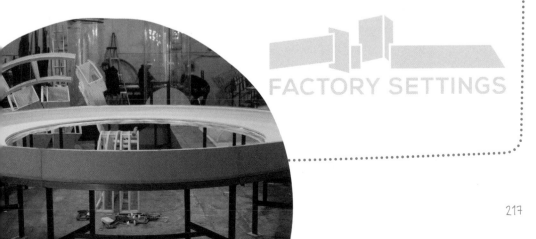

FACTORY SETTINGS

WORK WITH THE DECISION-MAKERS

When you are working with companies, it is always better to work with the decision-makers or as close to the decision-makers as is humanly possible. It saves time.

We all know that heart-sinking feeling when your client has to refer your work/budget or whatever to someone else further up the chain. It takes time, may change the game, mean you have to redo things because their internal briefing wasn't quite right, etc. etc. etc. So try to have the decision-makers in as many of the key meetings as you can.

HAVING BIG COMPANIES AS CLIENTS

Although there is a degree of cachet having big companies as clients, they aren't always all they're cracked up to be. It can be a mixed blessing, to be honest.

While they are less likely to go bust, they can have excruciating payment terms. For example, I understand that a well-respected retail pillar of our UK high streets does not pay its suppliers for 90 days. If this type of activity is hitting you hard, it can be worth looking at invoice factoring.

Big companies may demand

NEW WAYS OF STRUCTURING A CONSULTANCY CONTRACT

case study

When two ex-colleagues set up their creative business consultancy, we talked about what a 'contract of opportunity' might look like, and reframed their contract accordingly... The main clause we added was about 'permission'.

When working on a client's business, if the consultancy team saw an interesting commercial opportunity that the client had not identified and was outside the actual work scope outlined in the contract itself, the 'permission' clause allowed the consultancy team to bring it to the client's attention, presenting it to them at a separate meeting.

By turning their idea into a presentation, the consultancy retained the copyright of this commercial opportunity pending further commercial discussions, and did not pass any ownership across to the client. Could you adapt this idea to suit your business?

One day I received a telephone call from a small, early-stage animation company. They were being asked by a big broadcaster to supply animated inserts for a children's series, and had just received the contract from this big corporation. They were aghast at how it insisted they hand over the IP to their characters, and all the other terms seemed to go against their interests or give them no future stake in what they were creating. It made them feel like children in a world they didn't really understand.

So we sat down to unpack the contract, to think through what would be beneficial for *their* business and how this would translate into revised contract terms that would be acceptable to both parties.

We came up with a host of ideas, such as should the broadcaster want to develop the characters from the animated section of the programme separately, the copyright to any further exploitation would sit with the animators, so this would have to be discussed separately. Another said that if the broadcaster wanted to make a further series of the same show, they may not take the animation work to any other studio. And so on.

These were presented to the broadcaster in an email and a telephone discussion, with a clear explanation as to why they were not just signing the contract but wanted significant changes.

To the delight of the animation company, the broadcaster's business affairs manager understood the fairness of the new terms and agreed to them, sending a revised contract by return. Both parties were happy.

exclusivity of product or service, which could, if not carefully managed, damage your relationship with other companies. You then need to consider whether it is worthwhile developing a tweaked range just for them.

And the person who is buying from you may change not once, but several times during the course of your relationship with the company. It can make sense to ensure you establish contact with your buyer, but also with other people in their team, or department. I also always find out who in the Accounts Payable department is responsible for paying my invoice!

A 'CONTRACT OF OPPORTUNITY'

Although I am not a lawyer, I have seen all sorts of different contracts during my career. They are written to protect both parties regarding what they have agreed to buy/sell/do/produce and so on, to ensure both sides deliver. However, they can also be very defensive. Written in legal terms, there is almost never a statement that both parties are **partners** in the undertaking covered by the contract, both wanting the best possible outcome for themselves and each other.

So how can you make your contracts more positive, more proactive? Is it possible to do this in your industry?

CONTRACT KICK-OFF

This is going to sound unbelievably obvious – but a contract is not a contract until it has been signed by **both** parties.

Until that point, it is only a **draft** contract – so open to negotiation.

Large organisations will frequently send smaller companies quite onerous contracts. Heavyweight documents written by big, expensive law firms. These are designed to protect the interest of the big company only and they insist that you, as the smaller party, fall into line. In the creative and media world that I largely work in, this happens all the time.

However, the more exclusive the service that you are supplying to the large company, the greater your ability to negotiate the terms of the contract.

And if you are freelance or self-employed...?

A friend of mine was sent a contract for a global company that she was about to join, working for them three days a week. The remaining days she was running her own small business.

Under the IP clause in her contract, it stated unequivocally that **all and any IP** she produced would be owned by the company.

She asked me what to do. I told her to question it firmly as it was unfair. But a 'take it or leave it, we're not changing' response came back from HR. Not helpful.

I looked at the contract in detail and realised that it was outmoded and wasn't fit for purpose in the changing ways we are now working.

So Sara and I unpacked it together, rewriting the IP clause to say that 'yes, of course, any IP developed during the 9–5 hours/three days per week Sara was actually working for the company would belong to the company'. But work outside of these hours or for her own venture in the remaining four days each week would remain hers.

There were various other points we highlighted and tweaked to ensure both the company and Sara were being fair.

The latest I heard was that not only does she now have the contract she wants (and needs) but the company is changing their global staff contracts to reflect today's fast-changing working practices.

SYSTEMS, SYSTEMS, SYSTEMS

One of the easiest ways of helping your business ensure consistency across projects, people and suppliers – which in turn can lead to greater management control (and on to better profitability) – is to work out a clear action list at key points in your relationships.

So when a new member of staff starts – do you have a dedicated member of staff to go through health and safety, the staff handbook, etc.?

If you are working with a new client, is there an 'onboarding' process that you take them through, to ensure both parties know what to expect of each other and when? Do you have very clear T&Cs so everyone knows where they stand re: payment, responsibilities, IP ownership, making changes? And is there an agreed internal format for closing a project when it is complete?

All of these may seem onerous to develop, but they quickly become part of the company ethos and way of working, save time and arguments, and allow real clarity.

COLLABORATING

This can be a wonderful experience or a total can of worms...

And it mostly happens with other companies that you know in the middle circle. It can bring all sorts of interesting ways of working within your grasp. It can be around marketing, new product development, shared space, resources or people.

You can collaborate with colleagues or other freelancers, with clients, with suppliers, with schools or universities, with tech providers or your competitors. The list is endless.

If two people or organisations feel the other is worth linking to, collaborating with, and it is of mutual benefit to **both** – then go for it. But you **have** to be really clear about what the other's aims and desired outcomes are. And only collaborate with people you really trust. Misaligned collaborations are horrible and painful for everyone. But good ones can work on so many levels and bring benefit to both parties, often outside of the expected areas.

One of the easiest ways to find out the pros and cons is to talk to other people who've experienced collaborations – good and bad. They will happily eulogise about the joys of working closely with another business, or tell you their horror stories and what to look out for.

But this can be a brilliant way of extending your reach, finding new joint markets with your aligned ambitions – it's really worth exploring.

The Outer Circle

The people and organisations in the outer circle are those you are trying to win over to work with you... They represent your opportunities – whether as customers, clients, influencers or suppliers, potential staff or collaborators.

This is the space that feeds both the middle circle and the inner circle. Sometimes you will know who these people are, but mostly you won't. Yet you have to reach them, you have to touch them, you have to make them want to connect with you in some way or other.

This is the circle that the bulk of your marketing needs to connect with.

If you want to attract new and different types of clients, you have to go to places where they congregate – networking events, talks etc.

The Foremost Five

As I've been working with companies, I've come to realise that there are five key areas of business opportunity that can be easily identified. Each allows you to do new and different things to build your business. (And yes, I realise that no.1 below should fit into the middle circle...)

1 PAST/EXISTING CLIENTS
If you read the business planning section at the beginning of this book, you should already be well under way with finding new sectors and ways of working with past and existing business clients.

If you have just dipped in here – read the paragraphs on pages 27 about 'Clients/customers who've paid you' and 'What you've been paid to do'. Ensure you apply this thinking to all your past and existing clients, because once you are in a relationship with a client, it can be hard to change the terms of engagement.

2 FUTURE CLIENTS

Now, this is where you can really start revamping your business – if that is what you want to do. With your future clients, you can set up completely new ways of working.

They may have found you on social media, may have looked at your website, or may ask you to come to talk to them about a project. All of them offer you a chance to reframe your business – perhaps you want to change your contract, the ways you charge, the services you offer. Or you want to ensure you are seen as a partner alongside them.

Ensure that you clearly put this out there on all your marketing and other touch points where future clients may see you.

3 COMPETITORS

Don't overlook the value that your competitors could have to you – not only helping you see a trend they have identified and you haven't, but also as a potential market for something you have developed in your own company.

Perhaps you have created an online tool that helps your team do their job better, or you have improved an ingredient or invented some machinery. Yes, these can give you a useful commercial advantage, but could you also sell this to them as well as the end user? Then, as they grow, so too will you.

Or you could have come up with

New buyers in your marketplace will welcome support in understanding how best to work with you

something that solves a pinch point in your industry's working practice, which you can offer to everyone else for a fee.

4 NEW BUYERS

New buyers are recent entrants to the business-to-business market you may work in, who may be relatively inexperienced or have less money to spend than your past and existing clients. Think of creative ways that you can work with them to help them build their ventures, rather than just charging them at your current rate.

And finally...

5 NEW AUDIENCES

A new audience is a group of people to whom you may not have sold before. For example, if you generally sell your products or services to other businesses, can you offer anything to the people in the street through retail or direct to the consumer? The internet allows all businesses to access a global market – so are you able to make the most of this?

case study

TAXO'D

Dave Legion is a freelance designer and animator. Or, more correctly, I should say Dave Legion *was* a freelance animator.

Although he had tried to map the money he might owe on tax in a spreadsheet for a couple of years, in early 2014 he once again faced paying his self-employed tax bill to HMRC. And yet again he realised he'd failed to put aside enough money during the previous year to settle his tax bill, because he had absolutely no idea how much he needed to save. He was not alone – many of his friends and colleagues, also freelance or self-employed, faced the same annual shortfall.

As Dave admits himself, being both number and letter dyslexic did not help! So Dave decided to solve his problem once and for all.

He designed a simple mobile phone app that calculates tax as you earn money. And it shows it on the screen throughout the year so you know exactly how much money you need to have saved to pay your tax bill.

Called TAXO'D, you press the + symbol when you invoice, and the – symbol when you have to spend money on a business expense. The app then does the calculation. This makes it all seem simple.

Four years on, Dave is only just launching it, as he wanted the workings to be clever, intuitive and useful. The app will not only calculate your tax but also has the capability to file your accounts with HMRC. And it is packed with easy to find information and supportive advice, no matter what industry you work in. www.taxodapp.com

case study

SERENA – A LIFETIME IN THE FOOD INDUSTRY

Serena had arrived at the point many of us reach in our late 40s/early 50s, questioning what the future might hold for her. What would the next step on her rather disjointed career look like? In fact, she'd never even thought of it as a career – just a series of things she did to earn money. She felt lost, uninspired and lacking in self-confidence. So we talked and drew up the top half of the business map shown earlier in the book.

What emerged was extraordinary. But she couldn't see the value in it, until we really began to unpack it.

Serena loves food, cooking, ingredient provenance and small suppliers. Her 'CV' involved catering for small events, working for the Royal Warrant Holders Association, working for a whisky supplier, getting 90% of the way through her Master of Wine exams, launching a small Cornish pasty business that supplied both Harrods and Waitrose, producing dinner party and other event food for high-net-worth individuals, starting her own small but award-winning meat smokery. All while having three children.

With this career map forming the springboard, we came up with a raft of ideas as to what she was uniquely capable of doing.

As we worked our way through the Foremost Five, we realised her past/present client list was huge. Her future client list encompassed a range of sectors. There was much she could offer other food industry ventures – her competitors – and as for new buyers/audiences? Well, the list was endless.

As I write this, I don't know what her final choice of business(es) will be – but something tells me she'll be just fine!

So, even if you are self-employed or freelance, don't overlook the Foremost Five!

Let's talk about...

Tapping into pools of hidden talent

Two of the most amazing talent banks we have in the UK are hiding in plain sight. They are skilled, enthusiastic, efficient and love being in a team. And they are often over qualified or prepared to put in hard graft to do a thorough job. Could you use them as a powerful resource for your company?

The first of these talented groups is to be found at every school gate in the country. They are the mothers and fathers who either choose or have to stay at home to look after their children. However, many dream of being able to work part-time doing something where they are valued and that can also help build for the longer term – whether skills, relationships or whatever.

If you need part-time help for your company, really do look at how you could access this talent bank. It could be book-keeping or legal help. It could be marketing or digital help. For example, Digital Mums helps train experienced ex-marketeers to transfer their talents to the digital space while at home looking after children.

The second group who we often overlook are those who are incapacitated or disabled in some way – or are looking after those who are unable to care for themselves. Yes, they may be unable to work in a way

familiar to us, but they need outside stimuli and they want to contribute just as much as the next person. How can you access this pool of talent, who may well have the time and the skills to really contribute to your business in unexpected ways?

Mistakes

There isn't a person, a company or an organisation that hasn't made a mistake somewhere along the line. I have, you have, so has every other company you trade with. Some have been small and doubtless some will have been very much larger, with serious consequences.

What matters about mistakes, once the failure has been dealt with as quickly and adeptly as possible to sort out the issues, is that you **learn** from them.

Finding out why a mistake happened and looking at putting checks/balances in place to ensure it doesn't recur is crucial. And helping your team understand how to avoid it in the future, whether through training, revising your systems, implementing a different process or changing how you behave is all part of embracing that mistake and growing from it.

Having a big 'mistake map' up on the wall to show what mistakes were made (how, when), and the actions you've all taken to ensure you factor out each cause, can be a useful diagram to highlight what went wrong and how you are supporting your team to avoid repetition.

Listening

When you go to the hairdresser or to the barber for a haircut, shave, colour or whatever – how much of your life story do you share with them as they practise their skills on you? Probably quite a lot. In fact, they will know a huge amount about you, your circumstances, your preferences, your plans – knowledge built up over several years of listening. For them it fills the time, but also will potentially give them a picture of what style is right for you.

Listening is a vital part of business, whether for a consultant or a supplier, and one I certainly don't always use enough. It can be done in a café, in an office, travelling to a meeting and is often best in 'downtime' rather than in focused meetings. Careful, engaged listening can allow you to hear the undercurrents in someone's life, your business relationship, their concerns or indeed opportunities. It can help you understand their motivations, discover subtle changes or give valuable insights.

And it's free.

Apprentices

As a business owner, one of the best things we can do is to help those wanting to come into the workforce get a toe in the door. It brings diversity from a different age group, a new attitude, a different mindset. And with the apprentice schemes available, it's even easier.

Yes, there will be a financial cost. But by choosing the right young person, by giving them the opportunity to learn, grow and thrive, listening to their ideas, valuing their contribution, you help them and your company.

So ask yourself if you could create an opportunity for an apprentice. How fab to give someone a launchpad into their career!

Belief and validation

As I sit writing these paragraphs, I feel very sad.

I work with some of the most talented people in the UK. I am incredibly lucky. But often they will contact me with deep concerns about their abilities, their self-belief at rock bottom.

Working for yourself or running your own small company is hard. Make no mistake about it. You have to find your own clients. You have to put yourself on the line with every client. You have to have huge reserves of self-belief to draw on to keep you going, to face challenges alone.

This morning, one of the most talented women I know sent me an email questioning her own ability. That made me sad. I am the person she turns to for validation and to build her belief in herself, her capability to move forward with her dynamic business vision. This is a woman who has put together mind-blowingly complex contracts for global corporations. Way more complicated than anything I've ever done. But I believe in her. And she knows it because I tell her regularly.

If you are struggling with confidence in yourself, belief in the business you are building and your sense of worth, find yourself a business coach, or work with a confidence coach. If that costs too much, find a local business support network. Sharing a problem or finding out you are not the only one facing it can be really helpful.

And remember – just as you may need validation occasionally, help validate others in their work too. If someone you come across has done something amazing and seriously smart with their business, give it a shout-out on social media.

Identifying bottlenecks...

How many times in your career have you recognised that something's got stuck on someone's desk? Yours, a client's, a supplier's?

Bottlenecks are a real pain. They prevent growth by just putting a roadblock in the way.

If it's your desk causing the roadblock – no one can deal with it but you. Either delegate, allow someone else to work closely with you to share the load, or train someone up to handle the issues. There's no point in fudging it.

Sometimes the bottleneck is in your process, or maybe it's someone else in your team... If that's the case, time spent solving it is really worthwhile. Everyone in your process, your company, your orbit will benefit from unblocking it. And it can be startling how much growth freeing it up may allow.

Often, clients cause roadblocks due to their approvals or procurement processes. If this is having a detrimental impact on your growth and evolution, there are two good ways to deal with it.

The first is to ensure you have sufficient other projects flowing round the block to remove its impact on your cash flow. You have to manage it effectively from your end.

The second is to address it directly with the client, outlining the problem to effect a better solution. I'm often told this is not possible – yet mountains can be moved...

Unique skills

If you or your team have some unique skills – talk about them. Celebrate them. Inside the company, but also with your customers, your potential customers, your networks.

As a nation, the British, it isn't 'done' to talk about yourself, to 'big' yourself up. But sometimes this is hiding your

case study

MANUFACTURING COMPANY

I get around. Some of my clients work in beautiful spaces, some in shared workplaces, some from home. Others work in really awful spaces. But I also have clients who, by the nature of their work, are in an environment that is noisy, dusty, with a workshop, paint-splattered and filled with machinery. That's fine. But this often leads to the office space, the communal areas, the entrance not being cared for either.

I've been working with a company for several years. They are a fabulous company, they're growing, their team is amazing – dedicated, professional, funny and a delight to work with. Yet their offices are horrible. They know their offices are horrible. I know their offices are horrible. The loos are hideous.

The two directors have listened to me endlessly banging on about how their business would thrive even more if their environment was sorted. To be fair, they said they wanted to get other aspects of the business right before they did this as it involved building a mezzanine and a major refurb. As I write, this is finally underway.

Their staff is hugely excited, knowing how this investment is really in them, in their space, and their comfort. And everyone knows it will trigger growth in such a range of ways.

They will be able to welcome clients to their premises now. They will feel smarter, walking the walk as well as talking the talk. They will be seen and known to be an employer who cares.

light under a bushel when allowing that light to shine will help boost you and how you are perceived in a really good way. Two quick stories...

Oliver is an expert on biophiliac interior design – how natural materials, light and planting can have a positive impact on living and working conditions.

He is one of the world's leading practitioners, but never said so in any of his marketing. Having recognised this unique expertise, we added it to his marketing. Quietly. He now signs his emails 'Global Expert in Biophilia Design'. It's on his website.

Ben is one of the few people who

have choreographed big machinery to music for public events. Whenever he talks about it, people are fascinated. What a unique and fabulous skill to celebrate!

Employment policies

This paragraph will probably be skipped over on reading that title! But for your business to develop and grow, you **have** to put all those different policies required by law or your industry in place.

While this may not seem relevant to a book on growth – it is. Not having the right policies in place means that if something goes horribly wrong, you could be shut down. And quite rightly. A company, an employer or a small venture that hasn't identified risks or doesn't care enough about the people on its premises and their well-being doesn't deserve to be growing...

Whether it is the non-negotiable policies such as health and safety, your own company and office risk assessment, diversity or whatever – take the time to get these in place and then review them regularly. Ask a team member or other third party to check them out to ensure they are fit for purpose and can be reliably turned to if things go wrong.

The other, hidden benefit of putting all these policies in place is that it makes you think about your company as a 'proper' business. It puts you on a more solidly professional footing in your own eyes. Odd but true.

Is your working environment hobbling your growth?

Let's be quite clear here. I think that having a rubbish-strewn, uncared-for, hideous working environment inhibits company growth.

It will mean you feel bad when you get to work. Your team feel they don't matter because you are asking them to work in an unpleasant place. Whatever you do won't have that great edge to beat your competitors. Whereas a good, clean, well-presented environment gives off all the right vibes.

All it takes is a coat of white paint, and some thought.

What don't you know?

There is a simple series of questions...

- What do you know? This is information you should use to advantage.
- What do you know you don't know? If you are aware of gaps in your knowledge, find an expert to help you, or encourage a team member to extend their own knowledge to fill the gap.
- What don't you know you don't know? Obviously you can't answer this, but it's why having an outsider come in to look at your business can be really enlightening, as they will be aware of different things from you.

Your goals

Your people

By dipping in and out of the this section of the book, you should now be able to start setting yourself some clear goals in terms of what you want to achieve through working with the different people in your sphere.

Write them down here. You can have big, ambitious headline goals for the next 5 years – but to achieve these you will need to have smaller, closer goals for the next 6–18 months.

BIG GOALS

1 ....

2 ....

3 ....

6–18 MONTH GOALS

1 ....

2 ....

3 ....

Carry these forward to the GOALS section at the end of the book, when we will look at how to make a plan.

As long-standing partnerships with the staff owning the business, this has now been acknowledged in a name change to John Lewis & Partners and Waitrose & Partners: can you credit your team more fully for their contribution?

4

MARKETING

Marketing can be as simple or as in-depth as you want. It is about reminding your existing customers of what you do, and telling potential customers about your products/services to encourage them to buy from or work with you. And it's a mixture of art and science.

As with the section on this book about people, I am no marketing expert. There are lots of good books on the subject. Lots of workshops on the internet you can take part in, courses to do. Use them.

But below is a range of ideas that have appeared on my radar, that I use, that have surprised me with their easy effectiveness... Choose the ones that feel right for you.

BUSY MARKETING

If you are working really hard on a range of projects, one of the first things you overlook is marketing yourself. After all, your order book is full, so why focus on bringing in more work?

What you forget to identify is that the current work probably took 3–6 months, maybe more, to come to fruition – your lead pipeline.

You need to keep that pipeline

full while you are also busy delivering projects. So carve out a few hours every week, either in your diary or one of your team's, to ensure you keep selling yourself. It can be simple - a 'boast' about a current client project, or it can be a regular newsletter as part of your longer-term marketing strategy. But you **have** to keep doing it.

PUTTING YOUR BUSINESS IN CONTEXT

OK – what does this mean? And why can it make a difference to you?

Understanding where your individual services, your products or your company sit in the wider marketplace is important to grasp. It affects how your customers will engage with you, buy from you, talk about you.

Most people are pretty unimaginative and follow a fairly safe choice. They don't want to rock the boat, put their head above the parapet, as it may endanger their job or set them apart from the norm.

So it is really key to help them see the value of working with you – to their industry, their sector, their company, their team, their boss and themselves. It is as much about the intangible benefits this can bring, allied to the actual benefits. You have to explain, to show them, market to them. Be inventive and forward-looking... Show them what is potentially on the horizon that could impact them positively or negatively.

Audience or market?

Your audience and your market, while seemingly two similar ideas, and which do overlap, can be very different and need to be treated differently when you are marketing to them.

Let's look at who might make up each group.

YOUR AUDIENCE

Your audience is everyone you want to be able to tell about and influence their thinking around your brand and what you do.

It's not just the people who might buy your product, but the decision-maker holding the purse-strings, the person writing the social media posts your buyer might read, a company who might be a supplier to you in the future, someone who is able to refer work to you.

Just as you need to understand who your market is, understanding your audience is critical too.

Draw up a big list of **everyone** that you see in your existing audience – those who you want to know about you and what you do. Just list their names. This is List A, and should just be a 'top of the mind' list you can add to whenever you have a moment.

Now you Split **List A** - **Who** - into different groups that might have areas of similarity to create **List B** - **Why**.

These might include groups or sectors such as:

- future suppliers
- journalists or social media influencers who could write about you
- those who influence the buying decision from you, but aren't your direct customers (for example, if you are a driving instructor, a young learner's parents might be the influencers, whereas your actual customer is the learner).
- places where you do/could talk, show what you do, attend an event.

Write up as many areas as you can. Some may be sectors that you want to approach straight away while others will be groups that you just need to keep in mind as your business grows.

The next list asks **how** you should reach List B.

List C – **How** – Do you need to do anything different for one audience than for another? Is it more successful? By pulling these apart, it allows us to see more clearly where the audience is and where we need to focus better.

Take different colour pens and highlight the areas, the reasons, the ways on each list you think need greater attention, or have been most successful. Can you apply what you did here to other sectors on List A? Should there be other reasons on List B that you need to target – perhaps something you've

seen or heard working successfully in a friend's business?

Developing the right audiences for your business can have a real and cost-effective impact on your growth and also on your resilience. It's ensuring more people than just you are 'working' to inform others about what you do.

YOUR MARKET

So we've talked about your audience, but who is in your actual 'market'? Who are you trying to get to buy from you and how can you best make this happen?

Of course, your best market is always that place you already have clients… And the best target market is selling to your existing client list. So considering them is of prime importance.

Draw up exactly the same three lists for your market as you have just done for your audience.

List A – Who?
List B – Why?
List C – How?

Try to come up with very unique approaches to each section of your target market to make them really want to bring their business to you.

Let's go back to the analogy of the driving instructor. As we saw, a person might have their parents as the influencer in the decision, but learning to drive is about two people sitting in a car together with one teaching the other to drive.

There are lots of driving instructors to choose from in most locations; it is an expensive process and it can be hard for a learner to know who will be right for them. The other issue for you, as the instructor, is that once you have taught someone and helped them through their test, most learners will not become repeat customers because they will have passed their test. You therefore need to have a high level of success in attracting customers to generate the income you need.

By breaking down your target market into the above list, you can really think about who could be in your market and what additional ways you can make your service stand out for them. Perhaps not just for young learner drivers, but by offering other services that pull in other markets.

It is likely your marketing will need to look at ways alongside word of mouth/ recommendation models. You could start a young driver programme at a local school/college to help young adults be driving aware (and have you at the front of their mind as an instructor). You could run a film club around driving movies, talking about the vehicles used and the different driving skills needed for each – offering a membership and discount on a course of lessons. You could write advanced driver articles or blogs about 'coming back to driving' after living abroad, illness or whatever.

INSPIRING YOUR CLIENTS

One of the best ways to work with clients is to help them achieve the goals they've set themselves.

How often do you ask people you are working with, or for, what their ambitions and goals are? What they are looking to achieve? If they share this info with you, ask them how you can help with this, where their pinch points are... How can you solve this for them?

Quick tip... By putting yourself in your customer's shoes, and 'mapping' their customer journey with you, new ideas may emerge. So let's follow that journey... from the moment a customer starts becoming aware of your company, through the quoting, purchasing, working with you and leaving. Map it out on a big piece of paper. How do you think they feel at any point? Do they have concerns, anxieties, needs that you can help alleviate? Can you make the experience smoother, more inviting?

Another benefit in mapping this route a customer takes is that it may identify additional services you hadn't thought to offer.

case study

A few years back a TV production company I know brought in a new book-keeper. Having been well trained by past employers to ensure they paid suppliers in a timely manner on 30 days, as was standard practice in most other businesses, the book-keeper changed the production company's systems to match her experience.

After about six months, one of the TV production company directors started to hear rumours about the business being in trouble, when nothing was further from the truth. They were heaving with business.

Determined to get to the bottom of this misinformation, which could prove damaging, lots of questions were asked about how people had heard this 'news'.

It came to light that as a company, because they were financially secure through receiving money up front for their commissions from their broadcasters' clients, they had always paid their suppliers within seven days of receipt of invoice. This meant suppliers loved working for them, they were trusted and could always get the teams they needed at short notice ahead of their less financially astute competitors. And they were also often offered preferential terms.

But by shifting payment terms to 30 days – although an industry standard – the book-keeper had totally undermined this respected company practice, fundamentally changing the dynamic between the company and suppliers. Without realising.

Needless to say, the director asked her to revert to their better model and soothed the suppliers' ruffled feathers.

Gina spotted a really interesting gap in the specialised communications market in which she worked. She identified that more trained practitioners worked for in-house teams across her specialism than worked in external consultancies, but no one was focusing on developing training programmes and support for them and their unique needs. Sure, they could go to big corporate industry events alongside their fellow consultancy teams. But whereas consultancy teams got continually updated thinking and experience from their range of clients, this was often overlooked for in-house teams. So she built her business around providing training, courses, team building and other forms of support solely focusing on in-house practitioners. Simple but smart.

It's a simple question but will help you really hear what they are trying to do, where they want to go.

GOOD CUSTOMER SERVICE ALWAYS UNDERPINS A SUCCESSFUL COMPANY

(And the same goes for how you treat your suppliers...)

Whether you are selling lottery tickets or running a taxi service, the way you treat customers will always be able to set you apart from your competitors. It allows you to build loyalty, add value and gain referrals.

This is often referred to as 'the customer experience' by big brands and companies, which sounds so detached.

And who else do you want to feel good about the service they receive from you? Treating suppliers well can be as important as looking after your customers. After all – if it wasn't for your suppliers, you wouldn't be in business...

GAP IN THE MARKET

The best place to position any business – new, growing or established – is to find a gap in the market and offer a product or service that fills it.

Yes, sure, we all know that – but sometimes we forget. Or the gap is closing and we haven't seen the threat. Or our competitors are addressing it better. Or a new gap has emerged that we are uniquely positioned to fulfil by pivoting our business...

Every six months, sit down and have

a look at how gaps in your market are changing. Are they endangering you, or do they represent an opportunity for you, or more worryingly for a competitor? Or can you support another company to fulfil them, through advice or some financial support? Taking this stance keeps you plugged in, stops complacency and refreshes your thinking.

GO HUNTING

It's rare that a company opens its doors and work just flows in. It can happen, but not often. We all have to focus on marketing to ensure potential clients and customers hear about us, and are attracted to buy. Marketing comes in all sorts of forms – I am not an expert, so will not unpack it here.

However, one of the questions many of us overlook asking is: 'Who do I really, really want to work for?' It could be a company, an underdeveloped market, an industry. You then have to actively go after it in a structured way, hunting it out. Sometimes this can be as simple as picking up the phone and asking to meet those you'd like to work with. They might be flattered and invite you in, or they might feel less impressed by your cold calling and refuse to meet you.

I love working with creative people/ businesses, so I set up my company focusing on how to help them. Of course, I work with a range of other companies in other industries too.

But I actively seek out, 'go hunting', across the creative sector. It doesn't matter what area of creativity – I find it all fascinating, touching as it does on all sorts of other industries, ways of working, financial models and international opportunities.

PROACTIVE, NOT REACTIVE

Which one are you?

And does it matter if work's coming in anyway?

Well yes, it does.

Being proactive wins business, makes you a company good people want to work for, keeps you on your toes **and** makes you more profitable.

Let's see the flow of how this works...

Rather than just waiting for the phone to ring, or the order to pop into your inbox, you write a list outlining who you'd like as your next **three** clients. It could be the next three people to walk past your shop, it could be two big companies you met at an exhibition and one you've just heard of doing something interesting in Bristol.

Do they know about you? Why you rock what you do? What you offer and how good that is? If not – why not? And how do you get that message across?

What would you have to do, not only to grab their attention but to get them to work with you? What does your team think? Ask them to contribute too.

First, think about what they might buy from you. What need of theirs could

DESIGN COMPANY – 3 DIRECTORS: 3 MARKET SECTORS

case study

One of the design companies I was coaching a few years ago has three directors. They admitted that their new business development process was largely reactive – they never went out proactively to seek work, finding it challenging and having some degree of uncertainty around how to go about it. They would wait for the phone to ring – which luckily it did, fairly frequently. They felt they needed to instigate change in a demanding market, yet still wanted to appear different to their competitors.

As I got to know the directors better, I realised they had very distinct sets of interests. Each of their passions lay in totally different areas. In our discussions around new business development and who to target, I realised their ambitions for target clients were totally individual too.

So we focused on these passions. As a potential client, we reasoned, you would much rather be approached by someone who really, really loves what you do, the area you work in, the market you are looking to grow.

By really unpacking the past clients list (see page 27) and their passions, skills and talents list (see page 28), we wrote up a business development ambition list for **each** director. We ensured they had the marketing collateral they needed. Back-up case studies from past projects were written to enhance their expertise. The website was relaunched to focus on the breadth of their past scope, but with the wording subtly tweaked to point readers to the right director.

New business development became a joyful experience rather than a scary-looking chore.

you fulfil? Are you up to the job? Do you need to bring in some more team training, tweak your offer? And if you don't need to do anything extra, but just get your name in front of them – what new marketing initiative should you be implementing?

Or is it simpler than that... How about you pick up the phone and ring them, asking for a meeting for some advice. Nothing is more disarming than asking a person, a small business, a big company for advice – because most individuals want to help and you are appealing to that side of them, rather than overtly selling. It allows you to meet them, talk to them more widely than selling. It could be questions about new trends, training programmes they could offer your team, etc. But what you are doing is making yourself known to them, interested, available, informed.

By doing and thinking about all of the above, you will have already shifted from that reactive state of mind. Keep doing this exercise every week. If you run a team, get two different members of the team to do it.

But it has to be followed up by concrete actions – you can't just understand what you need to do, then leave it. Write the action list and make it happen. This change in attitude will impact every area of your business. It gives you a shot of energy that permeates throughout the team.

DEVELOP PERSONAS FOR YOUR TARGET CUSTOMERS

In tech and app-building companies, developers come up with 'personas' for their key potential clients. It has always surprised me that more companies don't do this too. It's easy, free and can give you fab insight into the behaviours, habits, personalities of your potential clients, which can inform how you market to them.

A 'persona' is literally a person – real or imaginary – with a story written around how they interact with your business. It's a good idea to have five or six to draw on. The aim is to be able to put yourself in their shoes to better understand their motivation, the ways they engage and so on.

COMPETING CLIENTS CONUNDRUM

There is an intriguing conundrum, particularly in the world of creative

Who are the influencers in your market?

Whether the influencers are on social media, in your direct network, in your town, or within your industry, it's really important to understand who these people are, make sure you are on their radar and engage with them in some meaningful way. They are the ones who can amplify your marketing, giving it a whole new reach.

However, influencers are only about spreading the word... the correct positioning of your business can only be done by you, so use influencers wisely and thoughtfully.

GROWING YOUR BUSINESS

COMPETING
CLIENT
CONUNDRUM

Information Lake

Client puts ——→
brief to agency

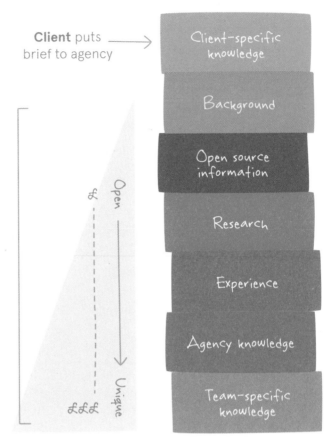

Client-specific knowledge

Background

Open source information

Research

Experience

Agency knowledge

Team-specific knowledge

As this information is not exclusive to that client, where else does it have value? What other clients, markets, companies, reports, etc. could you generate work from?

£££

£

Open

Unique

agencies – when clients do not want any of their direct competitors handled by 'their' agency. While you can understand the need for secrecy, would you ever go to a dentist who didn't look after other people's teeth? Or give your car to a mechanic who didn't look after other cars?

One of the ways around this problem is to look at the world opened up by the research/legwork you need to do to

handle their business and see to whom else it might have value. These could be in a range of interesting and related fields, away from direct competitors (see the diagram above). Try to aim for two or three target clients per new client.

This process works for all sorts of other companies too. When you learn about a new industry, have an additional understanding or an added skill – think about who else would value it.

SKIMMERS, DIPPERS, DIVERS...

This model is particularly useful when trying to work out how your website and social media are working. Look at the diagram below:

The Skimmers are the general audience that come to your website or engage with you in some way or other. They are like the window shoppers in a street. Not particularly interested or engaged.

The next level down is full of Dippers. They are willing to engage with you in some way and immerse themselves in your offer for short periods of time. A bit like someone coming into a store and browsing.

Then you get the Divers, who really want to interact with your business, whether through a purchase or through 'liking' a post or tweet. They can have a big impact and can become ardent fans and influencers.

The Dippers and Divers should generally make up around 15–20% of your audience...

So how can you harness the Divers to help you convert the Dippers to be more engaged, to purchase, to grow your business? Look at how other companies pull you in when you are in one of these areas... What can you learn from your own experience as a customer?

HOW DO YOUR CUSTOMERS FIND YOU?

This sounds such a very basic question... But you'd be surprised by the amount of businesses that have never identified this key metric and what it can tell you about tomorrow, about next year.

One of the best ways to grow your

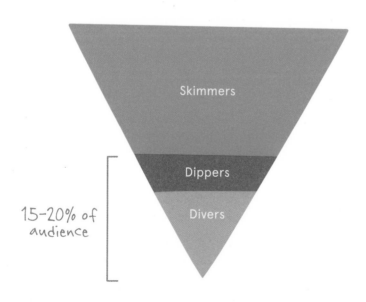

15–20% of audience

Quick tip... Try this simple survey. Take a short period of time – say today, this week, this month... Look at all the prospective and actual clients you meet, are working with, or have a trading relationship with during that time frame. Ask them how they heard about you, why they like you, who else they considered instead. Then ask them how you could have made this easier for them.

Draw up a list with the top-scoring 'routes to you' at the top... Is Facebook or another social media channel your best business-winning tool? Is it your location? Do your clients find you through referrals? Or has a report you've published attracted clients?

Now redo the list but based on the value of those clients' spend with you. Does the list change?

By doing this exercise regularly, you can see which of your marketing efforts are working, which represent best value, and in fact whether there are factors you had overlooked that are really contributing to your turnover, allowing you to give them some more attention.

business quickly is to do a simple review of how companies find you – and then be more in that place, or do more of what you were doing. But equally, if what you are doing *isn't* bringing you work, then don't throw good money after bad. Look at why not and change it.

Try doing this at regular intervals throughout the year. And map when there are busy periods for new business inquiries – why is this? A result of your marketing, something you posted on social media, or is there a strong buying pattern to what you offer?

BUYING CYCLES

Just as you have a pattern to your commercial year – such as a trade show, Easter and Christmas peaks, a summer fall-off or whatever – so too do each of your customers.

Getting to understand that cycle will help build your business. Try to discover when they are going to be in the market for new products, when their year end falls (they will have budgets either to spend or to rein in), what their purchasing patterns are, when they might be opening a new office or premises.

When a client recognises that you understand their business and can

THE DRIFTING BEAR COMPANY

case study

I first met the team from Drifting Bear at a business planning seminar in Bristol organised by the Crafts Council.

The founder, David, was working five days a week for a graphic design company, and during his evenings, weekends and lunch breaks was working on his own new personalised printed gifts business. It was obvious he had a vision for his company, and was looking to grow it substantially to employ both him and his partner, Tanya, full-time.

As the business evolved, the Drifting Bear Company started to sell merchandise through Not On The High Street's platform, along with other small makers. It helped grow their business substantially, bringing a hungry audience, the influence of TV advertising, and well-thought-through payment terms.

But David and Tanya also recognised that the competition between suppliers for best positioning on the platform was fierce.

So along with their own annual Product Development, Manufacturing and Marketing calendar, we developed a second that was focused exclusively on Not On The High Street's key dates.

They worked hard with their account manager to ensure they understood the trends shaping next season's buying patterns. New product development work was shown their account manager a few weeks before they needed it, with samples arriving perfectly finished and well presented. They tried to ensure at every turn that they had anticipated Not On the High Street's needs.

This calendar proved to be just as important as their own business calendar, as it led to a big increase in business as they became – and still are – one of Not On The High Street's top suppliers.

www.thedriftingbear.com

THE
DRIFTING BEAR Co

provide them with new ideas to fit their diary, you can grow to become seen as an integral part of their team and the 'go-to' supplier for their needs.

If you are selling direct to consumers in the street, think about when they might like to hear about your services... Perhaps at the end of the month, as payday approaches, when spring arrives. Whatever it is you sell, you need to recognise, understand and take advantage of that calendar.

I encourage people to have it up on the wall to refer to, reminding themselves of the pattern and to ensure they prepare well in advance.

WHY YOUR TEAM AND EXISTING CLIENTS ARE YOUR BEST MARKETERS

Rather than spend lots of money advertising in untested channels to potential audiences and customers you've never met, think how you can harness the power of your existing team and customers to market your business.

They have the potential to be your best advocates. How can you devise original ways so they can help you out?

But just as your team can help you win business, if they are not engaged with their jobs, are bored or are treated less than well, they can discourage business from walking in the door.

I once worked with a printing company. It was a hard gig. I found the management disconnected from the sales team, who had regular dealings with all of the clients. The sales team were smashing, fun, young and full of ideas. But the disengaged management never gave them any opportunities, never any credit, or thanked them for their efforts. A little more support, some incentives and opportunities to implement their ideas, could have easily doubled the venture's turnover.

WHAT ARE YOU HELPING YOUR CLIENTS ACHIEVE?

Talking about what you help your clients achieve is a useful strand in your marketing armoury. Don't just talk about what you do for them, but look at the bigger picture to see how you contribute to their end offer.

If you are a plumber working on contract for a bigger builder, piggyback on their marketing: 'We helped X give 200 people new homes last year. How can we help you?'

ADMIRATION MARKETING

What companies do you admire and why?

As you go through your day – from the moment you get up to when you go to bed – raise your antennae to think about what products and services you are using. How did that person or business market to you, how did they get to be in your life? Was it through marketing, through a well-timed email, through brilliant service?

Ask your team to do the same. See what the key factors that emerge are. It is likely that your customers will be influenced by similar things, so ensure you introduce these types of triggers into your marketing.

CUSTOMERS BUY BENEFITS...

Are you ensuring your marketing highlights the benefits rather than just the products?

I often use the marketing line developed for KitKat, the chocolate-covered wafer bar, to highlight this. The ad agency executive Donald Gilles at JWT Orland wrote the line 'Have a break, have a KitKat', positioning the bar in a different, less competitive space – people were buying 'stop time', not just the bar.

WHAT IS YOUR CUSTOMER'S PROBLEM?

And if you know – are you solving it? In what you offer, how you market to them?

In hot climates, biscuits with chocolate on the outside don't sell because the chocolate melts. By making a chocolate biscuit that encapsulates the chocolate on the inside, you have solved a problem and shown them how practically you can help them. While this may well be a 'product' innovation, you need to be telling your customers in your marketing that you have the ability to solve their problems.

CAN YOU POSITION YOURSELF AS A THOUGHT LEADER?

Being the 'go-to' person to advise, to talk at conferences, events or away days around your area of expertise is a really, really good way of marketing yourself and your business. Can you be the person that others within your industry will pay to hear speak, or to read what you've written? If so – fantastic!

By using your business plan from page 21, you can ensure you know what areas are unique to you, and can start developing unusual thinking and ideas in this space. But just having the ideas is not enough – you need to explore them, write about them, post them and get them out there. Otherwise no one will be aware of you.

FREE LOVE

Hmm – probably a bit of a questionable title for a marketing idea... but bear with me on this.

I get asked to give loads of talks around developing intellectual assets and IP. Each time I tweak the content to build in some new thinking, target it to the audience and add some fresh case studies or examples. But I always get sad when the event is over that the audience is gone (other than what goes on social media, etc.).

So I started to offer free talks to the various networks I contribute to. The offer goes along the lines of:

'I've just done this talk to X group about intellectual assets and IP. If you would like me to come to visit your company/group/network with the same talk, ping me an email.'

There is no catch. And at the end of the talk I don't do any selling. I thank them for their time and pack my stuff. I am just giving them freely something I think is hugely important they are across. It's about sharing information.

This free sharing has helped me talk to more people, has given me a wide group of contacts and has brought the subject to the notice of more companies than I can count. Its long-term value to my business is almost incalculable. And I still do it for free as and when I choose to. (It also brings me in clients – sometimes a year or so down the line.)

PIRATE TACTICS

I've always loved this approach...

If you have identified a weakness in your competitor, if that area is one of your strengths – emphasise it in your marketing. Not in any way critical of them, but just saying that you work in this way... It could win you a range of new projects.

SEND SOMETHING TANGIBLE

We've all forgotten the days when our postboxes were filled with endless mail-outs and catalogues for companies we no longer wanted to buy from. It's so much easier to unsubscribe from an emailed newsletter.

And that leaves a wonderful marketing opportunity just waiting to be seized.

If you run a small business, send your clients and potential clients something truly gorgeous in the post.

Due to our use of computers, tablets and smartphones, we are all suffering what I call 'sensory deprivation'. We are deprived of that wonderful touchy-feely moment when something arrived that had been thoughtfully designed, well printed, was useful and sat on our desks. Or someone wrote us a letter, or sent an invite or card.

Go back to that for your special clients, for the new clients you want to entice into working with you... What can you devise that is cost effective but delivers bang for your buck?

MAILING LISTS (OR DATABASES)

One of the most valuable assets any company has is the knowledge of who is buying from it. Who they are, what they buy...

For some the list is short, they know them personally, whereas for others the list is lengthy without any familiarity. It really doesn't matter where you are on this spectrum. What does matter is that you keep all of their names and their contact details in some form of list or database that is updated regularly.

You can use this list in so many different ways. Not necessarily to 'sell' to.

Let's think about who these people are and how they might prove valuable to you...

First, they are people who have spent money with you, so you can use them to do some audience/market research. Ask them for ideas about how you could improve your offer. Is there something they would like you to sell that's not available in the market, the area? Are there new technologies they would like you to engage with?

Or perhaps they would welcome being invited to test products for you? Or to join a fan club around your specialist area?

And the more names you have in your database, the more you need to ensure they are 'tagged' or labelled. This allows you to subdivide them into smaller groups very easily. My database is full of a wide range of subdivisions, such as how they found me, what they or their company do, the value of their contracts with me, whether they were a client or just made an inquiry, whether they are suppliers...

I've spent some time working out what were the best tags for me, and every so often add a new one, if I think it will have value.

Quick tip... Please bear in mind that if you hold customer or client data on a mailing list, there are clear privacy rules around what you can and can't do with it. You need to ensure it is looked after securely, particularly any personal or financial details. You may need to register with the Information Commissioner's Office and agree with their codes of conduct. If you are planning to market your mailing list to other companies, you need to ensure you have the permission of everyone on the list. (Remember those opt in/out boxes you tick about 'sharing your details for carefully selected third parties'? You will need to have a similar mechanism in place.)

New laws have recently come into force that insist on clear rules and structures around how you manage the personal data of your customers, giving them rights to be removed and to see what data you hold on them. Ensure you are aware of your responsibilities as a data holder, that it is stored safely and that there is an administrator whose job it is to take care of data for your company.

There is a variety of mailing list/CRM (customer relationship management) software that can help you to sort and use your database more fully. Before you buy or subscribe to it, really work out what you would like to do with all of the names and information you will hold and plan, not only for now but also for how you intend to grow your business.

BIG DATA, SMALL DATA... HOW ALL DATA CAN HELP YOU

We're all used to reading about the ways large companies are using big data to create predictive behavioural models to grow their companies based on how each of us, their customers, interact with them. References to big data are underpinned by serious computer number-crunching and the software teams to extract the trends and moves in their audiences, allowing them to harness their learning.

But don't think that because your company is smaller, with tighter constraints, you can't do the same – in your own way.

There are some very simple analytics that don't take much time or effort and with which you should be engaging regularly.

Google Analytics is the first. Really unpick where your audience is coming from, how they behave on your site, and do some simple work here. If you don't understand it, use the supportive help videos or articles to understand it. It costs nothing but could really give you valuable insights.

Even closer to home, however, is understanding and 'reading' the data/information that exists already within your own business – no matter its size. Just asking yourself very basic questions about where your customers are based, how they find you, their repeat purchasing habits, longevity of relationship and their lifetime value to you can give you surprising insights.

NEW BUSINESS PITCHING: WHY DO YOU WIN? WHY DO YOU LOSE?

It is rare that a company wins every single customer it goes after, whether you are a high-street store, run an e-commerce site, or are involved in some form of pitching/tendering process.

But your failure to win clients can hold some interesting intelligence to help you cut down on the losses and raise the percentage of wins. You just have to understand why.

And as Karla Morales-Lee, who used to run The Art of New Business, stated categorically: 'New business development is an art, not a numbers game' – and for most of us she is absolutely right.

Sometimes it might be obvious – price, location or limited skill in a key area. Make a simple map of all the reasons for the last month, quarter or year. Can you see a pattern emerging? Are the inquiries that fail to convert to new business growing or reducing, and what has changed this? Is there a tectonic plate shift in the market, a new trend, an emergent business disrupting your world that you hadn't anticipated? Are they offering something new or do they just have a fresher approach?

If you can't identify the reason, ask those who didn't choose to give you their business why that was. If you don't ask, you won't be any the wiser. If you do ask, you will gain valuable insight.

GROW YOUR OWN CLIENTS

Sometimes, heading out to the marketplace to attract clients can be relentless and needs a different approach... We are all hit by an endless stream of marketing messages – at home, work, playing, exercising – so ensuring that your marketing stands out can be hard work.

But suppose you could 'grow your own' clients? How much more fun would that be? This approach can and should be a part of your offer, whether it sits in the 'what you sell' or the 'marketing' section of this book... I'm not sure – so you're reading it here!

Quick tip... To help you understand your customers better and give you some basic data, create a questionnaire to gather information about all your clients, your potential clients, your past clients. Using an online tool like SurveyMonkey will give you simple analytics for each question. You can either ask your team to complete this in-house or send it to your clients to complete. This often throws up interesting and unexpected results, which can help guide you and your team to greater engagement with your customers.

Or if you'd like to have some rather more qualitative responses, brief a practised interviewer and ask them to talk to current and past customers about their experiences in doing business with you. Allow them the space to be honest, even if it is something that is hard for you to accept.

The cost of doing this type of research and data gathering can be kept low, but what it unearths can be so valuable for your team and what you offer.

Every small company needs to attract a mixed economy of clients – from young to older, small to large, across various sectors. However, often the smaller companies have less to spend with you, although the longer-term opportunity they may bring you when they reach maturity is interesting.

So in what ways can you find these early-stage companies, work with them, nurture them and share in their growing success? By doing this, you are helping your business, not for tomorrow, but for next year and the years after.

I heard about one accountancy company who had a forward-looking policy to do just this. When it moved premises, its new building had existing planning permission for a café on the ground floor. While the accountancy practice had no wish to go into the food and beverage business, they recognised that there has been a fundamental change in working methods in the economy. For some while, many small start-ups have been working in WiFi-enabled cafés or shared workspaces, to save on the cost of overheads.

The accountancy company realised that if they retained the café on the ground floor, they could provide a welcoming environment to encourage small start-ups who would be tomorrow's clients looking for financial advice, support and investment.

How can you make this happen for your business? It is not as hard as it may seem and certainly doesn't need you to buy a whole building!

SHORT + SHARP AND LONGER-TERM PROJECTS

Creating a mixed economy of different sized and value projects across all of your business is really worth doing, for a number of reasons...

Small 'starter' projects for clients can grow into longer-term engagements and relationships. They can also help to fill gaps in your work diary while clients are confirming quotes, making decisions or just faffing.

They have the added benefit of bringing in useful quick cash, when your other projects may have longer gaps between payments.

And they also give you a break and fill you with fresh ideas when the longer projects have lost their sparkle.

TALK ABOUT SOLUTIONS...

... to problems clients don't know they have or haven't got round to...

One of the key ways to catch a potential client's interest is to talk about solving a problem they haven't yet recognised they have. Trigger their interest by using terms and referring to emergent trends or areas they know they should deal with but have yet to do.

I often talk about how both innovation and IP are on so many companies' to-do lists but few really know what they should be doing, or how they should approach. Killing two birds with one stone by talking to me is an easy win.

TRUST

Building trust is one of the most important facets of your business – no matter what you do. Your customers need to be able to trust you to do what they ask – well and to the best of your ability. If customers trust you, winning more business from them will be easier, and winning new business from other customers will be easier.

But allow that relationship of trust to falter or break down and you can find yourself on a slippery downward slope, particularly with the echo chamber created by social media.

If you have an issue that interrupts the relationship of trust between you and a client, own up to it immediately and tell them what you are doing to put it right. Without delay. By doing this quickly, you help start rebuilding their trust in you.

BEG, BORROW, STEAL GOOD MARKETING IDEAS

We all sometimes run out of ideas to market ourselves. It becomes the bottom item on the to-do list, the thing we never get to. Recognise this behaviour? I do.

Next time you are surfing the net, or are travelling, or shopping in the supermarket with your brain in 'park'

mode, notice **what** you notice... Why did you stop there, what caught your eye, what feature sparked a few seconds' attention? If it clicked for you, can you adapt it in some way to work for your business?

Lots of people are paid huge amounts of money to capture our attention, sell us stuff, tell/remind us about services. And yes, sure, our businesses don't have the time, or cash, or need to advertise on TV... but we can steal some of the mechanics to apply ourselves. Obvious examples are loyalty cards... Six haircuts and you get 50% off the seventh. But what else is out there that you can adapt to your model?

FOOTPRINTS

Footprints tell you where you have been, the direction you have come from, and the direction you were heading in. Other people's footprints tell you that about them too.

From time to time it's instructive to capture some of this easy-to-find info in a map to see whether there is anything surprising for you to harness.

What would you discover if, over just one week, you/your team/your connections mapped your:

a. cultural footprint – all the cultural things you engaged with
b. brand footprint – all the brands you used
c. sporting footprint – all the sports

you participated in or watched or followed.

Create whatever footprints are useful for you and the commercial world you operate in. They can help you to see interesting new places to market what you offer, or behavioural changes in how your clients are shopping or relaxing to give you new ideas around shaping promotions and talking about your services.

Footprints may just be a short snapshot, but they can give you a quick, cost-effective insight.

We each have a range of different 'publics' that we want our marketing to appeal to – clearly defining these makes our marketing spend more effective

COST OF GOOD DESIGN VS BAD DESIGN

No one **ever** thinks they are buying bad design work, whether it's packaging, branding, the design of your store or shop front, or a website. But so often design is bought on price and not on whether it will achieve your visions for the company, taking you to the next level you want to reach with your business.

And good design – well-thought-through products, easy-to-follow communications, impactful branding that sets your company apart and conveys its unique position to your customers – costs the same amount as bad design. In fact, it is way more cost-effective, because bad design will *cost* you, lose you customers.

Hand on heart and being truthful – I am a passionate advocate of design. I see its intrinsic value in so many areas of our lives. Well-designed services, books, homes, furniture bring me utter delight. And when you are on the receiving end of good design, you understand what the company is conveying. It could be following signage through a museum, how well your favourite dress sits, the angle of the razor head as you shave. Good design will always build your business.

But bad design will mean your customers/potential customers drop out before they have clicked 'buy' on your website, or because of the poor quality of your packaging.

Quick tip 1... If you are thinking about commissioning some design work, the starting point is to write a clear brief about what your ambitions are for both the company and the project. What do you want those outcomes to be?

You may already know some designers that you want to ask to quote for the project. Great. If not, look at all sorts of websites, look for local companies, find businesses whose work you admire and ask for the details of their designer. Research a lot. Draw up a shortlist to quote, and meet with them to talk about your project. Work with those you think have the best grasp of your ambition and those of the project.

Good designers understand that you know more about your business than they do. But they also have outside perspective as well as experience across other industries, so they bring a wealth of useful knowledge along with their design skill to the table. Use it – it comes as part of the package. Value their input, their questioning, their creative abilities.

'PARTNER' YOUR CLIENTS – DON'T ACCEPT A 'PARENT/ CHILD' RELATIONSHIP

There is an interesting range of attitudes in commercial relationships – particularly when you offer a service.

If you go to a dentist, you expect him to be an expert. The same when you ring a plumber. You are paying a fair price for the work you require. You are equals.

However, there are times when clients try to push this relationship of equals to one of parent/child, where they are in control and 'know best'. This can be seriously damaging and undermining. I've lost count of the highly experienced, talented creative companies I've worked with whose big-brand clients treat them appallingly, forcing them into the role of a child who has to stand to attention every time they, the client, beckon.

So putting the notion of partnering with your clients fairly and squarely into your marketing materials or T&Cs is one way of clearly signposting your expectations of the relationship. It should be in your tone of voice, your expectations of terms – everything. Any movement away from this can then be immediately flagged and addressed.

Quick tip 2... Sometimes you can't afford the level of design or creative work your business needs. I hear this regularly. So this is where being inventive around business models comes in – Look at the pages on money and ways of charging for three different ways you and your design team could come up with new ways of rewarding the work they do.

This also helps you to build value into your service. You are an expert, not a supplicant.

WEBSITE AND SOCIAL MEDIA DELIGHT

I love a good website. Yes, I enjoy Instagram, Pinterest and Facebook pages, complete with all the riches you can mine, letting you build a great brand, but a well-constructed, beautifully thought-through website is a thing of pleasure.

Of course, you have to show your offer, to encourage potential and actual customers to engage with you and buy, but boy, is it also a whole lot more.

Your DNA, your raison d'être, your confidence, your character, your customer reassurance should be spread all over your social media and website. You can be you, delightedly exhibiting your best work, the pleasure you get in doing what you do, sharing the success you have brought to your clients, whether you are a food retailer or an electrician who's installed something smart that looks fab when lit at night.

So my question to you is: does your online marketing delight as well as inform those who visit? This doesn't involve complications but simply warmth, engagement.

If you are a builders' merchant, is the humour of your experienced staff reflected on your sites? It will certainly be part of the reason your customers keep coming back. If you are a freelance gardener, does your website show all the plants you love to care for, not just a list of services you offer?

UNDERSTANDING YOUR LEAD TIME

It's really useful to work out the 'lead time' for your business, as this will tell you when you need to get cracking on more marketing.

So what is a lead time? It is the time it takes from the first touch/connection with a potential customer until they walk in the door with a project.

For some businesses this can be really short, but for others there is a lengthy 'dance' to be negotiated before that work is confirmed.

Once you know what your lead times

Quick tip... If you realise you've got stuck in a rut on your website, ask one or two of your customers and suppliers why they love working with you. You're not looking for a testimonial (although these are always useful to have on your website), but comments about the DNA of your business. It could be that your café always has flowers on the table, or room for pushchairs, or fabulous-smelling soap in the washroom. It could be that your team worked through the night to help out with a tricky problem. These comments are part of the warp and weft of business life, but we overlook their value in showing who our business is.

are – and there may well be a mix of short and long – you can structure your marketing accordingly. If you are aware that it can be a six-month process to get just 20% of the people you connect with to buy, then you need to be working hard for nine or ten months ahead of time to ensure you are busy this time next year...

However, at times, in certain locations or via social media, other customers make decisions quite quickly. This is great and can be used to 'layer' your projects to ensure you mix longer-term and short-term.

There is a balance to be struck between the longer-term 'strategic' and the shorter-term 'tactical'...

BEING SEEN IN THE RIGHT PLACES

If your business is reliant on face-to-face marketing with your customers 'buying' you, you and your team – the people – have to get out there and be seen. Nothing will replace it. You need to go to where your clients are – whether that's a wedding fair for a dressmaker, a VR conference for a small studio, or maker fairs for handcrafters.

Even if your relationships are made online, they can be cemented face-to-face, and despite the internet this still has great value. After all, millennia of evolution have gone into each of us understanding how we read people, so don't dismiss this.

Of course, you can do lots online, using Instagram, Facebook and Pinterest, adapting your website, working with influencers, but this is just a different, digital version of being seen in the right places... For some it is the key to their business growth, whereas for others the face-to-face will never change.

ACCESS POINTS

Does your marketing material and website include all of the ways clients can access your service and buy from you? It's just worth checking.

Storytelling

Often people are surprised when I mention how important storytelling is to their business.

It is seen as a skill to entertain us at the theatre, on our screens, or help while away hours with children. But where does it fit, and how can you use it to benefit your company?

When you pitch for business, you are telling that target client a story. It's about who you are, what you do and for whom, but it's woven into a narrative of how the company has grown, what you love doing. It is the story of how you've arrived at this moment talking to them about solving their need. Good storytelling isn't just about the commercial but also about the contextual, the background, the hows and whys as much as the what.

It helps to build trust, mutual understanding and engagement.

Just as in a bookstore stories can be told through biography, history or geology, so too are business stories firmly based in fact.

Look at your set of annual accounts... What is that if not a story – told in numbers – of how your business performed this year against last year?

I went to a talk by one of the main buyers from London store Selfridges, who was explaining how she identified new suppliers they wanted to introduce to the food market. Yes, they had to have good-quality merchandise, well packaged, but for her, more important than anything, was the story behind the brand. How they'd got there and why they cared so much to want to produce this new range.

So what storytelling can you bring into your commercial world to help set you apart from your competitors, drive your marketing, raise your game?

Stories don't have to be big and lengthy, they can be short and sweet, but they do have to be honest. (We all know how cheated we feel when we buy into a story about a brand, a person, a business and it turns out to be untrue.)

YOUR BRAND MANIFESTO: WHAT IS IT? WHAT'S IN IT?

A brand manifesto is the summation of what you want to be and how you want to be seen. But it can help you in so many other ways too – the guy rope for

case study

I have my hair cut in Shaftesbury by a small salon called Right Over The Top. Their story is simple but delightful. Husband-and-wife team Andrew and Rachel have been styling and cutting hair here for over 30 years. During that time, all their clients have seen both their children, Josh and Harriet, grow from toddlers to adults. When both expressed interest in joining the business, Rachel and Andrew sent them to train at a world-famous salon in London, just as they both had when they were students. Now the younger team are working together with their parents in the salon. There is a delightful feeling of family, of perpetuity, of fun and laughter across generations – whether clients or stylists. This high-quality family engagement is the underpinning storytelling for the whole of their business.

Rethinking your storytelling and how you use your past life and experience is one of the simplest ways to make some big changes to your marketing approach that costs little, gives you a unique platform, but can help you form a strong bond with both existing and new clients.

And remember – the more stuff you do, the longer you have been in business, the more stories you have at your fingertips to share and tell.

www.rightoverthetop.co.uk

your marketing efforts, the key to talking about your business.

I pulled together the following list of things to include for a digital agency that was launching a product. Adapt it as you see fit, as it is just meant to give you some guiding points...

Let's suppose you are a company with a chocolate snack you are selling in the market.

The brand manifesto needs to have details about:

a. the actual product (e.g. a chocolate snack)

- What is it?
- What does it do?
- What customer need does it fulfil?
- Why did you devise it?
- How does it work?
- What is the competition?
- How are you going to sell the product?
- What is the pricing structure?
- How does the support mechanism work?

- How are you going to market the product?

b. the brand itself (e.g. Mars bar – 'A Mars a day helps you work, rest and play')
- What are you going to call your product?
- What sets your product apart from others in a similar space?
- Will your brand have a ser[...] purpose and intent that pec[...] use it/come across it can engage with?
- What sort of emotional engagement with your brand do you want your customers to have?
- What brand ID and messages do you

---

case study

WITHOUT STUDIO + YAWN

Design company Without Studio has in the past invested in one of its clients. On leaving the City, Alice approached Without to design the branding and marketing materials for a new range of lounge/sleepwear she wanted to produce. Under the brand name Yawn, she felt there was potential to offer well-made cotton pyjamas and robes for those times you just want to pootle around at home. As the Without team got cracking on the project, it soon became apparent that the level of work required to launch the brand was greater than Alice's budget.

But because both sides really believed in the project, and in each other, they came to an agreement that Without would become shareholders in the brand in exchange for the additional work needed. (This is sometimes referred to rather unappealingly as 'sweat equity'.)

This has worked well for both sides. However, an unintended positive consequence is how it looks as part of Without's pitch deck.

By incorporating their Yawn experience in their credentials slides (the presentation design companies do when pitching to new clients) as part of their commercial storytelling, it shows that the Without team has real commercial savvy beyond their core design business. They've got 'skin in the game', have products selling across the UK and Europe and are involved in the pain/gain of wholesale and direct trade, in the notably unforgiving clothing market. They use this to best advantage, highlighting different areas of the story depending on what type of company they are talking to.

www.without.studio and www.loveyawn.com

want associated with your product?

• Authenticity and meaningfulness to your target audience are key – who is/are your target audience(s)? And what will make your brand live up to these?

• You need to sum up the brand's values, hopes and aspirations...

• How will you encourage people (your customers) to engage with it (brand relationships are a two-way street)?

• These points are the sorts of things that can be incorporated in – for example – a design or marketing brief, encompassing a name, the logo for that name, the product screen interface as well as the personal satisfaction that you gain from the product.

If you run a small venture, you may have to run the marketing alongside every other role you fulfil, so try to make it a joy, a part of the everyday, rather than something big that gets put at the bottom of the list.

c. the company (e.g. Cadbury)

• How do you want your company to appear in relation to the product and its brand? Major weighting? Equal weighting? Lesser weighting?

• What is the character of the company and do you need to change any of its branding to fit with the product and its brand?

• How will you balance your existing company offer with your new product(s)/brand?

Obviously, each company and product is different, but the layers may well be similar to the above and this will give you pointers to think through.

BRAND DNA DECISIONS

When founders set up a company, it is frequently imbued with their very DNA. The way the company is, works, feels reflects their values and how they do business. As growth occurs, a decision needs to be made as to whether you want this DNA to continue, or whether as the founders leave, the DNA needs to change.

Often, it's a subtle mix of both... but whatever is chosen, ensure a positive decision is made around it.

case study

TURNBULLS

For nigh on 15 years, Charlie Turnbull has run a deli focusing on cheese in Shaftesbury, Dorset. He absolutely loves cheese. He knows more about cheese than anyone else I've ever met. He talks about cheese-makers as friends, inspires his customers to try new and delicious types, teaches other deli owners through to supermarkets how to look after cheese, is building a database around cheese provenance and lectures about cheese on cruise liners. He is also an international cheese judge. (Yes, I know – who knew there was such a job!) And all of this has grown out of him **being** the brand, of him absolutely focusing on his passion. But what is amazing is that this range of activity has grown from a single cheese shop in a small Dorset town, where someone passionate and ambitious was focused on being the brand.

Let's talk about...

Be the brand

You are the best advocate for your brand. Without doubt. Yes, all of your happy customers are brilliant advocates too. But no one 'gets' your brand like you do. You need to ensure you turn it to your best advantage and absolutely become the brand. Your enthusiasm, your care, your warmth and focus all need to be harnessed to bolster what you are building.

People buy from those they believe in and who they know will deliver. End of story.

Generosity

Generosity is greatly underused in the business world, but can enhance your reputation and win you business. That might sound a bit cynical – but it's true. Don't ever underestimate its power. So what do I mean by this?

case study

In the very early days of starting my current company, I was keen to test out my thinking. I felt I was offering something unique and needed to see whether it would work for small as well as larger companies.

So rather than cold-call companies asking if I could come to see them to just talk, I decided to sit in a local café to offer a 'free advice surgery'.

Worried that I might be sitting there alone for two hours, I joined forces with a local book-keeping company, thereby giving more reasons for people to pop in. And if no one turned up? At least we could talk to each other and drink great coffee.

I live near a small town in the middle of the countryside, so I put an ad in the local paper and flyers on the noticeboards in shops and post offices in the surrounding villages. A pretty limited marketing campaign.

To our amazement, 20 minutes before we were due to start we had a queue! And they kept coming.

I learned a lot that morning about how to structure my offer, about some really interesting enterprises trading in my home area, but also about how generosity can help you get answers. And two of the attendees became early clients.

Giving talks, writing for blogs, appearing on a discussion panel – all of these are ways of sharing your knowledge and experience for little or no reward. But they get you seen and heard and raise awareness of you and your company.

When you have a particular area of knowledge that can benefit other companies, what is the point of keeping it secret? Share it, send it out there into the world, let other people benefit. Be generous with it. Sure, tag it with your name, so people know who originated it. They will become your ambassadors in places and spaces you and your company may not even know about.

If talking or sharing your knowledge is not your 'thing', in what other ways can you be generous? Can you run events on your premises to help start-ups, parts of the community; can you offer an advice surgery?

case study

COURIER

Courier launched their media business in 2013. A well-designed, info-filled publication that emerged from the burgeoning start-up culture in London's East End, its original positioning was being the 'voice of start-up'.

But they realised that many readers in fact came from outside this grouping, from big companies, corporations, fast-growth SMEs (small and medium enterprises), all of whom wanted to be kept informed and in the loop. So, after some rethinking, the Courier team decided that they were going to own 'modern business'. This set them distinctively apart from their competitors and attracted the readership they were looking for, setting them up to approach advertisers and other contributors with a fresh proposition. www.couriermedia.co

Courier

Courier
STORIES OF MODERN BUSINESS

The Business of Design

Paulo ceramicists,
dic ingenuity and
next Ikea?

Work!

PATTERNITY

case study

Several years ago two individuals working in the creative industries, met through friends and realised they had something in common. A deep and abiding passion for pattern.

Roll the years on, and Grace and Anna are now regarded as experts around the world on pattern in its widest possible sense. The company they founded, called Patternity, is respected by fashion brands, science organisations, archives and design agencies, and their events around how patterns can impact positively on your life are attended by curious individuals around the globe.

They have studied how patterns in nature repeat themselves, observed patterns in our man-made environments, see patterns in our systems, our data, how we live, our psychology. They research patterns in behaviour, connections and construction for lectures and books; they design patterns for products and companies; their knowledge and love of patterns has allowed them to nurture and fulfil the deep curiosity they had for the world around them, turning this curiosity into a unique business.

www.patternity.org

PATTERNITY

Own something

*If I asked you to name **one** thing that you do really, really well, that is different from everyone else – what would that be?*

And if all your customers were asked – would they say the same thing?

By owning that core area of your business, you can make yourself distinctive, different, and in a space beyond your competitors – it gives you clear water.

Statistics (and how best to use them)

People remember simple statistics and numbers, particularly when they relate to their behaviour and help confirm their thinking.

So if you have some great numbers in terms of client retention, or how all your clients profit from working with your business – harness them. And have confidence in them – after all, they stem from your hard work. (But make sure they are correct!) I'd much rather engage with an organisation that tells me '90% of our clients have stayed with us for over five years', as it shows they care about longevity rather than just quick wins.

And you can have real fun with numbers too.... 'We laid 50 miles of domestic pipes last year, fitted 89 loos and 56 showers – in 75 homes' sums up an experienced plumber, so use these in your marketing, on your website or on a business card.

Your goals

Your marketing

By dipping in and out of this section of the book, you should now be able to start setting yourself some clear goals in terms of what you want to achieve through your marketing.

If so, write them down here. You can have big, ambitious headline goals for the next 5 years – but to achieve these you will need to have smaller, closer goals for the next 6–18 months.

BIG GOALS

1
2
3

6–18 MONTH GOALS

1
2
3

Carry these forward to the GOALS section at the end of the book, when we will look at how to make a plan.

5

GOAL SETTING

'**Whatever you can do** or dream you can do, begin it. Boldness has genius, power and magic in it.'

Attributed to Goethe

At the very start of this book, you were asked to write down your hopes and dreams. Perhaps you skipped that bit. But it's worth taking time out to think about what these might be.

Your hopes and dreams may be big things, or they may be small, seemingly inconsequential to others, but profoundly important to you. That is absolutely how it should be. They are *your* hopes and dreams – no one else's.

The reason for referring back to them now, at the tail end of this book, is that they can help determine the pathways you choose and the horizons you are looking for.

If living abroad is one of your dreams, then you need to start thinking about how you can internationalise your business, or how you can develop a product to export. Attend a few overseas events to get a feel, talk to others who have done something similar. Perhaps you are intending to make your company run purely on the cloud so it doesn't matter where you are based. There are so many ways you can do this now, that nothing need stand in your way, except planning it and executing that plan.

If greater financial security is one of your hopes – and it is certainly one for many people I work with – then lots of the ideas in this book should have triggered new ways of thinking about how you can achieve this.

But you won't achieve your life abroad or greater security unless you *act* on the plans you make. And drawing up the road map for those actions is vital.

QUICK GOALS

There are lots of ways to achieve things quickly. This book is peppered with them. So it may be that you have already implemented some of the ideas you've spotted – fab! They are intended as easy boosts to help you to grow.

Do keep a note of what you are doing and set yourself a goal for each idea you develop. It could be a schedule to ensure a new service is introduced within three months. Or a decision to update your work space before the summer rush. You might have decided to collaborate with a neighbouring store...

Whatever the idea, ensure you keep a note to work out where you are going, the timescales, what success looks like and what that success has helped you achieve. This will inspire you to continue, make you more adventurous and likely to try other things.

BIGGER GOALS

But if you have worked/are working your way through this book in a more consistent way – and we all do things differently – to achieve some bigger goals, let's look at how we get these underway...

First, pull together the following lists and diagrams you will have written up as you worked through parts or all of this book.

a. Your hopes and dreams
(see page 18)
b. Your strengths and opportunities
(see page 35)
c. Your vision(s) and USP
(see page 40)
d. Your Target diagram
(see page 143)
e. Any work you have done around SPICK that explores new potential revenue-earning opportunities

Lay all of them, or the ones you've done, out on the table in front of you – and stand back.

This is your future.

If you want it – it's there for the taking.

If you have followed through the different sections on 'What you sell', 'Value and finances', 'Your people' and 'Marketing', you may well have a list of goals for each of these areas. You will need these now, so lay them out too.

The Discovery Map diagram overleaf shows how all the different areas you've worked through hang together. Don't worry if you haven't done all of them, or if you just took a pick'n'mix approach to the book – that's fine. Then list the goals you've identified for your business.

Order: Then list the goals you've identified and put each one in the order that you want it completed.

Paid To Do

Feeds into:
- What you offer
- Value & Finances
- Your People
- Marketing

Passions, Skills & Talents

Feeds into:
- What you offer
- USP
- Marketing

Client List

Feeds into:
- What you offer (SPICK, Cake, IP)
- Marketing
- Value & Finances
- Your People

Recent Developments

Feeds into:
- What you offer (SPICK)
- Marketing

Business Plan

Strengths

Feeds into:
- What you offer
- Marketing

Background

Feeds into:
- Vision
- USP
- What you offer
- Value

Weaknesses

Feeds into:
- What NOT to offer
- People you need to support you

Opportunities

Feeds into:
- Everything

I **always** start by putting all my goals – new products/services, ways of charging, the team I need to bring in and so on – in the right order.

It will be a different order for every single person and business who uses this book – but you know something? By just looking at all these things, you've already decided you want to change, to grow, so now it's just a matter of implementing all the work you've already done.

Some goals will rely on other ones happening first. For example, you might want to enter a new market that will mean you need to hire additional expertise, but this can't happen until you have sufficient revenue to pay them or more space. So the goals will be ordered as 1) New market identification, 2) Research, 3) Increased levels of existing revenue to pay for the new, 4) New team hire and 5) New market entry.

Dates: The next step is to set some dates against each goal. Unless you really have a pressing need or circumstances dictate, don't be overly ambitious. It is better to do things well, giving them a bit more time to flower, than to push for unrealistic target times that you fail to meet. Missing them will leave you feeling frustrated.

Or you could go for a fast minimum viable product (MVP), where you get something launched very quickly to meet a market demand, and then improve it as you go. Many software/tech companies use this model as it allows them to try things fast, fail, retry. So don't feel everything has to be perfect before you launch.

So now you have a calendar of goals – likely to be covering the next 18 months in detail, with the next 2–3 years a little more hazy.

DEVISING YOUR INCREMENTAL STEPS

No big goal is ever achieved on day 1. Or even day 7. It is a process of getting there step by step.

We all know the childhood teaser: 'How do you eat an elephant?' The answer – 'One bite at a time' – is exactly the same way you will achieve your goals. You have to break those goals down into the steps you need to take this quarter, this month, this week to reach the goal. It is only by achieving the small things on a regular basis that you can reach the big goals you've set yourself.

It's a bit like running a marathon.

You don't just get up one morning, put on your running shoes and set off to run 26+ miles. You work out what you need to wear to make yourself feel comfortable. What you need to eat so you can ensure maximum nutritional value. Then you start by running short distances regularly, building your capability. Reaching your goals in business is no different.

Take a deep breath and let's get cracking...

If you've done the big Target diagram, you will have set yourself some fairly crunchy goals for the next three years. They may feel very big, ambitious and rather scary. But you **do** have the ability to get there. Have faith in yourself... and start working out the road map you need.

For each of the key lines on your target diagram, work backwards... What do you need to achieve in each quarter in Year 2 to get to the Year 3 total? What do you need to implement in each two-month block in Year 1 to set you on the right road for Year 2? And what are the actions you need to take each month this year to get you to Year 1's totals?

If the SPICK model threw up some interesting new products, how are you going to get these underway? Break each of them down into their smallest components and put them in a time schedule.

Just as you did with the goals themselves, pull all the goal breakdown

Quick tip... Remember to give yourself credit for small wins, whether it is a treat for you or your team. You are another step on the road towards those goals! It doesn't matter what the treat is – but taking time to give yourself a pat on the back, recognising your achievement, is key. As you get absorbed in the everyday and your ongoing growth, it's so easy to forget how far you've come. So acknowledge and mark it.

steps together and put them in the right calendar order. Identify the really big ones, highlighting those to ensure you keep them at the front of your mind.

So if I mapped out my business while writing this book – it would look like the diagram opposite.

Use the diagram below to help you out. Each step will involve a range of

factors and elements. It can help talking it through with a team, but if you're a sole trader, why not sit down with a friend to talk through your plan and help you sense-check it?

I often work through my plans with one or other of my children. They are useful supporters and critics. They know me and my ability to jump to

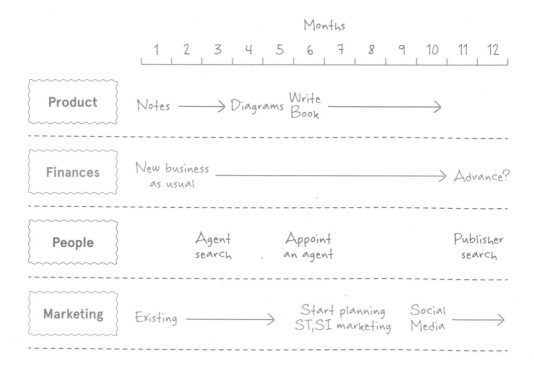

The process I used
to write this book...

Business Plan

Hopes/Dreams

- To help/have impact on UK small companies

Relevant Strengths

- Writing skills
- Experience with over 200 small companies in last five years
- Creative/IP/innovation/ financial experience
- Achieved growth for 180+ various companies in different sectors

Relevant Opportunites

- 4.7m companies of less than 10 employees in the UK
- Agility of small companies
- Limited government help
- Brexit triggering huge concerns

Product

- SPICK/CAKE/ new product

OFFER: Book & website to help small companies grow

GOALS: Write a book

Step 1: Analyse weeklys over last five years for all key notes: 27 notebooks

Step 2: Draw up key diagrams and write up theme

Step 3: Put all together

Step 4: Finish book

Value & Finances

- Target & market size
- Revenue models for book & web

GOALS: New revenue streams

Step 1: Maintain existing business

Step 2: Bring in X new clients

Step 3: Learn about publishing models/online value/deals/syndication etc.

People

- Who do I need to make this happen?

GOALS: Secure agent & deal

Step 1: Research

Step 2: Review People

Step 3: Select & deal

Step 4: Finalise publisher

Marketing

- How will I find my market?
- Real or digital world

GOALS: Grow awareness using social media (need to determine when deal done)

= Book

One of the great things about 'growth' is that, no matter what it means to you, it keeps you moving, inspired, engaged – stagnation is not an option.

the end result, forgetting about all the steps I need to take along the way. They pull me back, getting me to map the road more effectively.

It is useful to have just one key incremental step that you do each month. And no more than three big things you have to achieve in a year – because no matter how fast you want to reach the big goals, you still have to run your business alongside your growth plan.

Be prepared to flex and change too. External factors, whether local or national, may throw up once-in-a-lifetime opportunities or they may pose a threat. You have to be ready to flex and pivot your goals if needed. But don't let that deflect you. Adapt your plans, incorporate new steps and keep going.

And celebrate your achievements. If you succeed in achieving one of your key goals a little earlier than planned, give yourself a pat on the back.

One of my clients goes out to buy herself a new handbag, often in the colour she gave that particular goal on her big wall plan. It makes me smile when she comes to a meeting with a new red or blue bag. They represent real growth for her company. Her small team get treated too – perhaps not in handbags, though!

MEASURING YOUR SUCCESS: KEY PERFORMANCE INDICATORS (KPIS)

This is a term used in wider industry to measure how well you are on target to achieve your business goals.

Most people set these using financial terms, but they can really be in any area you want. It's good to have a mix of the financial, the more intangible and the practical.

Financial KPIs you may have set yourself as goals are likely to include turnover growth for the next two to three years, as well as improving your profitability as a percentage of this increased turnover. Another useful KPI is to aim to increase the average value of each transaction by a given percentage. An increase of just 10% over the year could make a big difference to your bottom line. Talk to other friends who have businesses to find out what KPIs they have set themselves.

One of the great things about setting targets for you, your team and the company is that once you have set them, it can make you really determined to reach them. It is about giving yourself a horizon to aim for – having that range of hills in the distance, setting your course and aiming for them.

However, it is vital that they stretch you but don't add absurd amounts of stress to you or the team.

The End!

But of course it's not – it's really the
beginning of your growth, new ways of
approaching your business, inventive
thinking around revenue models,
products and services you can sell,
different thoughts about where to
find customers...

Use this book as a companion to
your growth. You can refer to it regularly
– or just when you want a quick hit of
creative caffeine.

Good luck – I wish you well. Enjoy
the freedoms and opportunities that
working in a small business brings
you. There is nothing like it.

Erica

Appendix

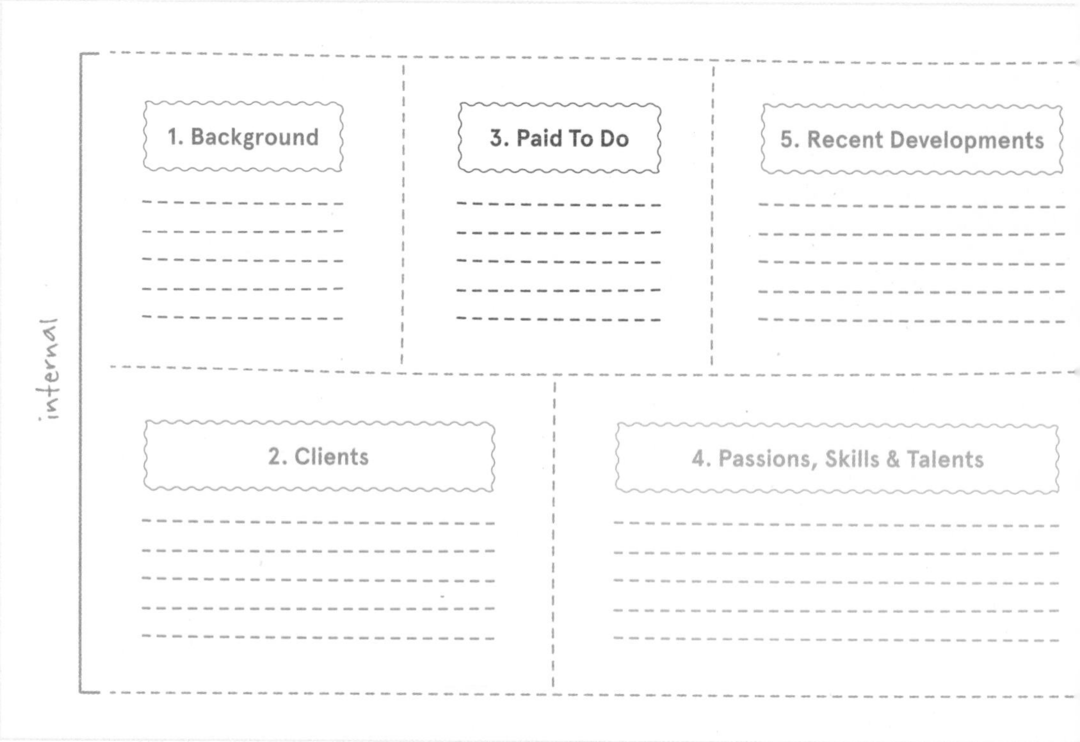

1. Background

3. Paid To Do

5. Recent Developments

2. Clients

4. Passions, Skills & Talents

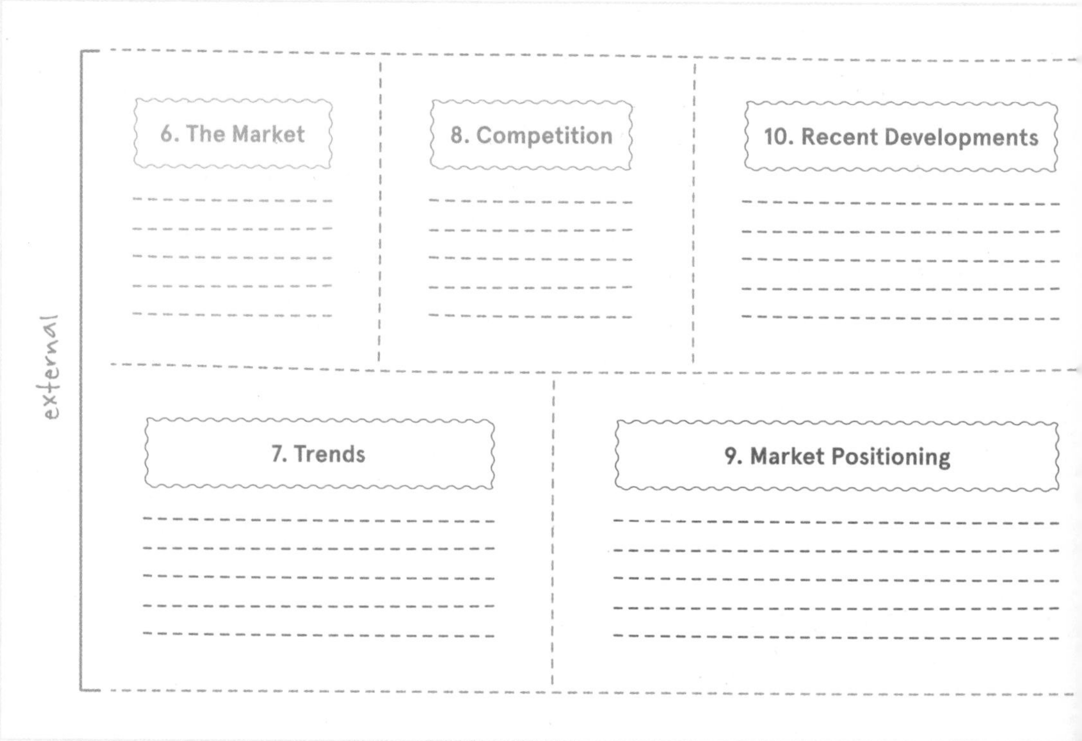

6. The Market

8. Competition

10. Recent Developments

7. Trends

9. Market Positioning

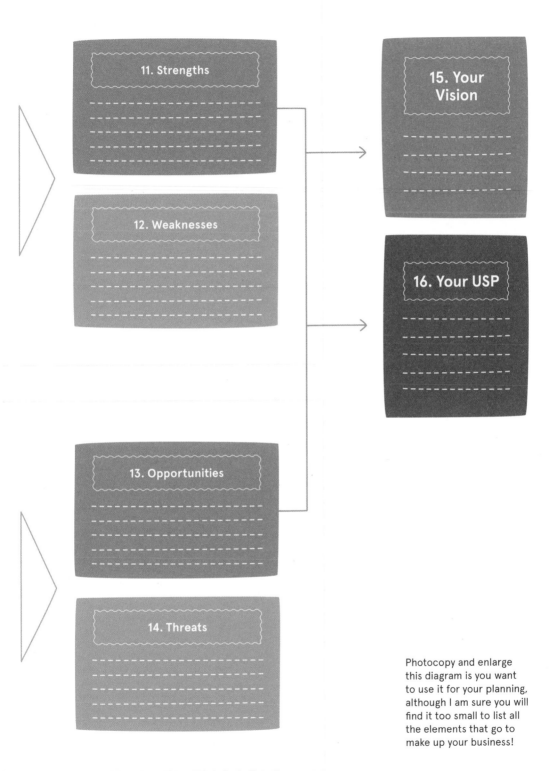

11. Strengths

12. Weaknesses

13. Opportunities

14. Threats

15. Your Vision

16. Your USP

Photocopy and enlarge this diagram is you want to use it for your planning, although I am sure you will find it too small to list all the elements that go to make up your business!

Notes

Photocopy or enlarge
this diagram to use
for your SPICK model.
Remember to put your
key revenue driver in
the far-left column.

Index

Page references in *italics* indicate images.

Picture credits

All case study images have been supplied and are used by kind permission of the companies mentioned and are their copyright.

Images on pages: 85, 86, 87, 88, 89, 90, 99, 132 © Shutterstock

Page 211 © Alun Callender

Acknowledgements

My past and present clients

When you start working with someone who will help your business grow, you probably don't expect to feature in a book you had no idea they might be intending to write... So I want to say a heartfelt 'thank you' to all of the clients, suppliers and advisors who I have worked with over the years. This book is as much their hard work as mine. If they hadn't walked their road and achieved what they did - their tales would not be mine to tell. It has been a joy to be part of your lives - we laughed, we crunched numbers, we drew up your daydreams on endless sheets of Magic Whiteboard, we devised hundreds of diagrams. (And this book was so nearly called 'Think about it this way...' the comment I apparently always use as I reach for my pad and pen to illustrate a different approach to solving a problem.) Thanks also to my coach, Clare Brigstocke - one of the very few people who has seen the story of my company, Lola, from the moment I first dreamed it up. Your challenges and support have always made me raise my game.

Alice Clarke
The design of all the diagrams and frameworks as well as the cover was done by Alice. Smart and talented, she has worked on several projects with me and always manages to make my scribbles look easy to understand. One hot summer week, she pulled rabbits out of hats against a deadline. I hope everyone who reads this book will appreciate what you have done. www.aliceclarke.com

Carly Cook
Agent extraordinaire who had the unenviable job of steering a rather wayward writer through the ups and downs of creating this book. I always appreciate your calm, honest advice, support and generosity. Thank you.

Gary Cook
Gary, who supplied the small line illustrations for the Cake section and others sprinkled through the book, is a talented artist who can be reached at www.cookthepainter.com

Lauren Lunn-Farrow
When I walked into the cafe and saw Lauren's beaming smile on our first meeting, I knew I had to work with her. Fun, incredibly hard working and dedicated, no-one could ask for a more 'on it' publicist. You rock.

David Rickard
My thanks to David Rickard, patent/TM attorney and IP solicitor, for kindly scanning the IP-related content of an earlier e-book of mine about IP that is incorporated here. You have always been so generous with your advice.

Austin Taylor
Austin worked magic across all the pages turning something that was a vision in my head into the enticing pages you see here. It was just thrilling to see each set of pages as they emerged from his desk, seeing an order and form to my words. You nailed it. www.bookdesigner.co.uk

whitefox
We did it! Thank you John, George and Kerr for getting me to this point, drawing on your years of publishing experience. It was a real journey but you helped me fulfil the lifelong dream of producing a book.

Notes

Notes